Rhetoric
in
Modern
Japan

Rhetoric in Modern Japan

Western Influences on the Development of Narrative and Oratorical Style

Massimiliano Tomasi

 University of Hawai'i Press

Honolulu

Printed in the United States of America

09 08 07 06 05 04   6 5 4 3 2 1

Library of Congress Cataloging-in-Publication Data
Tomasi, Massimiliano, 1965–
    Rhetoric in modern Japan : Western influences on the development of
narrative and oratorical style / Massimiliano Tomasi.
        p. cm.
Includes bibliographical references and index
    ISBN 0-8248-2798-8 (hardcover : alk. paper)
1. Japanese language—Rhetoric. 2. Japanese language—1868–
I. Title.
PL635.T66 2004
808'.04956–dc22   2003025832

Designed by University of Hawai'i production staff
Printed by The Maple–Vail Book Manufacturing Group

A Rika

e ai miei genitori,

Alfonso e Carla Tomasi

Contents

Acknowledgments

I am thankful to teachers, colleagues, and friends for their help. Professors Masumoto Masahiko and Fukuda Mahito were my graduate advisers at Nagoya University; I am indebted to them for all they taught me and for making my eight-year stay in Japan a memorable life experience. I am very grateful to Professor Rebecca Copeland of Washington University in St. Louis and Professor Judith Rabinovitch of the University of Montana for their invaluable suggestions and for their encouragement throughout the various stages of this project. I am also very thankful to Professor Suzuki Sadami of the International Research Center for Japanese Studies in Kyoto. I have benefited enormously from Professor Suzuki's expertise and assistance during my stay at the center. Special thanks also to Professor Peter Kornicki of the University of Cambridge for his extremely useful comments.

I would like to express my appreciation to Professor Brent Carbajal, chair of the Department of Modern and Classical Languages at Western Washington University, for his support and for all the time he spared from his busy schedule to engage in conversations about language and literature, Japanese and other. My gratitude goes also to Professor Joan Hoffman for her help throughout the years, and to Ms. Cheri Lashway, who, as a general reader, read the entire manuscript and made numerous critical stylistic suggestions. I have learned a great deal from Cheri's inspiring comments. Finally, I wish to thank everyone at the University of Hawai'i Press who assisted me with this project.

Many institutions have contributed financial support to this investigation. The Japan Society for the Promotion of Science provided me with travel and research aid during my graduate years at Nagoya University. A Western Washington University research grant enabled me to do research in Nagoya and Tokyo in the summer of 1999, while in 2002 a grant from the International Research Center for Japanese Studies in Kyoto helped me finalize the manuscript.

I would also like to acknowledge a number of journals where my work has been previously published. I thank the editors of *Monumenta Nipponica* for granting permission to reprint the articles "Quest for a New Written Language: West-ern Rhetoric and the *Genbun Itchi* Movement" and "Oratory in Meiji and Taishō Japan: Public Speaking and the Formation of a New Written Language" (chaps. 7 and 9), and the editors of *Japan Review* for granting permission to reprint the ar-ticle "Studies of Western Rhetoric in Modern Japan: The Years between Shima-mura Hōgetsu's *Shin bijigaku* (1902) and the End of the Taishō Era" (chap. 6). I also thank the editors of the *Journal of the Southwest Conference on Asian Studies* for permission to quote from my article "Studies of Western Rhetoric in Modern Ja-pan: The Years between Takada Sanae's *Bijigaku* and the Turn of the Century." Parts of this investigation have also appeared in other venues, albeit in substan-tially different form: chapter 2 includes material published in *Kokusai Nihon bun-gaku kenkyū shūkai kaigiroku* (Proceedings of the international conference on Japanese literature in Japan) and *Journal of Selected Papers in Asian Studies,* while chapters 6 and 7 contain sections of writings that appeared in *Nihon bungaku* (Japa-nese literature), *Kotoba no kagaku* (Studia linguistica), *Nagoya daigaku jinbun kagaku kenkyū* (Nagoya studies in the humanities), *PAJLS (Proceedings of the Association for Japanese Literary Studies),* and *Aistugia* (Italian association for Japanese studies).

This book is dedicated to my family: my parents, my brother, my son, and especially to my wife Rika, who has always supported me in my efforts over the years and across the continents.

Introduction

The Japanese quest for a new written language began in the early Meiji years. Increased exposure to the literary traditions of the West prompted scholars and intellectuals of the period to revisit their own literary heritage and to question the functionality of the currently predominant written expression, a static language that carried the legacy of centuries of literary practice but that was by then considerably different from the vernacular actually spoken by the people. Soon, these individuals began to envision the possibility of creating a simplified form of written expression based on spoken language and therefore more accessible to the masses. This idea, revolutionary in nature and seemingly impracticable to many, contained, already in its embryonic stage, the seeds for fierce academic debates and deep ideological conflicts. Not that the tension between traditional and more colloquial modes of expression had not already surfaced in premodern years; in fact, the presence of a more or less explicit discourse or metadiscourse that addressed the role of the vernacular in writing is detectable even before the Meiji era. However, the intensification of the debate on the question of language is a particularly significant phenomenon of the post-Restoration (1868) period. The critical reexamination of classical and pseudoclassical literary styles and the literary experimentation with the vernacular that followed became crucial traits of Meiji (1868–1912) and Taishō (1912–1926) academic discourse. The arrival of Western rhetoric in the early Meiji years added considerably to this process of renewal, contributing substantially to the creation of a new literary language in ways hitherto unclarified.

Previous scholarship has addressed several aspects of the rise of this new language. Prior analysis has treated not only the stylistic changes that occurred as a result of the exposure to Western languages and literatures, but also the parallel growing concern of the time for the creation of a literary medium capable of sustaining trends in literature that put growing emphasis on truth and the faithful reproduction of reality. The literary world of early Meiji faced a challenging task: to create a relatively simple written language that would ensure effective communication and at the same time be sufficiently refined for artistic achievement in writing. The dialectical relationship between this quest for a new form on the one hand and writers' aspiration to deliver a new content, along the tenets of current literary theories, on the other became one of the most crucial aspects of the literary developments of those years.

It is in the reexamination of the dynamics of this relationship that one detects the existence of a recurring theme in the critical discourse of the time that imbued every aspect of the debate on language: the question of rhetorical refinement. What is rhetoric and how should elegance in writing be defined? These very questions strongly characterized the Meiji and Taishō quest for a new written medium.

The understanding of the importance of rhetorical refinement in the debate on language leads in turn to another significant realization: the early inability of the Meiji *bundan* (literary world) to formulate a definition of rhetoric and rhetorical sophistication that could help bridge the ideological gap between the quest for a simple but relatively refined form and the drive toward the straightforward and unadorned content advocated by the current literary trends of realism and naturalism. Western rhetoric mediated between these two equally compelling pursuits, paving the way toward an acceptable compromise between classical and colloquial written styles.

But how and why is rhetoric relevant to the debate over the creation of a new written language and to the cultural and literary events of the Meiji era in general? It should be noted that a very significant portion of Meiji discourse centered on the issue of successful communication and the means to achieve it. Such discussion was often a metalinguistic operation, that is, a discourse concerning what type of language to use and how to use it, both in speaking and writing, in order to effectively communicate one's ideas and emotions. As a discipline that addressed the question of effective communication, rhetoric certainly held the key to many of the issues debated at the time. The oral dimension of rhetoric, in particular, was closely linked to the popularity of public speaking in Meiji Japan. The spread of oratory was one of the most significant phenomena of post-Restoration years, and although this proliferation has been addressed by previous scholarship, the framework of rhetorical inquiry has seldom been employed in the analysis. This book maintains that the history of oratory, and in particular public speaking, cannot be entirely separated from the history of Western rhetoric as a whole, but should be addressed as a constitutive part of its development. The popularity of public speaking was not only a social phenomenon that was supported by favorable political circumstances, but it also provided for the introduction of knowledge and the growth of a new awareness of the power and scope of the spoken language. This awareness grew parallel to and in conflict with the supremacy of the written language, which resulted in a relationship of friction and antagonism between the two. The conflict between the oral and the written medium became a recurrent theme in Meiji literary debates and is a point of chief concern in this book.

In addition, rhetoric's written dimension is inevitably linked to the literary developments of the period. It could not be otherwise, since literature is in part the very subject matter of rhetoric's discourse. If, as stated in many of the Western rhetorical treatises imported at the time, rhetoric taught how to discern beauty in writing, then it is logical to postulate that it must have played an important part in the debates that sought to discuss the aesthetic aspects of literary production. When Meiji literary discourse became earnestly engaged in the search for a new written language, rhetoric inevitably became a part of that process. On a broader scope, the search for a modern form of written expression was not a question that was necessarily confined to the specialized realm of literature. With the coming of the modern age and the increased need for an exchange of knowledge and information, the choice of words and style and the understanding of their relationship to the reader came to assume an unprecedented relevance, not only in the domain of literary production, but also in the realm of communication in general.

In a sense, however, this language-centered debate was especially pertinent to the field of literature. Centuries of literary tradition had reinforced the primacy of classical language to the extent that the vernacular was widely regarded as unsuitable for literary production. Classical language was perceived as elegant and changeless, whereas the vernacular was thought by many to be verbose and mutating, devoid of refinement and regularity. Although some scholars and intellectuals asserted the importance of the spoken language in literature, they faced strong resistance from those who argued in favor of the elegance and tradition of classical prose styles. This resulted in a dispute that became the core of a discussion addressing the feasibility of a modern form of literary language based on the vernacular: a debate, that is, on the nature of rhetorical refinement in writing.

Despite the likely crucial involvement of rhetoric in the academic debates of the time, very few existing works mention the existence of a tradition of rhetorical inquiry in modern Japan, and even fewer have considered its contribution to the literary debates of the period. As a result, Meiji and Taishō research on rhetoric has remained an obscure and unknown entity whose rightful place in the history of modern Japanese literature still needs to be elucidated. Such disregard for this aspect of recent Japanese literary history is in no way justified. If one considers that both the popularity of public speaking and the search for a new literary language have been major traits of the Meiji cultural and literary scene, it seems only logical to assume that there are important links between the social and literary developments of the period and the introduction of Western rhetoric. The large number of works of rhetoric published during the Meiji and Taishō years constitutes further evidence of the likelihood that the discipline played a key role in the academic and intellectual debates of the time.

Several factors have contributed to this paucity of interest. One may be found in the modalities by which rhetoric was introduced after the Meiji Restoration. The introduction of the discipline in some cases occurred as a result of the impulse to acquire Western culture, rather than from a thoughtfully motivated search for a source of knowledge to apply to native literary and cultural tradition. Ground-breaking works were often followed by redundant publications that amounted to mere translation exercises. Rhetoric became a corpus of scholarly production lacking in unity and coherence, being viewed by many as a marginal aspect of the process of importation of Western knowledge taking place during those years.

Another reason for the disregard of rhetoric among scholars thus far may lie in the discipline's recent rebirth in the West. Since the 1950s, rhetoric has found new relevance within a variety of fields such as linguistics, semiotics, philosophy, and communication theory. This engagement in multiple interdisciplinary issues has led to an increased interest among Japanese scholars in some specific aspects of the discipline, such as the internal mechanisms of rhetorical figures and their cognitive relevance to speech and literary production, which has paradoxically overshadowed efforts to reconsider the role of rhetoric at the time of its first importation to Japan.

A third and perhaps most important factor can be found in the widely accepted viewpoint that rhetoric was in a conflictual relationship with the literary trends that ruled the *bundan* between the end of the nineteenth century and the beginning of the twentieth century. According to this position, such a relationship prevented rhetoric from playing any kind of active role in the debate over the definition of literature and the creation of a modern literary language. This argument is crucial to the history of rhetoric in Japan and is discussed at length in this book.

This book seeks to reconsider the introduction of rhetoric into Japan and to clarify its interactions with the forces and synergies that shaped modern Japanese literature and culture. More specifically, it seeks to provide a historical account aimed at bringing to light the presence of distinctive features throughout the discipline's development. Ultimately, it aims to give modern Japanese rhetoric an identity of its own, denoted by both the achievements and the inevitable contradictions and failures that have characterized it.

Given the variety of meanings presently attributed to rhetoric both as a term and as a field of study, the first task of this book is to clarify the scope and boundaries of the domain that is specifically the object of this investigation. George Payn Quackenbos' *Advanced Course of Composition and Rhetoric,* a text widely read in Japan in the Meiji years, serves as a suitable starting point in that it conveniently illustrates the state of the discipline and its acceptation at the time of its introduction to Japan. According to Quackenbos, the word "rhetoric" originally

> had reference solely to the art of oratory; in this sense, moreover, we find it generally used by ancient writers. As, however, most of the rules relating to the composition of matter intended for delivery are equally applicable to other kinds of writing, in the course of time the meaning of the term was naturally extended; so that even as early as in the age of Aristotle it was used with reference to productions not designed for public recitation.
>
> At the present day, Rhetoric, in its widest acceptation, comprehends all prose composition; and it is with this signification we here use the term: in its narrowest sense, it is limited to persuasive speaking.[1]

Differently from Quackenbos' work, this investigation is concerned with both understandings of rhetoric: in its narrowest sense, that is, as the art of speech, and in its broadest sense, that is, as the art of composition. It is generally concerned with all those rules originally devised for public speaking that later came to be applied to the domain of writing. Consequently, it treats the various parts into which classical rhetoric was traditionally divided, namely "invention," "arrangement," "elocution (or "style")," "memory," and "delivery," and the general principles regarding the effective use of language, including the classification of rhetorical figures. Further connotations of rhetoric, most of which originated well into the twentieth century, are not considered here.

This book is thus divided into three parts: "The Tradition of Rhetoric," "History of Rhetoric," and "Quest for a New Written Language." "The Tradition of Rhetoric" sets the stage for the discussion by first providing an important overview of the chief theoretical points that have marked the historical development of rhetoric in the West. The section also addresses the existence of a tradition of rhetorical inquiry in Japan prior to the Meiji period, highlighting the presence of a broad range of misguided notions among modern scholars on the practice of rhetorical communication in premodern Japan.

"History of Rhetoric" chronicles the development of the study of rhetoric in Japan, from its introduction in the early Meiji period to its decline well into the Taishō years. Departing from the assumption, widespread among Japanese Meiji scholars, that Japan did not have a rhetorical heritage along the lines of Western tradition, the section focuses on the developments that took place after the Meiji Restoration. It comprises four chapters (chaps. 3–6), corresponding to the four main phases that, according to my investigation, have characterized the growth of rhetoric as a field of study in Meiji and Taishō Japan. Chapter 3 deals with the arrival of rhetoric, which was introduced mainly as the art of speech. Covering a period that spans from the Meiji Restoration to the end of the 1880s, the chapter discusses the rise of public speaking and the works of intellectuals and political leaders such as Fukuzawa Yukichi, Ozaki Yukio, and Baba Tatsui. Chapter 4 is concerned with the period extending from the end of the 1880s to the end of the century. Initiated by the publication of Takada Sanae's *Bijigaku* (Rhetoric) in 1889, this phase saw rhetoric come to be perceived as a system of rules and precepts for composition and literary criticism. The shift to a rhetorical investigation now concerned mostly with written discourse is analyzed in this section. Chapter 5 describes the changes that took place with the rise of rhetoricians such as Shimamura Hōgetsu and Igarashi Chikara and delineates the surfacing of crucial links between the discipline and the literary developments of the period. These vital links are detailed in the third section of the book. Chapter 6, covering the entire Taishō era, assesses the final stage of rhetoric in Japan, which then came to be mostly absorbed within the field of composition and studies of national language. Each of the four phases is duly contextualized so as to illustrate the existence of crucial intersections between the development of rhetoric and the social and literary events of the time. The question of language, in particular, is constantly held under consideration and constitutes a matter of high priority in the discussion of the content of each work.

"Quest for a New Written Language," the third section, discusses the debate over the creation of a modern literary language. It explores the collusions and conflicts characterizing rhetoric and its relationship with the *genbun itchi* movement (the movement for the unification of the spoken with the written language) and its call for a simplified written medium. The analysis considers one of the many aspects of the debate, namely the controversy over the role of rhetorical refinement in writing. The question of rhetorical refinement, it is argued, figured as one of the key issues in the literary discourse of the time, to the extent that it could be employed as an interpretative paradigm for the developments that took place throughout much of the Meiji and Taishō years. Attention is also paid in this section to the predominant literary trend of the period, naturalism. As Donald Keene has noted, "[i]f any movement in Japanese literature of the twentieth century can be described as central, it is doubtlessly Naturalism *(shizenshugi)*."[2] The movement's call for an unadorned writing style seemed to result in an impracticable coexistence with rhetoric and its teachings. This book illustrates how, on the contrary, the two were not necessarily in an antagonistic relationship. Furthermore, addressing the complex and conflicting relationship between the written and spoken mediums, "Quest for a New Written Language" also contextualizes the importance of oratory in modern Japan, clarifying its role as a tool for modernization and as an effective platform for the reappraisal of the spoken language. It discloses the process by which developments in oratory itself contributed to an ultimate resolution in favor of the final acceptance of a written vernacular.

The book concludes with an epilogue. Capitalizing upon the investigation's findings, this final section reaffirms Western rhetoric's significant role in Japan's modernization process. Whether in the field of politics, literature, or education, rhetoric is revealed as inextricably connected to the crucial developments that have brought Japan to the threshold of modern times. The epilogue highlights the existence of an important common denominator among recent studies on the development of modern Japanese literature: the recognition of the centrality of the question of language. In recognizing the *genbun itchi* issue as central to their investigation, recent critical approaches have challenged, even if only in a superficial fashion, the historicist view that held that language played a subordinate role in the literary discourse of those years. Concurring with these studies, this investigation seeks to reverse the notion of form as a merely passive component of the process that led to the development of a new literary language. Reiterating the crucial importance of the issue of rhetorical refinement in the literary debates of the time, the final section of this book shows the existence of significant convergences between rhetoric and the formation of modern Japanese narrative. As a result, rhetoric is propelled toward a theoretically ambitious dimension that does not confine the discipline to a question of a mere stylistic nature, but situates it squarely within mainstream contemporary discourse in the field.

PART 1
The Tradition of Rhetoric

1
Western Rhetorical Tradition
A Synopsis

No brief survey could do justice to the almost twenty-five-hundred-year history of rhetoric. So many authors and works have contributed to this field that it is impossible to cite all of them. The following synopsis is therefore intended to provide an overview of the essential themes that have characterized rhetoric and its development since the early ages as well as contribute a brief background to the discussion that will take place in the following pages. Priority is given to those aspects of Western rhetoric that bear important links to the development of studies of rhetoric in modern Japan.

According to an ancient tradition, rhetoric was first formulated by Corax of Syracuse in the fifth century B.C. Devised in order to enhance one's ability to defend or prosecute in court, it was transmitted to Greece by the sophist Gorgias of Leontini in 427 B.C. Gorgias (ca. 485–ca. 380 B.C.) captivated the Athenians with his embellished oratory style, spurring interest in the study of eloquence. However, it was in a dialogue titled with his name, *Gorgias,* that Plato (ca. 429–347 B.C.), speaking through Socrates, attacked the discipline, dismissing it as a mere form of flattery that was based on opinions and assumptions rather than philosophical truth. Plato's tone of inquiry is already evident in the opening exchange between Socrates and Gorgias.

SOC.: You are right there. Come now, answer me in the same way about rhetoric: with what particular thing is its skill concerned?

GORG.: With speech.

SOC.: What kind of speech, Gorgias? Do you mean that which shows by what regimen sick people could get well?

GORG.: No.

SOC.: Then rhetoric is not concerned with all kinds of speech.

GORG.: No, I say.

Soc.:   Yet it does make men able to speak.

Gorg.:   Yes.

Soc.:   And to understand also the things about which they speak.

Gorg.:   Of course.

Soc.:   Now, does the medical art, which we mentioned just now, make men able to understand and speak about the sick?

Gorg.:   It must.

Soc.:   Hence the medical art also, it seems, is concerned with speech.

Gorg.:   Yes.

Soc.:   That is, speech about diseases?

Gorg.:   Certainly.

Soc.:   Now, is gymnastic also concerned with speech about the good and bad condition of our bodies?

Gorg.:   Quite so.

Soc.:   And moreover it is the same, Gorgias, with all the other arts; each of them is concerned with that kind of speech which deals with the subject matter of that particular art.

Gorg.:   Apparently.

Soc.:   Then, why, pray, do you not give the name "rhetorical" to those other arts, when they are concerned with speech, if you call that "rhetoric" which has to do with speech?[1]

Socrates further questions Gorgias on the nature of his profession, discrediting rhetoric as a producer of belief rather than knowledge. Later, in an exchange with Polus, a disciple of Gorgias, Socrates denies that rhetoric is an art and depicts it as a mere knack through a memorable association of the discipline with cookery.

Soc.:   Ask me now what art I take cookery to be.

Pol.:   Then I ask you, what art is cookery?

Soc.:   None at all, Polus.

Pol.:   Well, what is it? Tell me.

Soc.:   Then I reply, a certain habitude.

Pol.:   Of what? Tell me.

Soc.:   Then I reply, of production of gratification and pleasure, Polus.

Pol.:   So cookery and rhetoric are the same thing?

Soc.:   Not at all, only parts of the same practice.

Pol.:   What practice do you mean?

Soc.:   I fear it may be too rude to tell the truth; for I shrink from saying it on

Gorgias' account, lest he suppose I am making satirical fun of his own pursuit. Yet indeed I do not know whether this is the rhetoric which Gorgias practices, for from our argument just now we got no very clear view as to how he conceives it; but what I call rhetoric is a part of a certain business which has nothing fine about it.

GORG.: What is that, Socrates? Tell us, without scruple on my account.

SOC.: It seems to me then, Gorgias, to be a pursuit that is not a matter of art, but showing a shrewd, gallant spirit which has a natural bent for clever dealing with mankind, and I sum up its substance in the name *flattery.* This practice, as I view it, has many branches, and one of them is cookery, which appears indeed to be an art but, by my account of it, is not an art but a habitude or knack. I call rhetoric another branch of it, as also personal adornment and sophistry—four branches of it for four kinds of affairs.[2]

Only at the end of the dialogue does Plato concede the possibility of the existence of a true rhetoric, one that is good and that takes into account the moral facet of the process of persuasion. This notion would later be addressed in one of his following works, *Phaedrus,* where Plato, again through the character of Socrates, argues that a true rhetoric, based on knowledge, should have a just purpose and be ethically and morally right. The orator should know the subject matter of his discourse thoroughly and have a deep understanding of human psychology.

Posed in these terms, rhetoricians faced the challenge of demonstrating with convincing arguments the possibility of a rhetoric that pursued truth rather than deceit and instruction rather than gratification. Aristotle (384–322 B.C.) accepted this challenge and systematized the discipline within a scientific-philosophical framework. In his *Rhetoric,* a treatise consisting of three books, Aristotle defined rhetoric as the faculty of discovering in every case the available means of persuasion. He identified three types of proof or persuasion: ethos (the persuasion arising from the qualities of the speaker); pathos (the persuasion resulting from the emotions of the audience); and logos (the persuasion deriving from the use of logical proof contained in the arguments made). He discussed the enthymeme as a means of logical proof, characterizing it as a method of persuasion that relied on probable knowledge rather than scientific truth. He therefore recognized the concept of probability as the essence of the art of persuasion. As Paul Ricoeur puts it, "The great merit of Aristotle was in developing this link between the rhetorical concept of persuasion and the logical concept of the probable, and in constructing the whole edifice of a philosophy of rhetoric on this relationship."[3]

Aristotle distinguished three types of speech: judicial (or forensic), deliberative, and epideictic (or demonstrative). The first type pertained to matters of forensic practice and referred to instances where the audience made the final judgment on the arguments offered by the speaker. The second type referred to speeches that encouraged the audience to take a course of action; it typically included the realm of political discourse. The third type dealt with praise and blame, such as in the case of ceremonial occasions.

Aristotle put much emphasis on the relationship between the speaker and the audience. He argued that the success of a speaker was determined also by his character and thus named intelligence, virtue, and goodwill as three fundamental prerequisites of the orator. Finally, he discussed the part of rhetoric that was most related to language and style: "for it is not sufficient to know what one ought to say, but one must also know how to say it, and this largely contributes to making the speech appear of a certain character."[4] He named clearness and propriety as the essential elements of style, since "if it [speech] does not make the meaning clear, will not perform its proper function; neither must it be mean, nor above the dignity of the subject, but appropriate to it."[5] As for language, he noted the following:

> Wherefore we should give our language a "foreign air"; for men admire what is remote, and that which excites admiration is pleasant. In poetry many things conduce to this and there it is appropriate; for the subjects and persons spoken of are more out of the common. But in prose such methods are appropriate in much fewer instances, for the subject is less elevated; and even in poetry, if fine language were used by a slave or a very young man, or about quite unimportant matters, it would be hardly becoming; for even here due proportion consists in contraction and amplification as the subject requires. Wherefore those who practise this artifice must conceal it and avoid the appearance of speaking artificially instead of naturally: for that which is natural persuades, but the artificial does not.[6]

And about metaphor:

> It is metaphor above all that gives perspicuity, pleasure, and a foreign air, and it cannot be learnt from anyone else; but we must make use of metaphors and epithets that are appropriate. This will be secured by observing due proportion; otherwise there will be lack of propriety, because it is when placed in juxtaposition that contraries are most evident. We must consider, as a red cloak suits a young man, what suits an old one; for the same garment is not suitable for both. And if we wish to ornament our subject, we must derive our metaphor from the better species under the same genus; if to depreciate it, from the worse.[7]

Aristotle cautioned against the indiscriminate use of metaphors, which "must not be far-fetched" and could cause ridicule if inappropriate. He underlined their ability to generate new knowledge by bringing into view similarities originally not apparent, since "we give names to things that have none by deriving the metaphor from what is akin and of the same kind, so that, as soon as it is uttered, it is clearly seen to be akin."[8] Metaphors were, from this point of view, "a kind of enigma," and their effective use denoted cleverness. At the same time, however, metaphors had to be derived from what was beautiful either in sound or in signification, or to sight or to some other sense. For it did make a difference, for instance, whether one said "'rosy-fingered morn,' rather than 'purple-fingered,' or, what is still worse, 'red-fingered.'"[9]

Aristotle's *Rhetoric* can be considered the apex of the Greek rhetorical tradition. This tradition was transmitted to Rome around the first century B.C., where rhetoric soon became the central element of education. Among the most distinguished rhetoricians of the time was Cicero (106–43 B.C.). According to Renato Barilli, "Cicero's stature is such that it is no exaggeration to see his contribution as marking one of the greatest moments for rhetoric." In particular, "if the Platonic moment is one of negation, and the Aristotelian one of Olympian acceptance and systematization, Cicero's model marks the triumph of rhetoric, which with him is privileged and raised to the rank of art of the arts."[10]

Cicero wrote several works on rhetoric, the first being his *De inventione* (On invention), which was composed around 90 B.C. It was a juvenile work, and Cicero himself criticized it later as an incomplete treatise that had escaped from the notebooks of his adolescent years. The book contained, however, Cicero's celebrated defense of eloquence, a defense that evokes the moral-philosophical doubts on the nature of the discipline cast by Plato in his *Gorgias*.

> I have often seriously debated with myself whether men and communities have received more good or evil from oratory and a consuming devotion to eloquence. For when I ponder the troubles in our commonwealth, and run over in my mind the ancient misfortunes of mighty cities, I see that no little part of the disasters was brought about by men of eloquence. When, on the other hand, I begin to search in the records of literature for events which occurred before the period which our generation can remember, I find that many cities have been founded, that the flames of a multitude of wars have been extinguished, and that the strongest alliances and most sacred friendships have been formed not only by the use of the reason but also more easily by the help of eloquence. For my own part, after long thought, I have been led by reason itself to hold this opinion first and foremost, that wisdom without eloquence does too little for the good of states, but that eloquence

without wisdom is generally highly disadvantageous and is never helpful. Therefore if anyone neglects the study of philosophy and moral conduct, which is the highest and most honourable of pursuits, and devotes his whole energy to the practice of oratory, his civic life is nurtured into something useless to himself and harmful to his country; but the man who equips himself with the weapons of eloquence, not to be able to attack the welfare of his country, but to defend it, he, I think, will be a citizen most helpful and most devoted both to his own interests and those of his community.[11]

In these first pages, Cicero also identified the parts into which the discipline was divided. *De inventione* covered only invention, but Cicero's distinction is nonetheless important because it shows how the division of rhetoric into five canons had already been accepted by his time.

The parts of it, as most authorities have stated, are Invention, Arrangement, Expression, Memory, Delivery. Invention is the discovery of valid or seemingly valid arguments to render one's cause plausible. Arrangement is the distribution of arguments thus discovered in the proper order. Expression is the fitting of the proper language to the invented matter. Memory is the firm mental grasp of matter and words. Delivery is the control of voice and body in a manner suitable to the dignity of the subject matter and the style.[12]

De oratore (On the orator), on the other hand, written around 55 B.C., is regarded as Cicero's most outstanding work on the subject. Cast in the form of a dialogue between Lucius Licinius Crassus, a former teacher of Cicero, and other prominent orators of the time, this treatise contained the philosopher's mature ideas on the nature of oratory and the prerequisites of the ideal orator. Cicero emphasized the need for the orator to be versed in a variety of fields of human knowledge. In the opening pages of the treatise, he argued that a distinctive style had to be accompanied by an understanding of human emotions, because "it is in calming or kindling the feelings of the audience that the full power and science of oratory are to be brought into play."[13] Humor and wit, knowledge of history and the law, as well as control of the body, gesture, and intonation of the voice were among the necessary elements that in his view made this art so difficult to master. These and other requirements of the ideal orator would later be discussed in detail by Crassus in the central section of the first book.

One point that stands out from this work is Cicero's partial dismissal of rules and increased emphasis on the importance of knowledge and practice. Through the character of Crassus, Cicero argues that writing in particular is an essential practice for the ideal orator. This close link between writing and eloquence would be reiterated by the other outstanding rhetorician of the time, Quintilian, and would become an important feature of the rhetorical theory of the period.

> [H]e too who approaches oratory by way of long practice in writing, brings this advantage to his task, that even if he is extemporizing, whatever he may say bears a likeness to the written word; and moreover if ever, during a speech, he has introduced a written note, the rest of his discourse, when he turns away from the writing, will proceed in unchanging style. Just as when a boat is moving at high speed, if the crew rest upon their oars, the craft herself still keeps her way and her run, though the driving force of the oars has ceased, so in an unbroken discourse, when written notes are exhausted, the rest of the speech still maintains a like progress, under the impulse given by the similarity and energy of the written word.[14]

Another major work of Latin rhetoric was the anonymous *Rhetorica ad Herennium* (Rhetoric for Herennius), the oldest extant treatise covering all five parts of rhetoric. This work, long attributed to Cicero, was characterized by an extensive treatment of style, covered in Book 4. Style was divided into Grand, Middle, and Simple. According to the author, an appropriate style should have three qualities: taste, artistic composition, and distinction. The latter of these qualities could be achieved through the employment of rhetorical figures, which were therefore discussed at length. Figures were divided into figures of speech and figures of thought, for a total of sixty-four figures. Albeit extremely important to convey a special effect to the style, the author cautioned that if "distributed sparingly, these figures set the style in relief, as with colors; if packed in close succession, they set the style awry."[15]

The treatment of style provided in *Rhetorica ad Herennium,* and in particular the detailed handling of figures, would set a standard for centuries to come. An additional salient aspect of this work is the elucidation of memory and delivery, neither of which were thoroughly discussed in Aristotle's *Rhetoric.* The author noted that "many have said that the faculty of greatest use to the speaker and the most valuable for persuasion is Delivery. For my part, I should not readily say that any one of the five faculties is the most important; that an exceptionally great usefulness resides in the delivery I should boldly affirm."[16] Denouncing the fact that this facet had been generally disregarded in the literature on the subject, the author went on to discuss such items as voice quality and physical movement. At the end of his deliberation, he turned to memory, that is, "the treasure-house of the ideas supplied by Invention . . . the guardian of all the parts of rhetoric."[17] He divided it into natural and artificial and provided a discussion that concluded Book 3.

Quintilian (ca. 35–ca. 100) is the other outstanding rhetorician of the period. In his *Institutio oratoria* (The institutes of oratory), a treatise comprising twelve books written between 92 and 95, Quintilian formulated a detailed pedagogical program for the education of the perfect orator, and his greatest contribution is probably in this area. The structure of his work is described in the opening pages of Book 1.

> My first book will be concerned with the education preliminary to the duties of the teacher of rhetoric. My second will deal with the rudiments of the schools of rhetoric and with problems connected with the essence of rhetoric itself. The next five will be concerned with Invention, in which I include Arrangement. The four following will be assigned to Eloquence, under which head I include Memory and Delivery. Finally there will be one book in which our complete orator will be delineated.[18]

A monumental treatise covering all five of the parts of rhetoric, with a substantial treatment of style (including rhetorical figures) and incorporating the generally overlooked sections of memory and delivery, Quintilian's *Institutio oratoria* could be considered the conclusive product of Roman rhetorical theory. One of the crucial elements surfacing from the work is the reiteration of the moral purpose of oratory. According to Quintilian, the perfect orator "should be a good man, and consequently we demand of him not merely the possession of exceptional gifts of speech, but of all the excellences of character as well."[19] He is a servant of the people whose interests are placed before his own welfare. Character, firmness, and moral stature are important prerequisites to his formation.

Overall, Roman rhetoric further contributed to the canonization of the five parts of the discipline and attributed renewed relevance to the sections concerning memory and delivery. Cicero and Quintilian, in particular, provided more detailed schematization, at times reinforcing the theoretical tradition inherited from the Greeks and at times adding new elements or giving priority to certain parts over others. The rules that applied to effective speaking also applied, by extension, to elegant and correct writing, particularly when concerned with the rhetorical theory of style, that is, the appropriate and elegant usage of words, the *ornatus*. Already in the early centuries A.D., the growing emphasis on the *ornatus* contributed to the narrowing of rhetoric's scope, which gradually came to be perceived as something mostly concerned with polished writing. That is to say, the central core of the theoretical discourse on rhetoric shifted from the original external purpose of persuasion to the intrinsic stylistic quality of the discourse.[20] This shift in rhetorical inquiry from spoken to written discourse is also a major trait of the development of studies of rhetoric in modern Japan and as such is a chief concern of this book.

The centuries that immediately followed Cicero's and Quintilian's works saw the Christianization of rhetoric. As George Kennedy noted, the acceptance of classical rhetoric by figures such as Augustine (354–430), author of *De doctrina christiana* (On Christian doctrine), "contributed to continuation of the tradition, though the functions of the study of rhetoric in the Church were transferred from preparation for public address in law courts and assemblies to knowledge useful in interpreting the Bible, in preaching, and in ecclesiastical disputation."[21] The scholarly production of this time included works by grammarians Boethius (ca. 475–ca. 524), Cassiodorus (ca. 490–ca. 585), and Isidore of Seville (ca. 560–636), who all made contributions to the rhetorical apparatus inherited from the preceding age.[22] After that, "the transmission of rhetorical tradition through the times of decadence, the Dark Ages (the tenth and eleven centuries), does not suffer any setback in its network. At most there is an impoverishment, a sort of drying up, meaning that, with this, rhetoric is progressively reduced to a body of rules. Instead of introducing radical innovations, the various 'renaissances' that occur will consist of new formulations of the old baggage of notions, now put forward with more eloquence, a deeper thrust and conviction."[23]

Two important developments need to be mentioned among the many that characterized the years between the beginning of the Middle Ages and early modernity. The first is the rise of rationalism. Descartes' rejection of the concept of probability labeled rhetoric as a discipline unable to produce truth and one that should be considered unreliable. The second development is the spread of Ramism. French philosopher Peter Ramus (1515–1572) separated "invention" and "arrangement" from rhetoric and placed them under the domain of dialectic, depriving the discipline of the canons that, through their close link to logic, had guaranteed the validity of much of its scientific framework. He thus redefined rhetoric as a discipline that was concerned only with style and language. The most tangible consequence of this operation was the relegation of rhetoric to the realm of "elocution." Rhetoric became a crystallized body of rules teaching stylistic flourishes, and this is reflected in the publication of works that, in those years, put sole emphasis on the stylistic aspect of the discipline.[24] It is in this direction that rhetoric's decline unfolded, albeit not without distinction. As Tzvetan Todorov noted, rhetoric "produced—through a final effort more powerful than any that had gone before it, as if to try to stave off imminent extinction—a body of reflections whose quality is unmatched."[25] This final effort materialized in the works of such rhetoricians as César Chesneau Du Marsais (1676–1756) and Pierre Fontanier (1768–1844), whose respective works on rhetorical figures, *Des tropes*

(On tropes, 1730) and *Les figures du discours* (The figures of discourse, 1827), became a distinctive feature of rhetoric's twilight.

Important developments, however, were taking place elsewhere, especially
in Great Britain. James L. Golden and Edward P. J. Corbett have identified four
main movements in the British rhetorical tradition between the seventeenth and
nineteenth centuries that constitute significant contributions to the evolution of
Western rhetorical thought: the neoclassical, the belletristic, the psychological-
philosophical, and the elocutionary. These advancements are of particular relevance to this book because modern Japanese rhetoric drew consistently from the
British tradition.[26]

An author widely cited by Japanese scholars of the Meiji era is Hugh Blair
(1718–1800). Blair was one of the most representative rhetoricians of the belletristic movement, and his *Lectures on Rhetoric and Belles Lettres,* first published
in 1783, is said to have been a long-time best seller both in Britain and the
United States.[27] A work divided into forty-seven lectures, partially rendered
into Japanese in 1880, *Lectures on Rhetoric* embodied the essence of the belletristic movement, which was the shift toward a conception of rhetoric that embraced the realm of literary criticism. Many of the concepts discussed by Blair,
such as taste and sublimity, reoccurred significantly in the works of rhetoric of
Meiji Japan, and the formulation of a belletristic rhetoric that combined disciplines like literature, linguistics, and aesthetics characterized much of mid-Meiji
Japanese scholarly production on the subject.

The developments in the psychological-philosophical tradition are also important for Japanese rhetorical investigation during the Meiji period. Among
the representative authors of this movement is George Campbell (1719–1796),
whose *Philosophy of Rhetoric,* published in 1776, is considered by many to be a
watershed distinguishing between premodern and modern rhetorical theory.
Drawing from the theories of mental and psychological associations of John
Locke and David Hume, Campbell articulated a rhetorical theory that put
much emphasis on the faculties of the mind—understanding, imagination,
emotions, and will—and the understanding of human nature. The argument
that the mind tends to associate ideas that bear some type of resemblance, either
through similarity, contiguity, or a relationship of cause and effect, was a distinctive feature of his work and had considerable influence on the theory of
figures of such Japanese rhetoricians as Igarashi Chikara.[28]

The British elocutionary movement was equally important. It was characterized by a renewed emphasis on the last canon of rhetoric, which is delivery.
Elocutionists—Thomas Sheridan's *A Course of Lectures on Elocution* (1762) being
perhaps one of the most representative works—focused on the study of vocal

expression and gestures, including the positions and motions of feet and arms. For reasons that are not clear, they employed the term "elocution" in place of "delivery," creating considerable semantic ambiguities over the use of the two terms.[29] Several early Japanese publications on oratory contained detailed treatments of this aspect of rhetoric, thus displaying an important link to this tradition. Interestingly, the elocutionary movement was characterized by a growing interest in the study of language and pronunciation. It became popular at a time when increasing opportunities for public speaking turned the question of language into a crucial issue for the achievement of effective communication. It was, in other words, closely linked to the formation of a standard language and the correction of dialects, a point also touched upon in this book.

Finally, a few words should be said about nineteenth-century authors and works that in many cases represented the only primary sources available to Meiji rhetoricians and provided invaluable access to the vast tradition of Western rhetoric. Alexander Bain's *English Compositon and Rhetoric* (1866) is perhaps the foremost of these studies, "for a great deal of what has been taught in traditional composition courses derives directly or indirectly from Bain's work."[30] A leading advocate of association psychology, Bain (1818–1903) has been regarded by many not only as the father of paragraph theory, but also as the main person responsible for the classification of discourse into the four forms of description, narration, exposition, and persuasion.[31] This classification became a standard feature of many late nineteenth- and early twentieth-century English and American books on rhetoric, to the point that Adams Sherman Hill, professor of rhetoric at Harvard University, "added sections on the forms of discourse [to the revised 1895 edition of *The Principles of Rhetoric and Their Application*] because practically every textbook of that period was including them."[32]

The core of Bain's contribution lay in the new psychological orientation he gave to the study of rhetoric, particularly in his formulation of laws of mental association. Of course, as Frank D'Angelo has also pointed out, the shift to a psychological orientation in rhetoric and composition had already taken place in the eighteenth century with rhetoricians such as Hugh Blair and George Campbell. Bain did nothing but follow this tradition, basing his theories on faculty psychology and on the primary laws of associationist psychology.[33] Nonetheless, Bain's definition of human thought as being the result of the three intellectual properties of discrimination, retentiveness, and agreement can be considered a distinctive trait of his work. Bain maintained that such properties constituted the basic activities through which humans perceive and understand reality. These features operated through the principles of contrast, contiguity, and similarity. Bain proposed that these properties could be employed as parameters on which to base a new classification of figures. Thus he placed figures such as antithesis under the property of discrimination; metonymy and synecdoche under that of retentiveness; and metaphor and simile under that of agreement.[34]

Bain's *English Composition and Rhetoric* was extremely influential not only in Great Britain, but also in North America. In a 1973 article, Ned A. Shearer quoted a doctoral dissertation by Harold M. Jordan that stated that Bain's book was used, in the last decades of the nineteenth century, at more than twenty institutions, including Harvard, Cornell, Northwestern, and Brown.[35] As will be discussed in this book, Bain's work also played a crucial role in the development of rhetoric in Japan. Kikuchi Dairoku's translation, *Shūji oyobi kabun* (Rhetoric and belles lettres, 1879), the first work to address rhetoric as a field concerned with literature and literary criticism, largely drew upon Bain's work, and several leading literary figures such as Tsubouchi Shōyō often made mention of it.

Two other important works of the time are Adams Sherman Hill's *The Principles of Rhetoric and Their Application,* first published in 1878, and John Franklin Genung's *The Practical Elements of Rhetoric,* published in 1886.

Hill was the fifth Boylston Professor of Rhetoric and Oratory at Harvard, a position he occupied from 1876 to 1904. A Harvard graduate and practicing journalist, Hill put much emphasis on style, grammatical purity, and word order. His book "became one of a few . . . which shaped early twentieth century perceptions of what the study of rhetoric should be."[36] Indeed, this work, translated in Japan by Sassa Masakazu (Seisetsu) in 1901, epitomized the changes that had taken place over the century. When the professorship was established in 1806, rhetoric was still largely concerned with oratory, but by the time Hill retired, its focus was only on written discourse. The term "rhetoric" fell out of fashion, and the discipline often came to be referred to as composition, in some cases becoming absorbed into English departments. Ronald Reid notes that the first three Boylston professors (i.e., John Quincy Adams, Joseph McKean, and Edward T. Channing) taught "in an age when almost every student was destined for one of two professions—the ministry or law, both of which involved the practice of public speaking. But the new trends . . . brought budding chemists and physicians, engineers and technicians, businessmen and administrators, scholars and poets to the university. Many of these students would never give a speech in their lives."[37] This emphasis on writing rather than oration deeply affected the Japanese perception of rhetoric at the very end of the nineteenth century, leading to the publication of an increasing number of rhetorical treatises that focused on composition and largely ignored public speaking.

Genung (1850–1919) studied in Germany and taught at Amherst College. His *The Practical Elements of Rhetoric* was "another of the late nineteenth-century texts that greatly influenced the teaching of composition in American schools in the early twentieth century."[38] Like most of his contemporaries, Genung did not discuss delivery in his work, which had now come to be an independent field of study as a result of the elocutionary movement.[39] He also put much emphasis on style and the appropriate use of language. A synthesis of classical rhetoric via eighteenth-century belletristic and epistemologic theories, *The Practical Elements of Rhetoric* was widely read in Japan; both Fuzanbō's *Bunshō soshikihō* (Principles of organization in composition, 1892) and Takeshima Hagoromo's *Shūjigaku* (Rhetoric, 1898) drew largely upon this work.

One last work widely cited by Japanese researchers was George Payn Quackenbos' *Advanced Course in Composition and Rhetoric,* first published in 1854. Intended for use in the study of rhetoric in both schools and colleges, this was one of the most well known textbooks of nineteenth-century American rhetoric. Quackenbos belonged to that generation of scholars still largely indebted to the British rhetoricians, and for this reason, perhaps, Alfred Kitzhaber did not include him in his list of the "big four," which included, by contrast, Hill and Genung.[40] Nonetheless, *Advanced Course in Composition and Rhetoric* was one of the first books to be available to the Japanese readership and thus played an important role in introducing Western rhetoric to Japan. It figured, together with Bain's *English Composition and Rhetoric,* in *A Select List of General Works, Comprising English, French and German, Imported and Published and Stationary, Z. P. Maruya & Co.* of 1883, the oldest extant catalogue of foreign books published by Maruzen.[41]

At the end of the nineteenth century, rhetoric appeared as an old and crystallized system of rules. However, developments took place in the twentieth century that revived interest in its study. For example, in 1936 British scholar Ivor A. Richards opened his *The Philosophy of Rhetoric* by suggesting that rhetoric "should be a study of misunderstanding and its remedies."[42] Two decades later, Belgian philosopher Chaïm Perelman reexamined the question of persuasion and elaborated a theory of argumentation that put renewed emphasis on discursive techniques and the adaptation of the message to the audience.[43] Other scholars, such as those who converged in the so-called Group μ of Liège, developed a rhetorical theory that focused on the taxonomy of figures and that attempted "to set forth the basic principles by which all figures of language and thought are derived and can be described."[44] This latter approach implicitly meant an increased narrowing of the scope of rhetoric to the canon of elocution, something that has been strongly criticized by some.[45]

It is, however, this interest in figures that has characterized recent Japanese scholarship in the field. Several works have been published that discuss metaphor, metonymy, and synecdoche and the mechanisms regulating the creation and employment of tropes in various types of discourse.[46] Such a renewed attention to rhetoric has nonetheless not yet led to a reassessment of the impact the discipline had at the time of its introduction to Japan. A handful of significant studies have appeared, but these do not fully address the relationship between rhetoric and the important events that took place in the Meiji and Taishō eras, such as the spread of public speaking and the formation of a modern literary language.[47] The influence that rhetoric had on these and other consequential issues is the object of this book.

2

Japanese Rhetorical Tradition Prior to the Meiji Era

> It is important to note at once that rhetoric is an entirely Western phenom-
> enon. As far as one can judge from surviving evidence, the Greeks were the
> only people of the ancient world who endeavored to analyze the ways in
> which human beings communicate with each other. There is no evidence
> of an interest in rhetoric in the ancient civilizations of Babylon or Egypt,
> for instance. Neither Africa nor Asia has to this day produced a rhetoric.
> —James Murphy, *A Synoptic History of Classical Rhetoric*

Renowned scholar of rhetoric James Murphy could not have been any closer to or further from the truth. Indeed, the issue of whether the Japanese, for example, had an interest in rhetoric prior to the Meiji period is a controversial one that has no easy answer. Certainly the question has begun to attract the attention of scholars in recent years. Studies in contrastive and comparative rhetoric have sought to address the existence of a rhetorical tradition in civilizations other than the Greek and the Roman, suggesting the possibility that rhetorical systems might exist that reflect the way other civilizations think and communicate. Comparative rhetoric, in particular, is, according to George Kennedy, "the cross-cultural study of rhetorical traditions as they exist or have existed in different societies around the world."[1] It has at least four objectives: the identification of distinctive features in different rhetorical traditions; the formulation of a general theory of rhetoric that will apply to all societies; the development of test structures and terminology that can be employed to describe rhetorical practices cross-culturally; and the application of the knowledge thus gained to cross-cultural communication.

One of the major methodological concerns for this type of investigation is the risk of employing Western concepts and categories to describe rhetorical practices in non-Western cultures that have not developed an extensive terminological repertoire in the field. The definition of rhetoric as the art of persuasive speech or elegant writing could also be a reductive one, because it would confine the sphere of rhetorical signification to these types of communicative acts. Yet, as Kennedy points out, if one considers rhetoric in a broader sense as being, for example, the art of effective expression, then it becomes evident that traces of rhetorical and metarhetorical discourse can be found in any type of civilization.

A few works have thus sought to identify the existence of a rhetorical tradition in Japan. These, however, have so far originated from outside the field of Japanese literary studies. They have emerged from the field of rhetoric itself, where, due to the increased interest in intercultural contact, steps have been taken to investigate the process by which different cultures conceive and practice rhetorical communication. Michael J. Day's *"Aimai no ronri:* The Logic of Ambiguity" is perhaps one of the most representative efforts in this field.[2] His work is extremely indicative of the present state of scholarship on the subject; at the beginning of his doctoral research, the author realized that "nothing of any length on Japanese rhetoric in English" was available, and "although many books have been published on differences in communicative styles between the U.S. and Japan, most lack academic rigor in that they fail to give much of the historical, cultural, and psychological background of discourse practices."[3]

Much to his credit, Day postulates the possibility of the existence of a rhetorical tradition in Japan, a tradition deeply rooted in the country's religious, philosophical, and ethical heritage. He also partially dismisses the opinion of those who had previously described Japan as a "rhetorical vacuum." According to John Morrison, "a rhetorical vacuum did exist in Japan prior to the 1950s; the art of persuasion apparently has had no tradition in Japan as in the West." Morrison recounts how "[i]n 1950, President Martin Clark of Osaka Bible Seminary proposed a basic speech course for the seminary but could not find one speech text written in Japanese, whereupon he adapted a classic American text to his needs" and affirms that "some 1350 years of recorded history up to and roughly including World War II evidence no rhetorical tradition."[4] As will become evident from this book, Morrison's article clearly overlooks not only the existence of a substantial native tradition of oral arts, but also the large number of treatises and manuals of oratory published in Japan throughout the Meiji and Taishō periods.

While *"Aimai no ronri"* and similar studies are commendable and effective attempts to draw the attention of rhetoricians to non-Western rhetorical traditions such as that of Japan, they also suffer from a deficiency that drastically limits the scope of their undertaking. These studies rely almost exclusively on English secondary sources, drawing at most from Japanese scholars such as Satō Nobuo who while responsible for the renewed interest in rhetoric seen in Japan in the last thirty years have focused mainly on rhetorical issues of Western origin rather than the rediscovery of native rhetorical practice.[5] These studies also do not seem to consider that early classical Japanese poetry already shows substantial evidence of a refined linguistic and aesthetic awareness, an awareness reflected in an established repertoire of poetic forms and rhetorical techniques that are distinct traits of classical Japanese literary production. Furthermore, these studies overlook the vast amount of scholarly production in the field of rhetoric that took place during the Meiji period, thus losing an important interlocutor in their search for native practices of rhetorical communication.

Interestingly, Western scholars have not been the only ones to disregard Japanese native interest in rhetoric. Leading Meiji Japanese rhetoricians themselves dismissed the quality and relevance of Japan's premodern rhetorical tradition. Shimamura Hōgetsu argued that no tradition of rhetorical study existed except for a few treatises on *waka* and haiku poetry and the works by such Confucian scholars as Ogyū Sorai (1666–1728), Rai San'yō (1780–1832), and Saitō Setsudō (1797–1865). Likewise, Igarashi Chikara indicated Kūkai's *Bunkyō hifuron* (Secret treasury of poetic mirrors, 819) as the only work worth mentioning and maintained that, as far as prose was concerned, only during the Edo period (1600–1868) could one see significant works by such scholars as Kamo no Mabuchi (1697–1769), Motoori Norinaga (1730–1801), Tachibana Chikage (1735–1808), and Ban Kōkei (1733–1806). A few years later, Sassa Masakazu confirmed this view and, addressing the question of composition, criticized scholars of Japanese studies for having traditionally considered prose a mere appendix of poetry.[6] Apart from these few but authoritative claims, not much was said about pre-Meiji interest in rhetoric, and it was common practice to regard the Meiji period as the beginning of rhetorical studies in Japan.

The same can be said for oratory. As will be discussed in chapter 3, the leading role played by educator Fukuzawa Yukichi in spurring interest in the art of speech during the early Meiji years reinforced the widespread notion that Japan did not have a tradition of public speaking prior to the Meiji era. Several factors were understood as the causes for such an extensive disregard for public speaking. In the 1880s renowned orator Baba Tatsui wrote that the political life of the nation had always been determined by the art of war rather than the art of speech. According to political activist Shiroyama Seiichi, formal education in

Japan had given priority to written rather than spoken language, resulting in a disregard for oral communication.[7] Diet representative Komuro Shigehiro observed that East Asian culture had always placed a negative connotation on the practice of oratory, and religious leader Katō Totsudō argued that communication in Japanese cultural history had never taken the form of speech making, but had instead been limited to individual conversations *(danwa)*.[8]

As will be discussed below, the Japanese were not totally indifferent to speech making or to rhetorical sophistication in writing; on the contrary, they had a remarkable tradition in the study of the effective use of language, both in the oral and written domain. However, the absence of a system of study in the field prompted the Meiji community of language and literature scholars to regard such a tradition as peripheral to the rising interest in rhetorical science that followed the Meiji Restoration. Today, many concur regarding the presence of a substantial tradition in rhetorical inquiry in pre-Meiji Japan, albeit mostly limited to Chinese and native poetics.[9] In fact, as Linda Chance has rightly observed in her study on Kenkō's *Tsurezuregusa* (Essays in idleness),

> As far as we take rhetoric to mean the artful use of complex language, Japanese literature is filled with it, and modern critics can make a habit of talking about little else. Insofar as it means communication through words, it is a basic element in waka, which after all frequently accompanied letters and were intended to produce real results in readers, such as capitulation to a seduction, or even just a letter in response. . . . The denial of rhetoric in the zuihitsu form and in other general discussions of the Japaneseness of Japanese literature was thus always an aberration strangely at odds with the bulk of what the literary tradition had to say about itself.[10]

Indeed, one can find examples of rhetorical inquiry as early as the Heian period (794–1185), a thousand years before the arrival of Western rhetoric. Among the works written in *kanbun* (Sino-Japanese style) is Kūkai's *Bunkyō hifuron*. A collection of excerpts from Six Dynasties and T'ang poetic treatises, *Bunkyō hifuron* was completed in A.D. 819. As Richard Bodman explains, only very few of its sections "are directly attributable to Kūkai's authorship. His major role in compiling it was to edit and rearrange the material and to provide it with suitable headings. While he sometimes included complete Chinese works in the text, in many cases he would divide an original work into pieces which would be scattered under a number of headings."[11] *Bunkyō hifuron* was divided into six sections that covered a variety of topics, including a treatment of Chinese tones and rhymes, guidelines on the composition of couplets and the prosodic errors to be avoided, and a discussion of literary theory.[12] Thus, for example, the book titled "Heaven" discussed the harmonization of tones in poetry and distinguished and discussed seven kinds of rhyme, while the book titled "West" identified and discussed twenty-eight kinds of fault in poetry.

Some sections of the work were distinctively the product of Kūkai's own research. In the book "West," which discussed the faults in poetry, Kūkai claimed the originality of his contribution. He observed that there had already been many studies by Chinese scholars on tonal arrangement, and names of faults and errors appeared copiously in treatises. For example, "each expert set his own standards, each man defined his own faults; they merely competed for literary laurels and in vain devoted themselves to restrictions." The existence of such a large number of terms and definitions made, in some cases, "the reader doubt, and cause[d] the researcher much weariness. Now I have edited out this profusion and rewritten it concisely."[13]

Overall, *Bunkyō hifuron* was a manual for the composition of *kanshi* (Chinese poetry). *Sakumon daitai* (Basics of composition, ca. 1108), written by poet and bureaucrat Fujiwara no Munetada (1062–1141), was also a manual compiled for this purpose. It provided, for example, a detailed analysis of various aspects of *kanshi,* including a set of rules for the use of tone patterns within a poem. Ivo Smits summarizes its list of the "eight diseases," or faults, to be avoided, as follows.

1. The first two characters of the first and last couplets should not both start with a level tone ("Level Head Disease").
2. The last characters of two consecutive lines should not have the same tone ("Raised Tail Disease").
3. The second and fourth character of the same couplet should not both have a level tone ("Wasp's Waist Disease").
4. The second character of the first couplet and the fourth of the last should not both have a level tone ("Crane's Knee Disease").
5. A couplet should not end with three characters that all have the same tone.
6. One should not use two characters with the same meaning.
7. One should not wrongly use similar rhyme.
8. One should not use either too many or too few characters in a couplet.[14]

Smits indicates that Munetada also provided detailed explanations on technical aspects of certain poetic concepts, such as the methods of incorporating the verse-topic into the first couplet of the poem. He also notes that *Sakumon daitai* distinguished eight styles of incorporating a verse-topic, which were, however, not fully explained.[15]

Other works that followed included, for example, anthologies such as the

Honchō mudaishi (Non-topic poems of our court), a Japanese compilation of Chinese poetry assembled in 1164.[16] By this time, however, several works of poetics had already been written in Japanese. Among them, *Kakyō hyōshiki* (A formulary for verse based on the canons of poetry), written by bureaucrat and critic Fujiwara no Hamanari (724–790) in 772, is considered "the oldest extant piece of poetic criticism in the Japanese canon," although "it was evidently not the first."[17] As Judith Rabinovitch indicates, although influenced by Chinese poetics, *Kakyō hyōshiki* was an attempt to revitalize Japanese verse through the application of rules derived from the Chinese poetic tradition, partly modified and revised. The work, a general discussion of problems of rhyme and euphony, began with the following passage, where Hamanari clearly differentiated the art of poetry from the act of ordinary speech, arguing for the need of providing rules for poetic composition.

> Your subject, Hamanari, wishes to observe that poetry in origin is that which stirs the innermost feelings of spiritual beings and soothes the amorous hearts of men and gods. Rhyming verse differs from common speech in its capacity to inspire feelings of pleasure. . . . In recent times, poets have shown excellence in versification, but they seem to know nothing about the use of rhyme. While their verses may bring pleasure to the reader they have no knowledge of "poetic defects." When compared to the poetry of high antiquity, that of recent times possesses none of the grace of spring flowers, nor is it imbued with the flavor of autumn fruit to be savored by future generations. How can poetry stir the feelings and soothe the hearts of men and gods if it is not written in the Six [Chinese] Modes?[18]

The introduction was then followed by a discussion of seven kinds of poetic defects or faults. This section has been seen as deeply indebted to the well-known four tones and eight defects of the Chinese tradition, but according to Rabinovitch, Hamanari's poetic defects were concerned with two problems of a different nature: "(1) the excessive repetition of what Hamanari termed the 'basic rhyme syllable' in *tanka,* that is, the last syllable of line three, the first of two rhyme syllables, and (2) the repetition or overuse of other sounds, that is, any single vowel or the consonant-vowel syllable."[19] The seven poetic faults discussed by Hamanari are as follows.

1. Head-Tail defect: the final syllables of the first and second lines must not be the same sound.
2. Chest-Tail defect: the final syllable of the first line and the third and/or sixth syllable of the second line must not be of the same sound.

3. Waist-Tail defect: the final syllable of any line must not be the same sound as the basic rhyme syllable.

4. Mole defect: none of the five lines should contain a syllable having the same sound as the basic rhyme syllable.

5. Wandering Wind defect: this fault results when the second syllable of any given line is the same sound as the final syllable in that line.

6. Same-Sounding Rhyme defect: this fault occurs when the two rhyming syllables are identical.

7. Whole Body defect: there must not be two or more identical sounds anywhere in the poem, excluding from consideration the [sound used as the] basic rhyme syllable, which is one of two rhyme syllables.[20]

Another major feature of *Kakyō hyōshiki* is the discussion of poetic styles. Hamanari classified styles into three categories that included a variety of stylistic and rhetorical items, ranging from rhyme to structural irregularities. Thus the first category, "the implementation of rhyme," comprised two kinds of rhyme, "coarse rhyme and fine rhyme"; the second category, "irregular forms," consisted of seven kinds of verse; while the third category, "miscellaneous forms and styles," included ten types of verse, among which *tanka* (the short poem) and *chōka* (the long poem) were discussed. References made to figures of speech throughout the text demonstrated Hamanari's interest in the use of figurative language.

Also of extreme importance at this time was the *Kokinshū* or *Kokin wakashū* (A collection of ancient and modern poems). The first of twenty-one anthologies of classical Japanese poetry, likely composed circa 905, the *Kokinshū* consisted of 1,111 poems, divided and arranged thematically in twenty books. The collection was preceded by two prefaces, one in Japanese (called *kanajo*) by Ki no Tsurayuki and the other in Chinese (called *manajo*) attributed to Ki no Yoshimochi. The former is regarded by many as a milestone in the development of Japanese poetics, a text heavily responsible for the codification of a literary aesthetic that would deeply affect poetic production for centuries to come. In the preface, Tsurayuki (ca. 872–945) described the origin of Japanese poetry.

> The seeds of Japanese poetry lie in the human heart and grow into leaves of ten thousand words. Many things happen to the people of this world, and all they think and feel is given expression in description of things they see and hear. . . . It is poetry which, without effort, moves heaven and earth, stirs the feelings of the invisible gods and spirits, smoothes the relations of men and women, and calms the hearts of fierce warriors. . . . In the age of the awesome gods, songs did not have a fixed number of syllables and were difficult to understand because the poets expressed themselves

directly, without polish. By the time of the age of humans, beginning with Susano-o no mikoto, poems of thirty-one syllables were composed.[21]

After attributing to poetry the power to stir emotions in the human heart, Tsurayuki stated that there were six poetic principles, namely Suasive, Description, Comparison, Evocative Imagery, Elegantia, and Eulogies, for which he provided examples followed by brief explanations.[22] Then, after denouncing the state of decline of poetry, he reiterated in the final section of his preface its eternal value, sanctioning the authority and prestige of past literary giants such as Kakinomoto no Hitomaro and urging the new generation of poets to pursue novelty and originality.

> Hitomaro is dead, but poetry is still with us. Times may change, joy and sorrow come and go, but the words of these poems are eternal, endless as the green willow threads, unchanging as the needles of the pine, long as the trailing vines, permanent as birds' tracks. Those who know poetry and who understand the heart of things will look up to the old and admire the new as they look up to and admire the moon in the broad sky.[23]

Crucial to Tsurayuki's opening passage was the introduction of terms such as *"kokoro"* (heart), *"kotoba"* (words), and, later, *"sama"* (principle or style). The first two terms, in particular, constitute in Laurel Rasplica Rodd's view "the central value in Tsurayuki's poetic ideal, an ideal that was taken up and elaborated by his contemporaries and successors . . . a strong sense of decorous elegance which involved an emphasis on style, a proper poetic diction, an accepted range of forms and themes and virtuosity."[24] After a period that saw the predominance of Chinese poetics, Tsurayuki sought to elevate the status of Japanese poetry by providing an enduring aesthetic and a rhetorical canon that would constitute a model by which every poet would have to be measured. *Kokinshū* displayed a strong concern for the use of rhetorical devices as demonstrated by studies that have recently analyzed the occurrence of rhetorical figures such as *makurakotoba* (pillow word, a fixed epithet usually attached to certain nouns), *kakekotoba* (pivot word, a pun involving one word employed with two different meanings), and *utamakura* (names of famous places usually associated with poetry).[25]

The importance of this collection, however, is not limited to the emphasis on rhetorical skills and diction. As a text, its preface

> reveals the emergence of a critical consciousness, as distinguished from the earlier birth of literary awareness; it is an attempt to create a theory and prescribe a practice

for Japanese poetry that would entitle it once again to social acceptance, this time as an art on a level with Chinese poetry. The effort appears to have entailed an insistence upon an established poetic language with the prestige of tradition, and a channeling of individual expression to important but subtle adjustments of the relation between the originality of the individual poet and the conventionality of his prescribed materials.[26]

Fostering the rise of such a new critical consciousness, Tsurayuki contributed to the canonization of a repertoire of lexical and thematic forms that constituted the foundation of a new aesthetic and poetic standard. Thus "from the time of this anthology the good and the bad in poetry were selected and fixed, so that for the basic elements of poetry one should look only into the *Kokinshū*."[27]

"*Waka* had [thus] come to be dominated by the rules of rhetoric and decorum."[28] While the balance between *kokoro* and *kotoba,* in a broader sense corresponding to the categories of content and form, remained a crucial point in the critical consciousness of the time, aesthetic judgment was based largely on "how well the poet handled his materials and operated within the rules."[29] Any deviation from these rules constituted an infringement of rhetorical canons, which disqualified the poem and its author. As Edward Kamens points out,

> *waka* thrived for centuries after Tsurayuki and his fellow *Kokin wakashū* compilers . . . and so, ipso facto, did *waka* rhetoric. And one of several important factors that insured the long survival of the *waka* tradition was the constancy and durability of *waka* rhetoric, the continuous presence of a communally available repertory of figures.[30]

The years that followed *Kokin wakashū* were characterized by a substantial number of treatises on Japanese poetry. *Shinsen zuinō* (Newly selected poetic essentials, 1004–1012), by poet, critic, and bureaucrat Fujiwara no Kintō (966–1041), is considered one of the most significant works of the period. Displaying a strongly prescriptive character, *Shinsen zuinō* began with a definition of *uta* (poem), directing it to be composed of thirty-one syllables, the first three lines being called "the base" and the last two "the end." Poems resulted from a crucial balance between soul and form; the latter, in particular, "should sound pure and clear, or contain a quality of awesome beauty."[31] The use of *utamakura* was briefly discussed, and Tsurayuki was soon mentioned as one of the great poets of the past. Repetition and homophones were denounced as practices to avoid in the composition of a poem, although "if the poem is really first-rate, it is not necessary to follow these rules."[32] Kintō also warned against the use of rhyme and held that, as a general rule, rough and indistinct words should be used only if the poet had exceptionally fine judgment.

After significant poetic treatises by the poets Minamoto no Shunrai (1055?–1129?) and Fujiwara no Shunzei (1114–1204), who wrote, respectively, *Shunrai zuinō* (Shunrai poetic essentials, ca. 1115) and *Korai fūteishō* (Poetic styles past and present, 1197), the works by Fujiwara no Teika (1162–1241) occupy a place of extreme importance in the history of Japanese literature. Teika should be regarded as one of the most influential figures of the period, since "his various experiments with diction, rhetoric, and figurative language, as well as with new styles, modes and aesthetic effects, were widely imitated by his contemporaries."[33] Teika wrote several treatises, including *Kindai shūka* (Superior poems of our time, 1209), *Maigetsushō* (Monthly notes, 1219), and *Eiga taigai* (General rules of poetic competition, ca. 1222). In *Kindai shūka,* which was, as the title suggests, a collection of outstanding poems of the period, Teika offered a brief introduction concerning the state of poetry, which in his view had significantly declined since the age of Tsurayuki.

> The art of Japanese poetry appears to be shallow but is deep, appears to be easy but is difficult. And the number of people who understand and know about it is not large. Tsurayuki, in ancient times, preferred a style in which the conception of the poem was clever, the loftiness of tone difficult to achieve, the diction strong, and the effect pleasing and tasteful. . . . However, as the times have degenerated, so have people's minds; later poets have not been able to attain Tsurayuki's level, and their diction has grown even more vulgar.[34]

The preface also contained a brief discussion of the device of allusive variation (*honkadori,* additionally discussed by Teika in his *Eiga taigai*).

> The practice of taking the words of an ancient poem and incorporating them into one's own composition without changing them is known as "using a foundation poem." However, I feel that if one uses, say, the second and third lines of such a foundation poem, just as they are, in the first three lines of one's own poem, and then goes on to use the last two lines of it in the same fashion, it will prove impossible to make something that sounds like a new poem. Depending on the style, it may be best to avoid using the first two lines of the foundation poem.[35]

Compared to *Kindai shūka, Maigetsushō* was a much more extensive treatise that included a detailed discussion of language and poetic techniques. Addressing one of his students who had sent him a number of poems for correction and advice, in this work Teika first reestablished the authority of earlier anthologies by suggesting their perusal and the imitation of their styles as a valid means for the acquisition of poetic skills. He cautioned, however, against indiscriminate imitation because "there are words and effects that should not be reproduced under any circumstances. What I mean by these are words that are too close to the common and vulgar usage, or effects that are rough and frightening."[36] He then proceeded to identify the existence of ten different styles, the style of "deep feeling" being by far the most important. Next, he discussed the problem of poetic diction, placing emphasis on the appropriate choice of language.

> Another crucial matter in poetry is the choice of diction, for in language there are strong words and weak, thick ones and thin. It is extremely important in composing your poems that you distinguish carefully among your words and be consistent, following strong words with strong ones, putting weak words together with weak, mulling your composition over again and again so that it is neither too thick nor too thin, but smooth and flowing and pleasing to the ear.[37]

Balance and an appropriate and careful selection of the linguistic materials seemed to be two of the chief concerns in Teika's poetics. Interestingly, Teika believed that "there are no words that are intrinsically good or bad. Rather, it is from the effect of words when put together that such distinctions arise in poetic diction."[38] The beauty of the expression was thus not exclusively determined by a preexisting canon of privileged forms; the poet, through his skill and aesthetic sensitivity, could adorn the expression and thus mold the form through his own imagery. Nonetheless, Teika noted that

> one thing that is absolutely unacceptable in poetry is a self-consciously fancy verse. An ornate verse that just happens to come about of itself as a person is composing a number of poems may be allowed to pass, perhaps, but precious verses consciously contrived in a desperate effort to sound clever and original are extremely ugly and distasteful.[39]

Teika proceeded to discuss the method of using a foundation poem and sketched rhetorical guidelines that included prescriptions against the well-known poetic diseases, and the rhyming of syllables. On repetition, in particular, Teika stated that "it is permissible to use quite ordinary words over again many times, but in the case of unusual expressions that strike the ear, even though they may not be very long, it is quite unpleasant when phrases of two or three words are repeated many times over."[40] Finally, he suggested that a student should compose in the style most appropriate to him and not the one deemed best by his teacher, a statement that is proof of Teika's belief in the merits of individual or unique expression.

The son of Teika, Fujiwara no Tameie (1198–1275), also contributed significantly to the poetics of the period. His *Eiga no Ittei* (The foremost style of poetic composition, 1274) "enjoyed a much wider popularity and exerted a far greater influence on the development of Japanese classical poetry than other writings—Teika's *Maigetsushō*, for example—that today are recognized as the seminal works of traditional Japanese poetics."[41] Robert H. Brower indicates that Tameie's work was especially important for its characteristic treatment of the poetic practice of borrowing expressions from other poems. This practice, as seen above, had already been discussed by Teika, who had cautioned against its overuse. Tameie went even further in providing a list of expressions used by earlier poets whose borrowing was to be categorically avoided.

In an opening passage that reflected the didactical and prescriptive nature of his work, Tameie emphasized that practice was essential if one wanted to become a skilled poet.

> The composition of poetry does not necessarily depend upon talent and learning. However, although it has been said that poetry comes from the heart, without practice it is impossible to gain a reputation for skill. . . . First you must learn certain essential matters and then give expression to your own thoughts and feelings in each of your poems.[42]

Next, he proceeded to discuss a wide range of stylistic and rhetorical issues that included a treatment of topics, styles, and poetic configuration; the use of associated words and extra syllables; and the practice of repetition, poetic diction, and the rhetorical device of *honkadori*. Thus, for example, discussing the desirability of associated words, Tameie observed that "poems without such related words are poor. On the other hand, plainness and simplicity are also good. It is bad to try to exhaust the supply of associated words by cramming as many as possible into the poem." Touching on the use of extra syllables, he stated that "it is bad to make a point of adding extra syllables to a line when there is no particular need for them and your purpose might have been accomplished quite easily without exceeding the usual number." On the problem of repetition, he affirmed that "the unnecessary repetition of words and phrases is absolutely to be avoided," while in the section regarding poetic diction he maintained that "to employ a word or phrase that is no longer used in poems today on the excuse that it is in one of the old collections would surely subject you to derision."[43]

As my brief summary has thus shown, Japanese poets and critics of the classical period already shared a profound interest in rhetoric—that is, the process of communicating effectively and in a polished manner. The existence of a canonized poetic vocabulary; the employment of and continued reference to a codified corpus of figurative language; the didactic and prescriptive nature of some of the treatises; the existence of a significant metapoetic and metarhetorical discourse that addressed language and its use—these and other elements are proof of a highly developed critical consciousness and awareness of the power residing in the skilled use of the linguistic material.

This awareness was not an exclusive product of the era; it was already alive in the preceding period, the early classical age, the epoch of the *Manyōshū* (Collection of ten thousand leaves), a poetic stage characterized by abundant use of parallelisms, pivot-word associations, and a lyricism that defined rhetorical signification as a distinctive trait of that period.[44] At the same time, as Robert Brower and Earl Miner also indicate, the midclassical period, of which some representative works have been briefly discussed here, also had its own rhetoric. This was a time when poets and critics were able to capitalize on the inherited rhetorical and aesthetic sensitivity and give further impetus to their poetic creativity. Ultimately, as Amagasaki Akira has recently noted, for poets such as Tsurayuki the main concern was "through what type of rhetoric to express the thoughts harboring in one's heart."[45]

The works that appeared after the thirteenth century were mostly treatises on Chinese and Japanese poetics. It is not until the late Edo period that one begins to finally see the appearance of a few studies dealing with native prose.[46] *Kuni tsu fumi yoyo no ato* (Traces of generations of national literature, 1777) is generally thought to be the first work of this kind. The author, Ban Kōkei, provided the first historical overview of the development of native prose styles. He divided the classical period into three different phases, each characterized by distinct stylistic traits. To begin with, he identified *norito* (Shinto prayers) as representative of the archaic style of the first period. He then proceeded to recognize such masterpieces as *Tosa nikki* (The Tosa diary), *Ise monogatari* (The tale of Ise), and *Genji monogatari* (The tale of Genji) as models of the midclassical style of the second period. The third period, which in his view already contained premodern stylistic traits, included a wide range of texts that spanned the writings of Minamoto no Shunrai to those of Keichū (1640–1701) and Kamo no Mabuchi. *Kuni tsu fumi yoyo no ato* denounced the scarce attention paid to composition by Edo scholars of national language and literature, who devoted most of their time to the study of grammar and classical language.

Bunshō senkaku (Select models of composition) by Tachibana Moribe (1781–1849) was another important work of the period. Compiled in 1819 and posthumously published in 1886, it was the third of a three-volume treatise that included studies of *chōka* and *tanka*. According to Suzuki Kazuhiko, Moribe's research was extremely innovative in that it drew attention to a variety of new topics at a time when scholars, as mentioned above, were mostly concerned with word conjugations, particles, and the meaning of archaic words. Among such new items introduced by Moribe, Suzuki describes the treatment of the historical transition of prose writing; the analysis of archaic, classical, and pre-modern styles; the discussion of a number of rhetorical devices other than repetition and parallelism; and the attempt to provide a standard to differentiate good writing from bad.[47] Moribe should also be acknowledged for emphasizing the existence of obvious but crucial differences between poetry and prose. Prose, he noted, did not follow the five-seven syllabic pattern, and devices such as *makurakotoba* and parallelism were not as common as in poetry. Further, he claimed, prose was originally written in the spoken language and was innately refined from a rhetorical standpoint. This refinement, however, had gradually faded, and by the time of the *Kokinshū,* language had lost its original elegance.[48]

Other works that appeared during the Edo period include, for example, *Shōsoku bunrei* (Models of epistolary style, 1799) and *Bun no shirube* (An introduction to writing, 1826), both by scholar Fujii Takanao (1764–1840). Works by scholars of Chinese prose and poetry such as Itō Jinsai (1627–1705), Ogyū Sorai, and Saitō Setsudō also appeared. Equally important—albeit not necessarily works of rhetoric—were the writings of scholars such as Motoori Norinaga and Kamo no Mabuchi.

As for the oral dimension of rhetoric, Buddhist sermon preaching and a long history of the study and practice of oral arts such as *rakugo* (comic storytelling), *kōdan* (lectures), and *rōkyoku* (chanting of ancient tales) offer examples of a significant tradition of oratory in the pre-Meiji years. However, as many have noted, East Asian culture has not put much emphasis on eloquence. Instances in which "being eloquent" does not carry with it a positive connotation can be found widely, including in renowned literary texts.

> It is desirable that a man's face and figure be of excelling beauty. I could sit forever with a man, provided that what he said did not grate on my ears, that he had charm, and that he did not talk very much.[49]

In the Meiji era, the existence of proverbs such as *"shaberi jōzu no saiku heta"* (clever talk, limited accomplishment) and *"kuchi to saifu wa shimeru ga toku"* (mouths and purses are best kept shut) were held to attest to a general atmosphere of mistrust of speaking in public.[50] As one writer put it in 1910, "the Japanese have always been indifferent towards speech making, and as a result they have become the poorest [among peoples] at speaking."[51]

Nonetheless, the presence of a consistent body of Japanese verbal communication conventions cannot be denied. In fact, in recent years a crucial link has been established between Buddhist preaching and the development of oral arts such as those mentioned above, owing mainly to the extensive scholarship by Sekiyama Kazuo. In one of his major works, Sekiyama has indicated that while the original purpose of sermon preaching was to explain the sutras and dogmas of Buddhism to the people, the practice gradually came to display strong artistic and literary traits, giving birth to distinct popular narrative forms such as *setsuwa* (tales). These *setsuwa* can be regarded as the prototype of *rakugo*. However, of even greater relevance to this volume is Sekiyama's indication that effective preaching was strongly contingent on the speaker's skillful use of voice, melody, and intonation. Sekiyama holds that in order to persuade the audience, preachers developed special speaking techniques that included the use of gestures and body language in general, but also the employment of metaphors, parables, and karma tales. In his words, "sermon preaching studied and established the most suitable way of speaking to the Japanese people."[52]

Based on Sekiyama's new findings, recent scholarship on Japanese oral arts has begun to give a renewed emphasis to the importance of sermon preaching. In their study of *rakugo*, Heinz Morioka and Miyoko Sasaki, for example, provide a short summary of the development of Buddhist sermon preaching in Japan. The authors indicate how, already in the Asuka period (593–710), detailed sermon techniques had been introduced through the sutra collections with commentaries of the *Sanrin seppō* (The three-wheel sermons) and the *Jūnibunkyō* (Twelve great sutras). At the time, the art of preaching included "various voice variations (*shiben hachion*, '4 modulations of fluency, 8 pitches') and the presentation of parables and karma tales."[53] Morioka and Sasaki also mention Buddhist priest Ryō Kōsō (502–557), thought to have brought the Chinese oratorical art to Japan; according to him, they note, *shō* (voice), *ben* (modulation in fluency), *sai* (talent), and *haku* (knowledge) were essential for persuasive speaking.

Later centuries saw the increased secularization of sermon preaching. The Kamakura period (1185–1333), in particular, saw the establishment of two schools, the Agui and the Miidera, which according to Sekiyama developed preaching styles that not only profoundly affected subsequent preaching, but also influenced other forms of oratory, even recent discourse.

Sekiyama identified five steps in sermon organization characteristic of the Agui school, which had Chōken (1125–1203) and his son Seikaku (1167–1235) among its most prominent members. These steps are *sandai* (introduction), *hōsetsu* (explication), *hiyu* (metaphor), *innen* (karmic tales), and *kekkan* (conclusion). While this five-step configuration is already reminiscent of the precepts involved in the organization of a speech in the Western rhetorical tradition, one scholar has argued that in fact significant similarities with Western rhetoric can be found not only in this type of sermon organization, but in the whole process that governed the practice of preaching. In "Buddhist Preaching: The Persistent Main Undercurrent of Japanese Traditional Rhetorical Communication," Satoshi Ishii argues that preachers of this school developed a principle of subject choice, based on human destiny and the transmigration of body and soul, that closely resembled the Western canon of invention. Ishii also sees the above five-step sermon organization as equivalent to the Western canon of disposition where the materials are carefully arranged. Elocution, or the choice of language and style, is also in his view clearly distinguishable in this type of sermon preaching, since "Agui preaching is audience-centered, stressing the listeners' understanding and emotional acceptance of the sermons. Consequently, one of the preachers' main tasks was to choose simple common words and phrases to explain difficult Buddhist terms and thoughts."[54]

At the same time, Ishii notes, preachers memorized and employed a variety of metaphors and puns that were intended to attract the attention of the audience. Finally, the precepts set forth regarding delivery and memory, the fourth and fifth canons of Western rhetoric, are also discernible, according to Ishii, in the practice of Buddhist preaching. Preachers were trained to improve and refine their voice and facial expressions and to memorize the subjects, ideas, and topics to use in their sermons.

Overall, many sources provide evidence of the importance of sermon preaching throughout the history of Japan's social and cultural history. Renowned scholar of Japanese literature Konishi Jin'ichi quotes from Zen monk Kokan Shiren (1278–1346), who complained about the increased secularization of preaching. The following passage indirectly shows the importance of skilled preaching, which has the power to move the hearts of the people.

> Because good preaching presents difficult philosophical systems in easily understood terms, enlightens and instructs us on several levels, moves countless people, and clears paths on which we would otherwise stumble, its effects are wide-ranging and its influence splendid. Nothing is more beneficent than preaching. Unfortunately, as soon as a monk begins to reap financial gain from his sermons, he is likely to forsake the pursuit of truth. . . . [Preachers] today speak only of what interests their audience. They put on odd performances, shaking their heads and bodies and making their voices sound seductive. Although their sermons are replete with parallelism, the

content is either maudlin or laudatory. The sponsor of the service is always mentioned, together with a guarantee that he or she will be enriched by the Buddha. Preachers make such strong appeals to the emotions that they are often quicker than the audience to weep at their own anecdotes. How shameful it is that the transmission of pure Truth has become degraded to an art practiced by deceitful actors![55]

More recent Japanese cultural history also provides evidence of the central role played by preaching and the art of oratory in general. In her study on Shingaku, "a system for cultivating the mind that became popular in the less-educated sectors of Tokugawa society," Janine Anderson Sawada makes frequent references to instances that show the social importance of certain forms of oratory in premodern Japan.[56] Writing on Tokugawa Japan, Anderson Sawada mentions the expansion of travel and the growing role of itinerant speaking, whether represented by preacher or storytellers. Among such itinerant speakers, she notes, were, for example, Shingaku preacher Nakazawa Dōni (1725–1803), known for his oratory skills, or new Shinto preacher Masuho Zankō (1655–1742), whose doctrines were, according to Peter Nosco, "concise and easy to understand, and his ability to communicate his message with such mnemonic devices as enumeration or puns probably made it more palatable to a broad audience of townsmen."[57] As Anderson Sawada explains, Shingaku members learned both through guidance from the master and group study. However, the movement became best known for its *dōwa* (talks on the "Way") that were addressed to the general public. Thus "*dōwa* used a plethora of analogies, metaphors, parables, popular tales, witticisms, Nō verses, and indeed any material that might effectively communicate its message."[58] Nakazawa Dōni was one of the key figures in the development of these talks. As Anderson Sawada concludes in her work, "the success of Shingaku preaching owed much to the rhetorical legacy of Buddhist preachers and storytellers who used idiomatic language and engaging metaphors to convey their teachings to large gatherings. [Ishida] Baigan's followers took advantage of this stylistic heritage to render the learning of the mind more palatable to common people than were Neo-Confucian scholastic presentations."[59]

Buddhist preaching did not fail to impress the first Christian missionaries either. Jesuit Luis Frois (1532–1597), who is said to have had unusual linguistic capabilities and knowledge of the Japanese language, wrote the following.[60]

When the signal was given by ringing a large bell three times, we knew that the preacher had entered and so we went up to the monastery. . . . The preacher was seated in a high chair so that everybody could see him and in front of him there stood a small table on which was placed a book. . . . His soft and mellow voice and the gestures which he made during the sermon were all worthy of note. His method of preaching was to read a passage from the book in front of him and then to explain it with such elegance that Father Gaspar Vilela (who could understand the sermon) and all the others present marvelled at his great skill and technique. We gained no little profit from this outing, as we learnt a great deal about how to preach to the Christians in accordance with their liking and language. Preachers in this country are generally eloquent and educated men and are venerated by the people even to the point of being worshipped in this life.[61]

In the same work, Frois also noted that it

would take too long to recount the disputes, arguments and questions of the hea-
thens here. Anybody fond of arguing has plenty of material here, although the form
of their arguments and their way of proceeding in them are very different from
what we learn in our studies. As many of them, especially the bonzes, are most eloquent in their speech, anybody who did not know about the basic principles on
which their religions are founded, might often well think that both we and they are
preaching the same thing.[62]

From rules for fashioning effective poems to the elements necessary for skilled preaching, it is then clear that Japan had a significant tradition in the study of rhetorical communication even before the Meiji era. For whatever reasons, rhetoricians during the Meiji period downplayed the existence of such a tradition, and so it is valid to consider the arrival of Western rhetoric as an appropriate starting point for the study of rhetorical inquiry in Japan. The existence of this pre-Meiji tradition and the modalities of its development fall outside the scope of this book.

This volume differs from any of the few studies conducted thus far in that it commences from a totally different premise. Rather than addressing the existence of a native rhetorical tradition during the premodern era, which is axiomatic, this book will attempt to assess the consequential impact that Western rhetoric may have had on crucial issues of a literary and linguistic nature during Meiji and Taishō Japan.

PART 2

*History of
Rhetoric*

3
The Golden Age of Oratory

Western rhetoric was first introduced to Japan as a coherent system a few years after the Meiji Restoration. Nishi Amane (1829–1897) introduced the term "rhetoric" to the Japanese intellectual audience by listing it under the entry of literature in his encyclopedic work *Hyakugaku renkan* (Encyclopedia, 1870). Rhetoric is there translated as *bunjigaku* and presented as something pertaining to the realm of both spoken and written language.

> There is an "oral" and a "written" rhetoric. "Oral" refers to spoken communication, while "written" refers to composition. In the West spoken and written language generally coincide, and since the spoken always abides by the rules of grammar, those skilled at speaking also excel at writing, and those that are skilled at writing also excel at speaking. However, our written and spoken language do not coincide at all. . . . Prose and verse, to which I referred earlier, are also part of rhetoric; and since all of today's writing is prose, the study of rhetoric becomes also essential.[1]

According to Nishi, rhetoric had ties both to oral and written communication. He reiterated this concept four years later, when he translated it parenthetically with the term *"bungaku"* as if to emphasize the discipline's close link to the domain of written discourse in general and literature in particular.

> Rhetoric is also called "eloquence" or "oratory." Even though the three are different in name, they are actually the same except that eloquence relates to talent. Oratory and rhetoric follow the same rules, their different names notwithstanding. It is only that oratory is spoken and that rhetoric is written.[2]

Nishi was instrumental in providing a definition of the term "rhetoric" at a time when not much was known about the discipline. Evidence shows, however, that the concept had already been introduced in Japan prior to the Meiji Restoration. A general outline of classical rhetoric can be found, for example, in the *Ra-ho-nichi taiyaku jiten,* also known as the *Dictionarium Latino Lusitanicum ac Iaponicum,* published in Amakusa in 1595. "Rhetoric," "eloquence," and "argument," as well as the five classical canons of rhetoric, are among the items translated and defined in this work. According to Sawada Akio, the fact that this dictionary also included references to Aristotle's *Topica* and Cicero's *De oratore* is indicative that those works had already been introduced to Japan by that time.[3] In fact, Sawada notes how existing literature by early Christian missionaries provides indirect proof that some classical treatises of Western rhetoric were already present in Japan as early as the sixteenth century. Jesuit Alessandro Valignano (1539–1606), for example, mentioned in his *Adiciones del sumario de Japon* (1592) that a collection of Cicero's works had been published in Nagasaki in 1592.[4] References to rhetoric can also be found in *Seiyō kibun* (Tidings of the West, 1715), a treatise drafted by the Confucian scholar Arai Hakuseki (1657–1725) after his interrogations of Roman Catholic missionary Giovanni Battista Sidotti (1668–1714). Other texts and dictionaries published in those years contained references to rhetoric, but these were mostly limited to brief definitions of a handful of terms.[5]

After the Restoration, Nishi's *Hyakugaku renkan* was not the only work to comment on rhetoric. The term appeared, for example, in Obata Jinzaburō's *Seiyō gakkō kihan* (Standards of Western schools, 1870), and it seems that rhetoric was already being taught at South University (Daigaku Nankō), the precursor to Tokyo University.[6] Nonetheless, Nishi's definition was crucial in that it fully reflected the state of the discipline in the West at the end of the nineteenth century, a field of study that had expanded to include literary criticism and covered all types of discourse, whether oral or written, persuasive or nonpersuasive.[7] At the time of its introduction to Japan, rhetoric was thus a discipline that could be applied to both written and oral discourse; paradoxically, this very trait contributed to the separation of the two domains of communication, which were often at odds in the course of rhetoric's history in Japan. The Japanese would in fact alternate in prioritizing one domain over the other, diminishing the possibility of considering and developing a rhetorical theory that addressed both. In the process of assimilating the various theories, they first turned their attention to the realm of oral discourse.

Fukuzawa Yukichi and the Introduction of Oratory

During the early 1870s, Fukuzawa Yukichi (1835–1901) was among the first to address the importance of rhetoric. He was, however, mostly interested in the oral aspect of the discipline. A prominent educator and propagator of Western knowledge, Fukuzawa had an extremely positive view of oratory, which he deemed necessary to help the well-meaning men of his time bring about solutions to urgent social, political, and economic problems. According to tradition, in 1873 he received a Western book on oratory from his associate Koizumi Nobukichi (1849–1894), a book that he later translated under the title *Kaigiben* (A handbook for meetings). The translation was divided into three parts: a preface, instructions on how to hold a conference, and the constitution of the Mita Oratorical Society (Mita Enzetsukai). In the preface, Fukuzawa complained about the lack of a systematic and orderly manner for conducting meetings, whether in the economic, political, or cultural realm.

> From the earliest times in Japan, whenever people have assembled to discuss some problem, nothing could be settled because of the lack of any set rules for discussion. This has always been true whether it is an argument among scholars, a business conference, or a municipal meeting. Unless an affair is organized, time and money will be wasted. Therefore, many things which could have been accomplished were not accomplished. . . . Today scholars claim that they are attempting to spread knowledge throughout the entire country; industrialists and businessmen claim that by forming companies, they are attempting to enrich the country; political speakers claim that by holding popular meetings, they seek to influence national affairs. All these signs of cultural progress are causes for rejoicing. But although the intentions are good, I have, in truth, yet to hear of these plans being accomplished. This is because although people know the importance of these goals, they do not know orderly methods for achieving them. And what is the most important method? It is actually this: a format for group discussion.[8]

The Japanese, Fukuzawa suggested, should take the West as an example and meet to discuss important matters systematically and to gather information. To that end, in *Kaigiben* he provided a summary of the rules and procedures to be followed in formal meetings, from the setting of a meeting agenda to the raising of motions and final deliberations. Hence Nishi Amane and Ōkuma Shigenobu later rewarded Fukuzawa with the title of "the ancestor of public speaking" in Japan.[9]

The view that Fukuzawa was the key figure in the spread of speech making has reinforced the assumption that oratory did not exist in Japan prior to the modern period.[10] As already noted in Part 1 of this volume, the notion that oratory made its first appearance on Japanese soil only after the Meiji Restoration had already gained currency during the first two decades of the Meiji period. This idea had an (unfounded) theoretical justification in the belief that the Japanese language was somehow not suited to public speaking, which accordingly hampered the expansion and practice of the art of speech. Political leader and intellectual Mori

Arinori (1847–1889) is said to have been one of the strongest advocates of this theory, which was in turn vehemently disputed by Fukuzawa, who stated,

> There is not the slightest reason why a person cannot speak before the public while conversing freely in the language of his own country. Furthermore, even in our own country, from ancient times to the present, excellent speeches have been delivered as a matter of custom. Have you not, all your lives, heard sermons by the priests of the temples? If you have never heard a sermon, then surely you have not found the tales of war or the droll stories told in storytellers' halls to be unpleasant. 'Speech' is another name for the methods that a speaker uses whenever he expresses his ideas before a large number of people. Would you say that the storytellers are capable of 'speech' and that we scholars are incapable of it?[11]

The Japanese in the premodern period were not, in fact, totally indifferent toward speech making. Sermons and educational lectures were not uncommon and served as an important form of social communication. Such forms of speech making nevertheless differed significantly in nature from oratory as it had been perceived and defined in the Western tradition.[12] The theoretical discourse on rhetoric in the West had emphasized the importance of persuasion and of formulating plausible and logically coherent arguments while stressing the psychological aspects of the process of communication. The idea of the free exchange of information associated with the notion of public speaking was likewise something new. To see Fukuzawa as the pioneer of oratory in Japan is thus justifiable. For these reasons, it is possible to accept the view that oratory did not constitute a relevant social aspect in Japan until the modern age.

The appearance of *Kaigiben* was certainly a significant step in the spread of public speaking in Japan. Yet Fukuzawa's contribution to the cause of the art of speech was not limited to the publication of his pamphlet. Stressing the educational aspect of speech making and debate, he encouraged his colleagues in the Meiji 6 Society (Meirokusha) to hold regular oratory meetings and practice sessions. He founded the Mita Oratorical Society and financed the construction of a hall built for the practice of speech (Mita Enzetsu Kaikan), thus contributing in a most concrete fashion to the spread of public speaking among students and intellectuals.[13]

Fukuzawa further advocated the importance of public speaking in his *Gakumon no susume* (An encouragement of learning, 1872–1876). In this work he writes,

> *Enzetsu,* or in English, "speech," is the art of expressing one's opinions before an assembly of a large number of people, or of communicating one's ideas at a meeting. Sermons delivered in Buddhist temples, and so forth, are types of public speak-

ing which have been presented without knowledge of this heretofore unheard-of art. . . . In the various Western countries, this art is widely known, and it is used in parliaments, assemblies of scholars, assemblies of merchants, assemblies of townsfolk, and even on minor ceremonial occasions such as the openings of businesses and shops. In fact, it is the custom to use this art whenever ten or more people congregate—to explain the purpose of the meeting, to give vent to various individuals' pet theories, and to express, in impromptu fashion, spur-of-the-moment ideas.

Arguing in the following pages that learning without practical application is equivalent to ignorance, he concludes,

> Therefore, the basic purpose of learning is not merely the reading of books, but in putting the mind to work. And there are various methods for the practical application of this work. There is observation; and there is reasoning, whereby one may evolve his theories through inferences based on truth. One cannot say that these two instruments of learning have already been exhausted. In addition to these, one must read books, one must write books, and one must converse with others and speak to them.[14]

Thus for Fukuzawa there was no learning without the exchange of opinions and ideas. Speech and debate were fundamental components of the learning process and a part of one's own education.

Fukuzawa is also credited with coining the term *"enzetsu,"* which, as in the passage cited above, he employed to translate the English "speech." According to his own account, he could not find an appropriate word at first, but then recalled that in the old Nakatsu clan to which he belonged there had already been instances in which the word had appeared, albeit with different Chinese characters.[15] He discussed the matter with some of his colleagues and eventually determined that this word would be a viable choice. Some sources suggest, however, that this term already existed during the Edo period. According to journalist and politician Ishikawa Hanzan (1872–1925), for example, the term can be found in some old court records of the *bakufu,* while the postwar researcher Saitō Tsuyoshi indicates that *rangakusha* (scholars of Dutch learning) used it as a translation of the Dutch *redevoering.*[16] Journalist and historian Miyatake Gaikotsu (1867–1955) was especially adamant in rejecting Fukuzawa's claim. He wrote that "if Yukichi sensei did not intend this to be a boastful hoax, he was displaying his ignorance of various ancient Japanese records. The word 'enzetsu' has been used in our country since ancient times," Miyatake claimed, providing examples from records that supported his theory.[17] It is widely agreed, however, that Fukuzawa was the first to employ *"enzetsu"* to indicate a form of communication that could be used for the exchange of academic and other knowledge and information. The choice of the term *"enzetsu"* suggests, incidentally, that he either had a reductive view of oratory or that he was interested only in one of its possible forms, namely speech. In fact, he did not discuss in depth the psychological or procedural mechanisms that underlay the act of oral communication; his focus was rather upon the social benefits to be gained by promoting debate and discussion. At the time of its introduction, therefore, oratory was seen simply as a practical means of exchanging information and opinions so as to spread knowledge and foster education among citizens. It was to take on further connotations through its association with the Freedom and Popular Rights Movement (Jiyū Minken Undō) in the late 1870s and early 1880s.

Oratory and Political Activism

The Freedom and Popular Rights Movement was a nationwide political entity that asked for freedom of speech and popular involvement in the governance of the nation. The movement had its roots in a coalition against the government formed by a number of political activists following the defeat in 1873 of the call for a punitive expedition against Korea.[18] One of its core leaders was Itagaki Taisuke (1837–1919), who helped establish the Public Party of Patriots (Aikoku Kōtō) in 1874, the Society of Patriots (Aikokusha) in the same year, and the Liberal Party (Jiyūtō), the first Japanese political party, in 1881. The movement also drew from several societies originally formed to discuss the law and to provide young lawyers with an opportunity for forensic practice, as well as "to mobilize a national protest movement against the Meiji government."[19] Among them were the Risshisha, which was founded by Itagaki Taisuke in 1874; the Kyōzon Dōshusha, founded in the same year by Baba Tatsui, Ono Azusa, and Kikuchi Dairoku; and the Ōmeisha, in which Numa Morikazu and Shimada Saburō played a prominent role.[20] All these associations employed speech making as the most effective way to spread their political views and ideas and counted among their members some of the finest orators and speakers in modern Japanese history. The members of these societies vowed to study and practice speech and debate; they believed that "in order to exchange knowledge and promote civilization, there [were] only two weapons—the press and public speaking."[21] In the latter half of the 1870s there was thus a rapid rise in the popularity of speech making. According to journalist Kawaoka Chōfū, Fukuchi Gen'ichirō and Numa Morikazu became the first individuals to give a speech in public when they lectured on French law in 1876. According to Haga Yasushi, however, the first public speech was given in Tsukiji, Tokyo, by Meiji 6 Society member Nakamura Masanao on February 16, 1875.[22] At the same time, in place of the academic lectures *(gakujutsu kōdan)* generally favored by the members of the Meiji 6 Society, the dominant form of oratory in the second decade of the Meiji period became the political speech *(seidan enzetsu)*.[23]

Oratory's growing popularity among politicians and popular rights activists at the end of the first decade of the Meiji period also spurred efforts to sum up and systematize the notions about speech making that had thus far circulated by word of mouth within academic and political circles. *Kōkai enzetsuhō* (A manual of public speaking, 1877), written by political activist Ozaki Yukio (1858–1954), was of key importance in this regard. The first work to introduce rhetoric as a coherent system to Japan, *Kōkai enzetsuhō* constituted a watershed between the early practice of oratory and its eventual development as a field of study in the late nineteenth century.

Ozaki Yukio entered what is now modern Keiō University in 1874. Aware of the outstanding reputation of the institution and fearing the scorn of his fellow students, Ozaki thought of a way that would prevent his lack of education from being exposed to others.

> After mulling it over, I came up with a solution—I would play dumb. At the time I thought it was an extremely fine idea. My lack of education and ability would be exposed as soon as I opened my mouth. It followed that if I avoided saying anything then I would never betray my intellectual shortcomings, and no one could ever reproach me for them. I believe my classical Chinese education had something to do with this decision to live the life of a mute. It had taught me to despise speech and men of many words, and to revere the ancient art of writing. Since I was brought up in this Chinese way of thinking, it was not surprising that I looked down on speech and spoke very little.[24]

From the beginning Ozaki appeared to have a particular relationship with public speaking; he was never, by his own admission, a talkative person and found it difficult to make friends and interact with people. However, his acquaintance and interaction with Fukuzawa Yukichi prompted him to slowly assume a different attitude toward speech making. He later acknowledged the influence of this man whose scholarly authority he had often challenged in his younger years.[25]

In 1876 he withdrew from Keiō University following a dispute with the school directors over the morality and discipline of the students. In the same year he entered the National Technological Institute to pursue a career as a dyer in Kyoto. However, he soon gave up the plan, left the college, and began to devote all his time to writing and translating. It was in this period that *Kōkai enzetsuhō* was published.

Kōkai enzetsuhō was a translation of a Western work on public speaking whose original title is not known.[26] Divided into eleven chapters, the work provided a short discussion on the origins and social functions of oratory and treated various issues related to the preparation and delivery of a speech, including a characterization of the ideal orator and basic notions on diction and body language. It called for logical coherence and clarity in the arguments made and for an appropriate and simple language that would facilitate understanding among the audience. It also included a brief discussion of figures.

Being mostly a Japanese rendering of a Western piece, the opening and closing chapters of the book were perhaps the most poignant in that they reflected Ozaki's own views on public speaking. In the first pages, Ozaki predicted that oratory would grow in popularity with the "democratization" of the political scene.

> We understand from the present situation of the world that public speaking will achieve prosperity and that there is no reason for it to decline. To give a couple of examples, as the National Diet is established, it will be necessary to give speeches there; as the judicial system is instituted there will be a need to make speeches; and as religion grows popular, temple sermons will prosper.[27]

With great political acumen, Ozaki foresaw the political importance of oratory in the social events of the early Meiji period. He went on to define it as the act of "speaking well and moving the hearts of the people, making them cry, laugh or get angry."[28] Here, two points are of paramount importance. First, Ozaki was evidently interested only in the art of speech, since he made no reference to the fact that rhetoric could have a wider range of application, extending to written communication. In fact, for him the term "rhetoric" referred to the realm of rhetorical figures, that is, the canon of "elocution."[29] And second, he introduced the novel notion that oratory had the power to appeal to the people's emotions. In fact, Fukuzawa's "public speaking" had been characterized mostly as a means for the exchange of knowledge and information. By contrast, Ozaki's definition revealed the true nature of the rhetorical process, which entailed the persuasion of the audience. Ozaki drew attention to the psychological element underlying the rhetorical process of communication and to the nature of rhetoric as the "art of persuasion," a powerful means to convince the audience of the truthfulness of the orator's arguments. Although this definition carried with it the possibility that rhetoric could also be used for unethical purposes, Ozaki countered this danger by insisting that the ideal orator was a just leader whose goals were the well-being and social progress of the nation. In fact, the orator had to be not only erudite and versed in several fields of human knowledge, but also a champion of liberty, one who had to "attain loyalty and patriotism, sincerity, and a true heart."[30] Ozaki thus contributed to creating a positive image of the orator as one committed to the well-being of his country and fellow citizens.

The closing chapter was a criticism of the state of oratory in Japan. Ozaki denounced the lack of a tradition of public speaking and forcefully reiterated the existence of a close link between freedom of speech and the progress and prosperity of a nation. By linking public speaking to the concepts of progress and social justice, he fostered a crucial ideological alliance between oratory and freedom.[31] In the following years various figures echoed the connections he had drawn, arguing that freedom of speech was a prerequisite for democracy and indispensable for the progress of society. In 1877 Nishi Amane gave a lecture at Tokyo University and indicated that all forms of speech—whether sermons, lectures, or public address—ultimately followed the rules of oratory. He explained some of the merits brought about by the practice of this art, among them the possibility of addressing a large group of people at one time, something not possible through private conversations, and the opportunity to express one's views.[32] Two years later scholar Nakamura Masanao (1832–1891) discussed the communicative aspect of speech making; argumentation, he held, was different from mere conversation in that it implied a process of persuasion of the audience. Nakamura particularly emphasized the importance of language as a component of speech making and as a necessary tool for the achievement of communication.[33] Following Nakamura, political activist Numa Morikazu (1844–1890) pointed to the importance of speech in sustaining public morale.

> I read in Western history that when Greece was about to be conquered, Demosthenes addressed the crowds in Athens, lifted their spirit in a blink of an eye, and expelled the approaching enemy, thus restoring the fallen nation. . . . This is probably when I first realized the importance of public speaking in society.[34]

Likewise, popular-rights advocate Nakae Chōmin (1847–1901) wrote that

> when bureaucrats seek to prevent freedom of speech, it is likely to have damaging effects. Those who seek the prosperity of the nation must communicate to the citizens either by writing or by speech the content of their theories and their reasoning. If bureaucrats try to obstruct the freedom of speech, we lose the opportunity to talk or write about our theories. In this manner, our ideas accumulate in our brains,

without the possibility of being written or talked about to others, and our descendents are not able to gain from the merits of our theories.[35]

Thus the call for freedom of speech as an essential element for progress and social justice became a consistent and recurrent element in the social discourse of the time. Among the individuals who strongly advocated the need for freedom of expression at the time was Ueki Emori (1857–1892). Ueki deserves special mention not only for his extensive activity as a leading spokesman of the Freedom and Popular Rights Movement, but also for his popularity as an orator and his contribution to the spread of public speaking in the early phases of its introduction. It is said that he became determined to pursue a political career after listening to a speech by Itagaki Taisuke in 1874.[36] Ueki became a habitué of meetings and lectures and often attended sessions held by the Meiji 6 Society and the Mita Oratorical Society. In 1877 he joined the Risshisha in Kōchi where he distinguished himself for, among other things, his oratory skills, becoming instrumental in the opening of political speeches to the masses.[37] Ueki grasped the crucial importance of speaking in public, and while his activity as an orator is already clear evidence of his remarkable contribution as an advocate of freedom of speech, many of his writings also reflected his strong commitment to this cause.

> Freedom is necessary for humans to live and work together; it is needed to develop knowledge, to better one's heart, and to realize all types of accomplishment. . . . Without freedom of speech, people, even if members of society, will not be able to cooperate and carry on their enterprises.[38]

Ueki was also one of the very few champions of women's rights. Said to have been significantly influenced by Herbert Spencer's theories, Ueki repeatedly postulated social equality for men and women. Beginning as early as 1880, he delivered speeches that addressed women's participation in the political life of the nation and discussed their legal rights as members of society. Ueki's interest in women's issues culminated in his *Tōyō no fujo* (Eastern women), a work published in 1889 that included essays on the family system, marriage, and the future role of women in society.[39]

The debate on women had begun in the early Meiji years. The intellectuals of the Meiji 6 Society were particularly active in the discussion; Fukuzawa Yukichi, Nakamura Masanao, and Mori Arinori all wrote on the subject, raising crucial questions on the position and function of women in the Japanese traditional family and society in general.[40] Their writings spurred interest in women's issues, and although the "debate was brief, and the arguments often contradictory," "it had a significant impact on Meiji society," prompting some women to push "the arguments of the Meiji thinkers to new conclusions."[41]

The popular rights movement provided significant opportunities for the articulation of women's aspirations and their call for social reform. Public speaking was again one of the most effective vehicles of communication, and women's participation in speech meetings increased rapidly. According to Tanaka Sumiko, a policeman's wife became one of the first women to deliver a political speech when she addressed a political rally in Nakatsu, Kyūshū, in March 1882.[42] A few days later, Kishida Toshiko (1863–1901; also known as Nakajima Shōen) took the platform for the first time. Japan's most celebrated female orator, Kishida played a crucial role in the rise of Meiji feminist discourse and criticism. She delivered her first speech, "Fujo no michi" (The way for women), at an Osaka political gathering on April 1, which immediately earned her the reputation of being a talented speaker. "Fujo no michi" was in fact only the beginning of Kishida's career as an orator. In the months that followed she embarked on a speech tour that took her to several towns in the region. She delivered at least three more speeches in Osaka during the month of April, after which she traveled to Okayama in May and Tokushima in June. She then continued to deliver speeches in the Kinki area and was in Kyūshū from November to December.[43]

Although widely recognized as one of the most talented speakers of her time, very few of Kishida's speeches still exist today. One of the most well known is "Hakoiri musume" (Daughters in boxes), which she delivered in Ōtsu on October 12, 1883.[44] Attacking the old practice of confining daughters to the household and to an existence tied exclusively to marriage, Kishida called for the need to provide women with a proper education that would enable them to be functional members of society. This speech caused her to be arrested for having allegedly covered topics of a political nature. She spent approximately a week in prison, after which she was released and later fined five yen.[45]

Kishida's speeches inflamed the crowds, prompting other women to organize public speaking societies. In October 1883 she helped organize the founding meeting of a Women's Lecture Society (Joshi Daienzetsukai) in Kyoto, an event that attracted more than two thousand women.[46] Kishida was overall a strong believer in the importance of public speaking.

> Through lectures we share knowledge and intelligence. Since the object of lecturing is the increase of human knowledge, it is quite logical to assume that we carry on this kind of activity for the good of the country.[47]

As Sharon Sievers has also pointed out, "the lecture platform provided by the

Liberal Party gave Kishida an unprecedented opportunity to communicate in plain, direct style with women in many different regions, representing the widest spectrum of age, experience, and class."[48] Many young women were fascinated by Kishida's eloquence. One of them was Fukuda Hideko (1865–1927; also known as Kageyama Hideko). Widely known for her work as a promoter of women's rights and for her involvement in the 1885 Osaka Incident in which Ōi Kentarō and others plotted to establish a reform government in Korea, Fukuda was in the audience when Kishida delivered her speech in Okayama in May 1882. She later recounted in her 1904 autobiography that she had been extremely impressed by Kishida's oratory skills.[49] She thus became involved in associations that practiced public speaking. By November of the same year, Fukuda's name figured, for example, among the members of a women's society that had been formed following Kishida's visit to Okayama and that included public speaking among its activities. In April 1883, Fukuda delivered a speech titled "Ningen byōdōron" (On the equality of human beings) at a political meeting organized by the popular rights movement.[50] And the Jōkō gakusha, the private school she co-founded with her mother in 1883, also included debating sessions in its curriculum.[51] It is then evident that oratory was viewed and employed by several women leaders as a critically effective tool in demanding better education, voting rights, and equal opportunities.[52]

As a reflection of the currency of the linkages between speech and social advancement, oratory flourished, making the second decade of the Meiji period a true golden age for speech making in Japan.[53] Increasing government efforts at censorship also provide evidence of this phenomenon. Initially, government censorship had targeted primarily the publishing industry through the promulgation of the Publication Ordinance (Shuppan Jōrei) of 1869. This ordinance represented a harsh blow to those who were calling for reforms and were making freedom of expression their main weapon in their political battle against the government. The two ordinances that followed, namely the Press Ordinance (Shinbunshi Jōrei) and Libel Law (Zanbōritsu) of 1875, were also aimed at controlling the press in the face of growing criticism from the Freedom and Popular Rights Movement. These two laws, which were reinforced by amendments in 1876 and 1880, empowered the authorities to control or ban any newspaper that published articles considered dangerous to public order or to the security of the state and provided penalties for "misrepresentation" and "defamation." Baba Tatsui provides an account in English of the developments that took place in those years.

> In 1878, this social or popular movement became more active. Public speeches were delivered and pamphlets published. Frequent meetings were held and every

favorable sign of progress was seen in these social phenomena. But the Japanese government began to perceive that if the popular movement was allowed to go on, the acts of their policy would be freely criticised by the people. Then they resorted to a course which was intended to discourage these enterprises. The newspapers were the first to meet with a check. Press laws and newspaper regulations were made and writers were imprisoned for a year or even three years for very slight offenses. But the government was comparatively careless as to the meetings and public speeches, because these were not at first as influential as the newspapers.[54]

As evidenced by Baba's passage, the fortunate omission of speeches from these laws further encouraged activists to turn to public speaking as an effective means of making their ideas known. Speech making became a remarkably strategic means of communication, at the same time making it possible to address a large part of the population that was unable to read newspapers and journals.[55]

Ozaki Yukio's definition of oratory as a potential instigating force of the masses on the one hand and the progressive involvement of prominent political and cultural figures in the debate concerning freedom of speech on the other became a direct warning to the authorities of a possible political destabilization of the country. The government, attempting to contain the euphoria that had been spreading since the booming of public speaking, opted for a hard-line policy against the advocates of freedom of expression and in 1878 passed the Regulation of Public Speaking Ordinance (Enzetsu Torishimari Rei) by which any person seeking to speak in public with the purpose of creating public disorder or instigating the masses would be prosecuted.[56] The regulation was subsequently followed by the Public Assembly Ordinance (Shūkai Jōrei), which was passed on April 5, 1880.[57] This ordinance was composed of sixteen articles establishing the procedures to be followed for registration and prior approval of any type of public meeting. It also prohibited outdoor meetings and contacts between different political organizations and empowered local authorities to dispatch police forces to meetings. The leaders of the Freedom and Popular Rights Movement strongly criticized the oppressive policies of the government; nevertheless, in 1882 the authorities passed an addition to the Public Assembly Ordinance that further restricted the freedom of speaking in public. This ordinance represented a final blow to all those who were advocating the importance of freedom of speech. Thus in the mid-1880s censorship intensified, and governmental suppression also began to affect speech making. According to Matsumoto and Yamamuro, the number of public speeches authorized in the country reached a peak of 13,212 in 1882 and subsequently gradually decreased each year thereafter, reaching 2,845 in 1885.[58]

Nonetheless, the interest in oratory was such that a large number of publications on the art of speech continued to appear.

Studies of the Art of Speech in the 1880s:
The Rise of a New Language Awareness

The popularity of speech making also spurred interest in the study of the principles of oratory, and the 1880s saw the publication of a number of scholarly books on the art of speech. Many of these, particularly the early ones, were translations of Western works. For example, Kō Ryōji's *Taisei ronbengaku yōketsu* (Essential principles of Western rhetoric), which appeared in 1880, was a translation of Hugh Blair's *Lectures on Rhetoric and Belles Lettres,* while Tomioka Masanori's *Benshi hitsudoku enzetsugaku* (The study of public speaking: An essential guide for orators) of 1882 was a rendering of Alexander Melville Bell's *Standard Elocutionist.*[59] Among such works was also Matsumura Misao's *Enzetsu kinshin* (The golden needle of speech making), which was published in 1881.[60] Matsumura's work consisted of a general introduction to oratory, a section concerning the use of body language, a short history of public speaking in the West, and a reproduction of the notorious Public Assembly Ordinance. In his preface, Matsumura bemoaned the lack of a manual of oratory, noting that the increasing number of publications in the field were merely reproductions of speeches by popular orators. It was in order to fill this gap, he stated, that he had decided to write a book that would explain some of the basic principles of public speaking. He went on to describe oratory as an art that centered on the process of communication between individuals. This notion was likely derived from Nakamura Masanao's "Enzetsu no shugi o ronzu" (A discussion of the principles of public speaking), which was reproduced at the beginning of the work. Matsumura emphasized that the art of speaking in public was an art that was concerned, by definition, with the audience. Two aspects were crucial to the effective delivery of a speech: the relationship between the orator's thoughts and feelings, and, in turn, the relationship between these two and language. Language had to be used in a manner consistent with the ideas and intent of the speaker in order to have an effect on the audience. The receiver of the message was ultimately the crucial link in the communication process. Accordingly, three points needed to be carefully considered: how to discern the audience's thoughts, how to express one's ideas in response to the audience's thoughts, and how to articulate one's argument so as to appeal to the emotions of the audience.[61] As Ozaki had earlier, Matsumura emphasized the significance of persuasion in the process of communication. But he also added another crucial element to the definition of oratory: it was, he declared, "the art of uttering language in an elegant way."[62]

Others at this time were already addressing the notion of elegance in language. In that many classical scholars viewed linguistic elegance as a prerogative of established literary modes, this issue figured centrally in debates over the feasibility of a written language based on the vernacular and, as such, intelligible to a larger section of the population. Scholars discussed whether the vernacular could ever become a refined means of expression, but they debated this matter primarily regarding written communication. *Enzetsu kinshin* was probably one of the earliest works to emphasize the notion of elegance in speech.

Another important translation was *Yūben bijihō* (Principles of rhetoric and oratory) by Kuroiwa Dai (Ruikō), published in 1882. With a preface by Suehiro Tetchō, *Yūben bijihō* was an adaptation of Quackenbos' *Advanced Course of Composition and Rhetoric*. In his preface, Kuroiwa noted that the recent popularity of public speaking and debate had led to a compelling need for a manual of oratory. Several translations published before that time had sought to provide guidance in this regard, but very few had focused on the problem of language and its usage. Hence, he had decided to translate Quackenbos' treatise to provide a useful guide on this very aspect: language.

The first chapter of *Yūben bijihō* was devoted entirely to oratory. Kuroiwa described public speaking as the act of expressing one's opinion in front of an audience in such a way as to produce an emotion in the listeners. He then reiterated the point already brought forth by Nishi Amane that in Western nations the language used in a speech could be used as well in writing. This argument suggested in part the idea, shared by many at the time, that the spoken and written languages were extremely close in the West, and this in turn prompted a legitimate debate on the issue of language in Japan. Kuroiwa understood that the language used in a speech was not necessarily the same language one would use in ordinary conversation. In fact, this language, he went on, had to be refined and elegant in order to be employed also in writing, thus making public speaking fundamentally different from native forms of oratory such as *kōshaku* (lecture, explanation) and *rakugo*.[63] Kuroiwa also observed that three forms of oratory were predominant at the time, namely deliberative, forensic, and pulpit oratory. He then addressed the act of speech making, giving an explanation of the six parts that, in his view, comprised the structure of a speech (such as the opening and concluding statements of an address).

Kuroiwa went on to provide one of the first detailed treatments of rhetorical figures. He defined them as a deviation from an ordinary way of expression, arguing that their employment gave prestige and elegance to the style, but also observing that they were not absolutely necessary to achieve beauty in writing. He discussed the nature and history of figures as well as the advantages deriving from the use of these devices, echoing the arguments made by Quackenbos in his work. He then went on to discuss style, harmony, and the ridiculous and provided a treatment of invention and arrangement in prose, that is, the canons of rhetoric dealing with the selection and disposition of the material to be used in composition.[64]

On the whole, a comparison between *Yūben bijihō* and *Advanced Course of Composition and Rhetoric* reveals the existence of several differences between the two works. For example, in the chapters on figures, Kuroiwa omitted the discussion of taste, which by contrast constituted an integral part of chapter three in Quackenbos' original work. The treatment of the ridiculous was also moved from his "figures" section to the end of the treatise, and the number of rhetorical figures explained was reduced from sixteen to ten. These and other minor differences were, however, also accompanied by more meaningful discrepancies. In fact, while Kuroiwa chose to begin his work with a chapter on oratory, no significant discussion of oral communication can be found in Quackenbos' original work, in which the first two chapters covered instead the history of the English language and punctuation. Kuroiwa's choice likely reflected the interest in oratory seen over those years. Nonetheless, *Yūben bijihō* also concealed a latent trait of the developing process of the discipline during the first decades of the Meiji era: the slow but certain transition to a rhetorical inquiry that would prioritize written over oral communication. According to Kuroiwa, *Yūben bijihō* was purposely written to address the (effective and refined) use of language. The pages spent on the explanation of figures, the final chapter on essential aspects of prose, and the choice of a Western work on composition such as Quackenbos' are indications that Kuroiwa's main concern lay in the realm of written signification.

Yūben bijihō thus epitomized the internal disciplinary transition that by the early 1880s was already shifting the scope of rhetoric toward the realm of literary production. To be precise, this approach had not been the first of its kind; three years earlier, Kikuchi Dairoku's *Shūji oyobi kabun* had sought to establish rhetoric as a discipline that addressed literature and literary criticism, but his attempt had not been successful.[65] However, as noted above, the overwhelming popularity of public speaking, which was at its peak at the time when *Yūben bijihō* was published, may have led Kuroiwa to begin his work with a treatment of oratory. Interestingly, this aspect can also be observed in other translations of the time such as the aforementioned *Taisei ronbengaku yōketsu*. This work was a rendering of Blair's *Lectures of Rhetoric and Belles Lettres,* which was originally composed of forty-seven lectures on different topics, ranging from language to style, literary themes, and eloquence. Despite the extent of the original lectures, Kō Ryōji translated only the section that pertained to public speaking, providing further evidence of the interest in oratory during those years, which persisted even as attention to prose rhetoric intensified.

Another point in *Yūben bijihō* that needs to be noted is the renewed stress on elegance and refinement in speech. This argument would be crucial, as will be discussed later, in the reappraisal of the vernacular that took place in the following years. Of course, not all the works that immediately followed necessarily developed this point. In fact, one begins to see the birth of a new genre among studies of this period that did not necessarily make the discussion of language a high priority. Such a new genre slowly replaced the large number of translations of the first decade, giving primary attention to the reproduction of the speeches given by Japanese personalities around the country. Kitaki Seirui's *Nihon enzetsu tōron hōhō* (Methods of speech making and debate in Japan), published in 1882, was a representative example of this trend. His work was divided into two parts, one addressing speech and the other debate. In the first section Kitaki gave a general explanation of speech making. He indicated the four essential qualities of the orator, namely scholarship, firmness, memory, and diction. He then provided a cursory treatment of diction and body language, together with helpful illustrations on posture and the position and motion of the hands and the lower limbs. Examples of speech making included Nakamura Masanao's "Enzetsu no shugi o ronzu" in the field of general scholarship and Numa Morikazu's "Kokuseiron" (On government) in the realm of politics. The second section contained instructions concerning how to hold a debate, from the choice of an appropriate place to the procedures needed to conduct a meeting. Here excerpts from the meetings of the Kokuyūsha and Ōmeisha societies were provided. Kitaki emphasized that both speech and debate were essential tools for the advancement of society and predicted their increased importance with the opening of the National Diet.[66]

There was as well, however, a growing effort by Japanese researchers to investigate the nature of oratory and to envision its possible application to the needs of Japanese cultural life, albeit not without a great deal of redundancy. The works published at this time included writer Yano Fumio's *Enzetsu bunshō kumitatehō* (Principles of arrangement in speech-making and composition). The work was a discussion of "argumentation" and the principles governing the organization of a speech. Comparing the assemblage of the various elements of an oral address to the construction of a house, Yano (1850–1931) defined argumentation as the process through which a speaker conveyed his ideas to an audience in a clear fashion. In his view, a competent disposition of the materials to be treated was the key to effective delivery of a speech and persuasion of the audience. Two points in this study are of special interest. First, Yano noted that argumentation did not exactly follow the principles of logic. In fact, the argument made by a speaker was in the first instance founded on the speaker's own subjective judgment. This was an important distinction because it struck at the core of the rhetorical process. Yano held that the persuasion of the audience was conducted on the basis of the plausibility of the arguments made and not purely upon demonstrable truths. Second, Yano indicated how the rules for speech making could be applied by extension to writing.[67] In fact, he kept referring throughout the text both to "readers" and "listeners," providing evidence that he saw the two realms of communication as closely linked. This was a most original realization that did not, however, receive much support. In fact, it took thirty years before another major work addressed oral and written communication concurrently.[68]

Although the works published between the beginning of the Restoration and the early 1880s had discussed the principles of oratory in detail, they had only marginally addressed the question of language. However, with the publication of Baba Tatsui's *Yūbenhō* in 1885, language finally came to be the object of deeper analysis. Baba (1850–1888) was certainly one of the leading protagonists of the cultural change that characterized the Meiji years. A strong believer in the importance of eloquence, he spent several years in England, becoming very proficient in the English language, as evidenced by some of his writings. His scholarly production includes *An Elementary Grammar of the Japanese Language,* written in England in 1873. In this work, he attacked Mori Arinori's criticism of the Japanese language, calling his ideas unjustified and extravagant, displaying the polemic vein that characterized much of Baba's political and intellectual career.

Upon his return from England in 1878, Baba became involved with the activities of the Kyōzon Dōshusha, where he introduced the practice of holding regular public meetings and lectures. This idea was not especially welcomed by the members of the society, leaving Baba and Ono Azusa as the only individuals responsible for giving lectures. Baba was not new to speech making, nor was he new to a society of this type. In fact, he had been very active in this respect while in London, having founded a club for Japanese students, where he would often give speeches and hold lectures. While in England, Baba had the opportunity to attend several public meetings and was favorably impressed by the power of eloquence. He considered "freedom of speech beneficial to the general interests of the nation" and held that eloquence was needed to educate the masses and to find a tool to appeal to their public opinion.[69] His deep involvement with the Kyōzon Dōshusha marked the apex of his career as an orator; journalist and historian Tokutomi Sohō, who often attended the meetings of the society, described Baba's skills as unsurpassed.[70] Even after the adoption of the Public Assembly Ordinance and the consequent dissolution of the society, Baba continued to give speeches widely, until he delivered his last lecture in Yokohama on July 29, 1885. This lecture was published as *Yūbenhō* later in the same year.

Yūbenhō was therefore the product of years of experience lecturing around the world and as such was very different in nature from Ozaki Yukio's *Kōkai enzetsuhō* or any preceding works. Ozaki, in particular, had published his translation at a very young age, with little or no actual experience in speech making. By contrast, Baba was an experienced, successful orator who once again utilized oratory for "the reassertion of his liberal convictions, as a medium for democratic propagandizing, and as a means of indirect polemic and reiteration of many of his already expressed ideas."[71]

Yūbenhō was divided into nine sections. The first three were a short history of oratory in the West. The fourth section, titled "Oratory," constituted the core of the treatise and addressed various issues related to public speaking such as "The Order of Argumentation," "Persuasion," "Style in Language," "Sound," and "Gestures." The last sections provided a brief historical account of oratory in Japan and a classification of the types of speech in fashion during early Meiji times. Each of these speeches followed a specific model, differing from the others not only for the audience it addressed, but also, mostly, for the type of language it employed. The first type of speech, which Baba called *eigakusharyū*, was characterized by the use of terms that resulted from directly translating English words into Japanese. Baba argued that this type of language, often found in the classroom, was very unnatural given the fundamental grammatical differences existing between English and Japanese. The second type, called *shinbunryū*, was modeled upon the editorials appearing in the press, especially in publications in the countryside. Baba denounced this type of language, arguing that it was characterized by a large number of Chinese characters and words difficult to comprehend. The third type followed a linguistic pattern largely adopted in *rakugo* and as such was referred to as *rakugoryū*. According to Baba, it was very effective and easy to understand, but nonetheless replete with colloquial expressions that were hardly suitable to speech making. The fourth type, *sekkyōryū*, referred to the style used in sermons. This type of speech, while also effective, tended to be condescending and as such needed be avoided, in Baba's view. Finally, the fifth type, *haiyūryū*, reflected a speaking pattern found among actors. He saw this pattern as dramatically very effective on account of the high-flown language it used, but at the same time this language tended to discredit the image and reliability of the orator because of its flamboyant nature. Baba suggested a syncretic approach, one that would consider the merits of each of these styles with the objective of creating a refined language intelligible even to a general audience.

Yūbenhō covered several chief aspects of speech making, including the need to understand the nature of the audience and how to appeal to their emotions. One of its merits, however, lay in the assertion that the language to be used in speeches had to be simple, clear, and appropriate, three obvious prerequisites crucial to the delivery of any type of speech, regardless of the style of language employed.[72] Following Baba, others added that language had to be not only correct and clear, but also effective, thus emphasizing the need for a competent and strategic use of language in order to appeal to the people and their emotions.[73] Furthermore, the debate slowly shifted to problems specific to the Japanese language. The "complexity" of Japanese, it was argued, derived from the existence of a large number of competing written styles; to develop a successful tradition of public speaking, it was therefore necessary to address this issue.[74] Many authors also warned against the use of homophones, abundant in the Japanese lexicon, and urged orators to avoid dialecticisms. As a standard language to be employed in public speaking, they recommended that spoken in Tokyo.[75] In these ways, Japanese scholarship on oratory in the 1880s contributed to a new awareness of the importance of the spoken language. This, as will be discussed later, would be an essential step toward advancing the debate on the creation of a truly standard national spoken language and a modern literary style.

Eventually, in the late 1880s, scholarship on oratory slowly began to show signs of exhaustion. At the same time, public speaking began to lose its vigor and popularity, due also to the pressure of government censors. The heyday of oratory can thus be said to have run from its introduction after the beginning of the Meiji era until the promulgation of the Constitution in 1889 and the establishment of the National Diet in 1890. These events were hailed among the successes enjoyed by the advocates of public speaking. However, ironically, the study and practice of oratory soon thereafter began to decline.

Interestingly, the year in which the National Diet was established also roughly coincides with the publication of Takada Sanae's *Bijigaku* (Rhetoric) and the beginning of a new disciplinary course for rhetoric, which began to be mostly viewed as a discipline concerned with writing rather than public speaking.

4
The Supremacy of the Written Medium

The early Meiji period was a time of fervent political and social debate, providing an ideal environment for those especially skilled or knowledgeable in the techniques of public speaking. Individuals such as Fukuzawa Yukichi, Ozaki Yukio, Kuroiwa Dai, and Baba Tatsui introduced rhetoric to the Japanese political and intellectual world in its original meaning, "the art of speech," encouraging public speaking-related activities and affecting the political and social life of early Meiji Japanese society. Rhetoric, in the form of public speaking, came to be hailed as a synonym for progress and justice and soon became linked to issues of freedom of speech and democratization.

By the end of the second decade of the Meiji period, several books on rhetoric had already been published, but these mostly dealt with oratory and did not consider the study of rhetoric as a field concerned with writing and literary criticism. However, one work, Kikuchi Dairoku's *Shūji oyobi kabun,* had already sought to address rhetoric in those very terms. Kikuchi (1855–1917), a mathematician, had been commissioned by the Ministry of Education to translate "Rhetoric and Belles Lettres," a piece that had appeared in William and Robert Chambers' encyclopedia, *Information for the People* (1867). This work was in turn largely based on Bain's *English Composition and Rhetoric.*[1]

Since "Rhetoric and Belles Lettres" originally addressed such topics as style, persuasive communication, poetry, and literary arts, Kikuchi, with this translation, was able to introduce essential new concepts regarding literature and prose writing, putting special emphasis on the written message. He provided a more in-depth treatment of the persuasive message, which had been only partially addressed by Ozaki, and also introduced a new terminology in the field of aesthetics, literature, and philosophy.[2] Most of all, Kikuchi's work redefined rhetoric as "a branch of knowledge and practice having reference to spoken and written compositions, and to the means of employing language so as to produce its greatest possible effects on the minds of men." The main consequence of this definition was the reiteration of the double connotation of the term "rhetoric," which, as already introduced by Nishi Amane, encompassed both the meaning of the "art of speech" and the "art of composition." However, none of the works that immediately followed addressed rhetoric in these terms. Instead, they mostly considered the discipline as the art of speaking in public. This was likely due to the fact that the early Meiji literary world did not have the theoretical means to absorb and elaborate incoming Western literary theories in so short a period of time. But another major cause probably lay in the increased interest in public speaking, which led many authors to prioritize the discussion of oral over written communication. Thus except for Shōyō's *Shōsetsu shinzui* (The essence of the novel, 1885–1886), which was, strictly speaking, not a treatise of rhetoric, more than ten years would pass before rhetoric was once again addressed as a field of study concerned with literature and literary criticism.

It is not a coincidence that *Shūji oyobi kabun* has been considered by many as an essential step toward the modernization of Japanese literature. Already at the beginning of the twentieth century, Iwaki Juntarō acknowledged the importance of this translation to the revolutionary changes that occurred in the Meiji literary world.[3] Honma Hisao stated that this work had played an essential role in the creation of modern literary theory.[4] Takaichi Yoshio argued that although doubts remained over the actual influence exerted on contemporary authors and critics, *Shūji oyobi kabun* was the first Japanese work to discuss "pure literature" and therefore was essential reading for any student of Meiji literary theory.[5] In more recent years, Yanagida Izumi has written that as a scholar whose expertise was not in the field of literature, "with this translation [Kikuchi] made an unexpectedly significant contribution to the development of early Meiji literary thought."[6]

Shūji oyobi kabun has thus enjoyed substantial recognition among scholars, some of whom have gone so far as to regard it as the beginning of Japanese literary criticism. This is especially so in light of the influence it is said to have exerted on Tsubouchi Shōyō's theory of the modern novel. It is well known that Shōyō (1859–1935) acknowledged Kikuchi's translation in a piece published in 1925.[7] While it is possible to speculate that this acknowledgment may have been the very reason for *Shūji oyobi kabun*'s later fortune, some scholars have discussed at length the clear influence of *Shūji oyobi kabun* over *Shōsetsu shinzui*.

Equally important is the direct influence of Alexander Bain's *English Composition and Rhetoric*. Shōyō acknowledged Bain's work as one of the few Western books available in the Tokyo University library at the time he was working on his treatise on the modern novel.[8] This has generated a debate concerning the extent of Bain's influence on Shōyō's thought. For example, Oshima Kenji has indicated that Bain's work was crucial to the development of Shōyō's ideas on a variety of key topics such as the definitions of art, novel, and realism.[9] And it seems likely that not only Bain's, but also other works of Western rhetoric, may have played a crucial role in the theoretical development of Shōyō's ideas.

One scholar that has put renewed emphasis on the existence of strong links between Bain and Shōyō's work is Kamei Hideo. Kamei has also pointed out that when Shōyō was a student at Tokyo University, W. D. Cox, who taught English there, published *The Principles of Rhetoric and English Composition for Japanese Students*. This manual, Kamei has noted, was inspired by Bain's *English Composition and Rhetoric,* and while it is not clear whether Shōyō took Cox's classes, it seems likely that he may have been under the influence of both works. Kamei also argues that Shōyō may have been influenced by other books such as Quackenbos' *Advanced Course of Composition and Rhetoric* and Hill's *The Principles of Rhetoric and Their Application.*[10]

Of course, one can easily cast some doubts on *Shōsetsu shinzui's* overall contribution to the modernization of Japanese literature. As Keene has indicated, Shōyō has been criticized in recent years for the shallowness of some of the ideas expressed in this treatise. However, "it is to be marveled at that he was able to derive from an extremely limited knowledge of Western literature (he mentions in *The Essence of the Novel* only eight English novels), and a knowledge of literary theory based mainly on some encyclopedia articles, a work that inspired a whole generation." In fact, "the decisions of Bimyō and Kōyō to make literature their life-work germinated in the stimulus provided by Shōyō's work."[11] Thus its importance "cannot be overstated."[12] If, as seems to be the case, Bain's and other works of rhetoric, including Kikuchi's translation, did play such a significant part in Shōyō's development of his theory, then it is possible to postulate that at this stage rhetoric had already begun to play an active role in the process that led to the modernization of Japanese literature and, very likely, the formation of modern literary language.

Takada Sanae's *Bijigaku:* Rhetoric and Literary Criticism

The publication of Takada Sanae's *Bijigaku* comes, then, to assume paramount importance in later developments both in the field of rhetoric and in literary criticism in general. Takada (1860–1938) entered Tōkyō Kaisei Gakkō (later Tokyo Imperial University) in 1876, graduating in 1882. In the same year he became a lecturer at Tōkyō Senmon Gakkō (later Waseda University). Takada was also the son-in-law of Maejima Hisoka, who was president of Tōkyō Senmon Gakkō the same year *Bijigaku* was published. Since Takada was already deeply involved in his job as contributor to both the *Chūō gakujutsu zasshi* (The central journal of arts and sciences) and the *Yomiuri shinbun* and was, furthermore, not necessarily an expert in the field of rhetoric, Hara Shirō speculates that Takada and Maejima's personal relationship may have been the driving force behind the publication of *Bijigaku*. In particular, Maejima's strong commitment to the Westernization of Japanese culture may have exerted a strong influence on the young Takada.[13]

Takada advocated the need to study rhetoric as early as 1887 in an editorial that appeared in the *Yomiuri shinbun*.[14] There, he complained that the large number of books published at the time were often marred by poor quality, which was caused not by a problem of content but by one of style. He observed that most authors had a poor awareness of the meaning of taste, which he understood to be the ability to distinguish between the beautiful and the nonbeautiful. Takada stated that such an ability was defined by Bain as the faculty to appreciate a work of art. This ability, although innate in all human beings, needed to be nurtured. Its refinement was, accordingly, the domain of rhetoric.

Comprising two volumes, *Bijigaku* sought to establish aesthetic criteria for the appreciation of literature, discussing the attributes of style and the nature of effective and elegant literary expression, and concurrently addressing general principles of composition. In his preface to the first volume, Takada discussed the motivation behind undertaking such a rhetorical treatise. In his view, several schools at the time already included the study of rhetoric through a foreign language, but few individuals really understood its rules and application. Hence the aim of his work, as expressed in the preface, was to explain those rules and to apply them to native literary tradition.[15] Takada went on to define the scope of rhetoric, mostly in terms of its dialectical relationship with the traditional heritage of native scholarship in the field. He acknowledged that Japan could boast of a long tradition in teaching composition and the appreciation of literature, but such a tradition had never constituted a "scientific" field. By contrast, Western rhetoric was a discipline that was scientifically sound and based on a system of rules that, if well applied, could benefit all of Japanese literature. The existence of such rules, he went on to say, was seen by many to limit the freedom of the writer, thus impeding the creativity necessary for the realization of a work of art. Takada rejected this view and hinted that those same rules could provide the standards for which the Japanese literary world was searching.

Rhetoric provided a reliable system of rules. Takada's argument in favor of investigating rhetoric had the potential to attract scholars of language, literature, and related fields. As the repository of centuries of Western theoretical thinking, rhetoric seemed to hold the key to the resolution of several issues, among them the conception of an aesthetic model to be employed as a reference in creating or discerning beauty in literature. Possibly, it could also be of help in addressing the creation of a new form of literary expression consistent with the calls for modernization made by new literary trends.

With such implications providing the background for his undertaking, Takada stated that as a discipline rhetoric was concerned at the same time with public speaking, composition, and literary criticism. He thus departed from the scholarship of the previous decade, which had perceived rhetoric largely as a system of rules for effective speaking. By moving away from the earlier school of thought, he provided a new perspective on the study of language and literature, which obviously correlated to rhetoric since they were the subject matter of its discourse. But most of all he reclaimed that written dimension of rhetoric, which had been disregarded after *Shūji oyobi kabun,* at a time when the debate on the role of literature and the creation of a new form of literary expression were becoming critical themes of academic discussion.

Interestingly, despite a definition of rhetoric that viewed it as an area of investigation covering both oral and written communication, *Bijigaku* virtually ignored the dimension of public speaking and became the first native work to address rhetoric solely as a discipline concerned with composition and literary criticism. In fact, the work did not discuss oral communication at all, which contradicted the definition provided early in the treatise. The major implication of the exclusion of public speaking from the scope of rhetoric was a sanctioning of the schism between the oral and the written dimension of the discipline. This schism would characterize the development of rhetoric throughout the Meiji period. From this point of view, *Bijigaku* may indeed be regarded as the beginning of a new phase in the history of Western rhetoric in modern Japan.

Takada's effort to lay the groundwork for future developments in the field was also characterized by his struggle to find an appropriate translation of the term "rhetoric," a translation that would encompass both of its main connotations. In his view, the term *"shūji(gaku)"* had been widely employed in past Japanese literary tradition, but it had never indicated a field of study simultaneously concerned with speech making, composition, and literary criticism. For this reason, he noted, he had chosen to employ the all-embracing term *"bijigaku."*[16] Ultimately, the strong emphasis on the discussion of style and taste seen in Takada's work contributed to the development of a special, new understanding of the term, one in which the very word "rhetoric" was used in a manner rather reminiscent of "aesthetics." Those treatises that later employed this term, Tsubouchi Shōyō's "Bijironkō" (A study of rhetoric) and Shimamura Hōgetsu's *Shin bijigaku,* retained this special connotation and discussed rhetoric more as a source of an aesthetic model than as a practical guide for composition.

Having provided a general overview of the purpose and scope of his work, Takada defined rhetoric as a science whose purpose was to enable people to choose the most effective means of expression and afford them the means to discern between the beautiful and the nonbeautiful.[17] He then defined taste as the ability to receive pleasure from the beauties of art, a definition that strongly resembled that of Bain. Takada went on to subdivide taste into "the sublime," "the beautiful," and "the ridiculous," providing a discussion that was predictably largely indebted to Bain, but also to Quackenbos.[18]

Next Takada turned to rhetorical figures. He defined them as "a means of enhancing the clarity and the effect of a linguistic expression, by replacing an ordinary word with a special one," adding that a written style that did not employ them could not be regarded as such.[19]

Such a definition of the rhetorical figure, probably borrowed from Bain, seemed to suggest the existence of two planes or codes in language: a "special" and an "ordinary" one. While it is true that the identification of two different planes in linguistic signification did not necessarily translate into the dichotomy "elegant versus vulgar language," which permeated the academic debates of the early 1890s, with the vernacularization of literary language causing much dispute among scholars and intellectuals, it may as well have been read in those terms. This being the case, Takada's definition of rhetorical figures may have intensified the conflict between classical and colloquial written styles that characterized the second half of the Meiji period. The social and political changes brought about by the Restoration and the new ideas introduced by incoming literary trends had inspired writers to seek a literary language that could better express the subtleties of human existence. Writers became increasingly engaged in literary experimentation, many of them opposing the employment of large numbers of rhetorical embellishments in favor of a more simplified literary style. Thus in regard to matters of literary style, the Meiji literary world became generally divided into two factions, one supporting the employment of established literary conventions and one calling for a radical abolishment of those conventions in favor of a more colloquial literary language. Advocates of the two factions confronted each other with more or less sound theories on the nature of language and literary signification. Ultimately, the debate was reduced in most instances to either encouraging or criticizing refinement in writing. The interpretation of the meaning of refinement and of rhetorical expression thus held, to a certain extent, the key to the solution of the dispute.

Because of its pronounced tendency toward categorization and dogmatism,

Bijigaku came to be identified by many as a product of traditional scholarship rather than the result of a process of innovation. In particular, one indication that the work was still a vestige of the past was its failure to address the *genbun itchi* movement. By 1889, in fact, several developments had taken place that should have prompted Takada to place the discussion of the *genbun itchi* issue at the forefront of his treatise. In the field of education, a number of textbooks had already been published that were written in the colloquial, while significant experimentations had also taken place in the press, albeit with mixed results. The mid-1880s had also seen the publication of important academic works by scholars of language and literature that cogently supported the call for a simplification of literary language, and in the very year *Bijigaku* was published, the debate on the feasibility of a written language based on the vernacular significantly intensified. In the field of literature, in particular, Futabatei Shimei and Yamada Bimyō had just caused a stir in the literary world with a literary language that broke with tradition and saw the vernacular as a possible appropriate means of literary expression.[20]

Despite the extreme relevance of the *genbun itchi* debate to the literary developments of those years, however, *Bijigaku* made no reference to the creation of a new literary language or to the debate over its feasibility. In fact, the examples employed throughout the book in support of its arguments came entirely from classical literature, leading many to erroneously identify rhetoric with purely premodern styles and literary conventions. However, it is fair to say that as the first native treatise on rhetoric in modern times, *Bijigaku* contributed significantly to the proliferation of studies of composition and literary criticism.[21] According to literary scholar Tsukahara Tetsuo, with the publication of this work rhetoric progressed through the early stages of its development to become an independent and established field of study. For scholar Namekawa Michio, *Bijigaku*'s influence on the development of writing education cannot be denied.[22] And for Hara Shirō, the publication of this work was more than an individual achievement: it was the result of the ongoing common effort of scholars at Tōkyō Senmon Gakkō to engage in a serious investigation of language and literature.[23] Interestingly, the publication of *Bijigaku* coincided with that period in the development of Japanese literature to which Nishio Mitsuo has referred as "the beginning of a new trend in writing and its investigation."[24]

Bijigaku's contribution reached far beyond the issue of originality, embracing a series of questions that were crucial to the cultural transformation of the Meiji years. Takada sought to introduce a new system of rules that would serve to redefine the heritage of Japanese literature. He believed that this new system of rules could provide a platform from which to address problems peculiar to the Japanese literary world, among them the creation of an aesthetic model for the definition of Japanese literary identity, albeit in Western terms. His *Bijigaku* was thus more the result of a syncretic assimilation of Western treatises rather than the original formulation of a uniquely Japanese rhetorical theory. It follows that the points discussed within its pages were likely dictated by the content of the original Western works, most of which drew from the British tradition. It could not have been otherwise, since rhetoric did not exist as an official field of study yet and still needed to be defined both in terms of methodology and investigative scope. As discussed earlier, the works published before *Bijigaku* were essentially manuals of oratory that did not consider rhetoric as a field concerned with literature, but only with oral communication. Takada's major achievement thus lay in his effort to reestablish the link first created by Kikuchi Dairoku between Western and native literary tradition. The main task of this endeavor was to determine whether and how Western rhetoric could be applied to issues peculiar to Japanese language and literature.

Rhetoric in the 1890s: The Conservative Years

The last decade of the nineteenth century saw the publication of several works on rhetoric, both in the area of oral and written communication. The field of investigation that was mostly concerned with literature and the written language began to move in two main directions, one emphasizing literary criticism, the other composition. In the former category were the works of the rhetoricians at Tōkyō Senmon Gakkō such as Shōyō and, in the following decade, Shimamura Hōgetsu. The latter category, in contrast, included works by scholars who moved in other academic circles, like that of Tokyo Imperial University, or those who did not necessarily view rhetoric as closely correlated to aesthetics and literary criticism.

Following *Bijigaku*, one of the first works to appear was Nakajima Kanji's *Bunshō kumitatehō* (Principles of arrangement in composition).[25] Published in 1891 and divided into two sections addressing, respectively, thought and writing, *Bunshō kumitatehō* was a discussion of the nature of thought, including its mental and emotional aspects, and the process through which it could be better expressed. In Western rhetorical terms, it was partly a discussion of "invention" and "arrangement," that is to say, the means to find and organize the materials to be presented. However, there was no definition of rhetoric within its pages, and the author himself emphasized the originality of his work.

Nakajima bemoaned the lack of a manual for composition written for pedagogical purposes. He noted that the field of composition had enjoyed some new developments in recent years but was still far from constituting an organized field of study. In particular, he regretted the fact that despite new discoveries in various areas of scholarly investigation, the field of composition was the only one that was still struggling with modernity.[26] With many examples from classical literature and a strong emphasis on *kanbun* in general, *Bunshō kumitatehō* was hardly even cited by its contemporaries, nor is it mentioned in recent scholarship, with the notable exception of Nishio Mitsuo, who regards it as one of the important works of the period.[27]

In the following year, another work was published that primarily addressed the problem of composition. Edited by Fuzanbō, *Bunshō soshikihō* (Principles of organization in composition) was part of *Futsūgaku zensho,* a collection of volumes that also included works on botany, geometry, psychology, and so forth. According to the preface, *Bunshō soshikihō* was largely indebted to Genung's *The Practical Elements of Rhetoric.* Divided into two sections, one on style and the other on invention, *Bunshō soshikihō* touched on some stylistic issues that are particularly relevant to this volume. Style was defined as a means to express one's thoughts through language, to be characterized by clarity, force, and beauty. Figures were defined as a deviation from the plain and ordinary mode of expression, for the sake of greater rhetorical effect. A comparison with *The Practical Elements of Rhetoric* reveals that *Bunshō soshikihō* adopted almost in full the definitions provided by the original Western work. On two points, however, the Japanese work differed from its Western counterpart. First, *Bunshō soshikihō* added that figures were indispensable to the sentence, a statement that had been made previously by *Bijigaku* but that cannot be found, certainly not in the same terms, in *The Practical Elements of Rhetoric.* Second, *Bunshō soshikihō* failed to indicate that a deviation from ordinary expressions in figurative language is not to be taken as an argument against naturalness, a point strongly emphasized by Genung in his work.[28] Thus *Bunshō soshikihō* proposed a definition of figures that shared Takada's view of rhetorical necessity without clarifying that the presence of such figures did not necessarily imply affectation in writing. This may have offered grounds for the further criticism of rhetorical figures as mere ornaments that produced only a pedantic and undesirable effect. Apart from that, however, the treatment of rhetorical figures was virtually identical to Genung's: they were classified into those promoting clarity and concreteness and those promoting emphasis. *Bunshō soshikihō* discussed a total of fourteen figures, four less than were discussed in *Bijigaku.*

Aside from its discussion of style, *Bunshō soshikihō* should be credited with offering one of the first treatments of "invention," which served to introduce new ideas about that part of the discipline concerned with discovery of the material to be presented. In fact, the second section of the book defined the various procedures involved in finding, sorting, and ordering the material of discourse. It also addressed the attitudes and habits needed for the improvement of the above activities, the three fundamental elements of "invention" (introduction, development, conclusion), and its relationship to different types of writing, namely description, narration, argumentation, exposition, and persuasion. From this point of view, *Bunshō soshikihō's* contribution was noteworthy, all the more so because it discussed a component of rhetoric that Takada had neglected and that only Takeshima Hagoromo's *Shūjigaku* would later discuss in 1898. Despite this contribution, however, *Bunshō soshikihō* shared with *Bijigaku* the failure to address the important changes taking place in the literary world. In fact, according to its preface, the written styles predominant at the time of publication were *wabun* (Japanese native-prose style), *kanbun,* and *wakan konkōbun* (a Sinicized Japanese prose style). The *genbun itchi* vernacular style was not even considered, and the examples used throughout the book were once again exclusively drawn from classical literature. This possibly led to a reinforcement of the notion that rhetoric was concerned only with traditional literary styles and, as such, antithetical to the development of a modern form of written expression free from literary constrictions.

This trait was common to most works of rhetoric of the time. Hattori Motohiko's *Shūjigaku* (Rhetoric), published in 1891, also dismissed the vernacular as a literary style. Hattori taught rhetoric at the Kokugo Denshūjo, a private school founded in 1870 whose faculty included Konakamura Kiyonori (1821–1895) and Kimura Masakoto (1827–1913). Hattori's *Shūjigaku* seemed to be largely indebted to Takada's *Bijigaku*. The treatment of style and taste as well as the definition of rhetoric as a science concerned not only with composition but also with discerning "good" and "bad" writing were reminiscent of Takada's conception. Figures were defined along *Bijigaku's* lines and also were to an extent described using the same terminology. Most interesting was the last chapter, where the author decried the lack of adequate manuals for the study of rhetoric and stressed its importance for the development of the art of composition. Hattori himself had accordingly devised *Shūjigaku* to support his lectures and to lament the lack of scholarship in the field.

Returning to the question of language, *Shūjigaku* interestingly defined rhetoric as a science that taught how to write well and that could be applied to the domain of oral communication in those countries where "the spoken and written language coincided."[29] Since the work did not ultimately consider the discussion of rhetoric as the art of speech, it is possible to speculate that it was indeed the awareness of the existence of a substantial gap between spoken and written Japanese that convinced Hattori to exclude this area from the scope of rhetoric. As is then clear, the exclusion of oratory from the domain of rhetorical investigation continued to characterize the scholarly production on rhetoric throughout the 1890s.

Later works confirmed this trend. Hagino Yoshiyuki's *Sakubunpō* (A manual of composition), for example, published in 1892, completely disregarded the domain of oral discourse and focused exclusively on writing.[30] This work contained a short history of Japanese prose and covered separately each of the four styles the author had identified as the most predominant of the time, namely *futsūbun* (standard written style), *sōrōbun* (epistolary style), *wabun,* and *kanbun.*[31] The section on *kanbun* made up one-third of the book, indicating the high regard for this style even at the end of the nineteenth century. Overall, the examples provided throughout the text were again limited to premodern literary works, and the *genbun itchi* style itself was again devalued and criticized as "verbose, vulgar, and without literary taste."[32]

Meanwhile, at Tōkyō Senmon Gakkō, Takada and his colleagues had been able to ride the wave of a growing interest in questions of style, criticism, and literary theory. Tsubouchi Shōyō further translated that interest into "Bijironkō," a series that appeared intermittently in the journal *Waseda bungaku* (Waseda literature) from January through September 1893. Shōyō had always shared with Takada a deep interest in rhetoric. Already in his *Shōsetsu shinzui* he had displayed important links to Western works of rhetoric such as Bain's *English Composition and Rhetoric.* And in an article that had appeared in 1886, he clearly advocated the importance of rhetoric in the process of searching for a new literary style.[33]

In the preface of his "Bijironkō," Shōyō warned readers not to think of rhetoric as a discipline concerned with composition. He held that rhetoric ought to teach how to discern beauty in literature rather than how to become skilled in writing, although rhetoric could be used as a tool to prevent poor writing. With this view, he distanced himself from the notion shared by some that rhetoric was mostly concerned with composition. Next, he complained about the lack of native scholarship in the field. He noted that a few works had appeared following the publication of Kikuchi's *Shūji oyobi kabun* and Takada's *Bijigaku,* but these did not, in his view, represent any significant scholarly achievement. Compared to them, he went on, Takada's study was by far superior. Yet *Bijigaku* itself was not exempt from Shōyō's criticism, and he denounced its strong dependence on Western sources and the repeated use of inappropriate examples. For these very reasons, Shōyō added, he had decided to write "Bijironkō" to complement his friend Takada's effort to establish the study of rhetoric in Japan.

Shōyō maintained that writing was the object of his rhetorical theory and that it comprised three fundamental elements, namely the intellect, the feelings, and the will. Writing could be divided into *koto* and *tsū, koto* representing the realm of particular types of communication such as legal or strictly scientific documents, and *tsū* representing writing in general. Literature was, according to Shōyō, part of the latter domain and was the very object of rhetorical investigation.

The classification of writing into the three elements of intellect, feelings, and will was already present in his earlier piece, "Bunshō shinron" (A new theory of writing, 1886), and closely resembled the following passage from Bain's *English Composition and Rhetoric.*

> In speaking there are three principal ends—to inform, to persuade, to please. They correspond to the three departments of the human mind, the Understanding, the Will, and the Feeling.[34]

According to Shōyō, each of these types of writing had an object, a channel, and a tool through which writers achieved their goal. Intellectual writing used the tool of speculative thought to stimulate understanding through the channel of argumentation. It was characterized by five elements, namely perception, memory, recollection, imagination, and reason, and could be divided into two main styles, description and argumentation. The goal of this type of writing was the transmission of knowledge, and it was considered especially useful for the conveyance of information. The emotional style, by contrast, appealed to the emotions by means of imagination through the channel of description. It could be divided into poetry (dramatic, lyric, and epic) and prose (or belles lettres). This type of writing did not have a real goal per se other than the transmission of the author's feelings. This was, for Shōyō, the domain of literature. Finally, the persuasive style sought to encourage the receiver of the message to take a concrete course of action through both speculative thought and the use of imagination. This final type was, however, never fully addressed, and the discussion thus remained unfinished.[35]

It is not easy to assess the contribution of "Bijironkō" as a work of rhetoric. Some scholars have suggested that it was an outgrowth of the ideas expressed a decade earlier in *Shōsetsu shinzui.*[36] Others have seen it as an extension of the *botsuirisō* (rejection of ideals) dispute with Mori Ōgai that immediately preceded the publication of this work.[37] As a textual entity, "Bijironkō" was certainly the outcome of Shōyō's long theoretical journey in search of a new definition of the function of literature. Such a journey did not necessarily hold the study of rhetoric as a priority of its investigation. However, it was nevertheless so closely linked to the field of rhetoric that Kamei Hideo has recently emphasized the strong dependency of *Shōsetsu shinzui* on several Western works already present in Japan at the time.[38] Regardless, "Bijironkō" shared with *Bijigaku* the important perception of rhetoric as a discipline having strong ties with grammar, logic, and aesthetics, while also having significant interdisciplinary ramifications in several fields of human knowledge. Shōyō clearly located rhetoric between the fields of national language and logic on one side and aesthetics on the other, enhancing the status of the discipline in the literary debates of the period. The idea that rhetoric was not a system of rules for composition but rather a field of study concerned with the discernment of beauty in literature was clearly at the foundation of both works. Rhetoric was not, for Shōyō, simply a "science that taught how to write well."[39]

Published in 1893, Ōwada Takeki's *Shūjigaku* (Rhetoric) reiterated rhetoric's proximity to literary criticism and elegant composition. This work was part of *Tsūzoku bungaku zensho* (A complete collection of popular literature), a collection whose purpose lay, according to the preface, "not in the encouragement of aristocratic literature but popular literature." The collection included a total of twelve volumes, all authored by Ōwada and including works on *kanbun, kyōgen,* and traditional and free-verse poetry. *Shūjigaku* was admittedly the attempt to apply the rules of Western rhetoric to native poetry and literature, another indication of how relevant rhetoric was thought to be in fostering literature during those years.

In the opening pages of his work, Ōwada (1857–1910) linked rhetoric to the domain of the *bibun* (elegant prose). According to him, rhetoric was a science that taught how to write well and how to touch the reader's emotions. It could be divided into the two activities of learning and criticism. The former was related to the creation of a beautiful literary style and presupposed the knowledge of grammar and the study of the appropriate rules of composition. The latter was by contrast concerned with the comparison and criticism of past and present literary pieces. Ōwada saw literary signification as distinctly divided into two planes of expression (and content), a higher and a lower one. The higher one was the domain of the *bibun,* which was in turn the object of the application of rhetoric. Rhetoric was thus limited only to elegant writing, a notion that implicitly excluded the analysis of modern forms of literary expression based on the vernacular. It is not a coincidence that the examples provided throughout were all from classical literature and that even the advertising section of the book spoke of a manual of composition for Japanese classical prose and poetry. Once again, rhetoric did not address the possibility of developing a literary style based on the vernacular.

An appendix followed containing examples of literary criticism on classical pieces such as *Genji monogatari* and *Tsurezuregusa.* This emphasis on classical literature as well as the redundant references throughout the text to traditional poetry is indicative of the fact that *Shūjigaku* mainly addressed a specific form of written communication, that is, literature, and more specifically, that generally referred to as "belles lettres." In the first pages of the treatise Ōwada defined rhetoric as a discipline that taught how to become skilled in writing, but his concern was clearly limited to literature and its appreciation. In fact, he addressed the issue of composition in another work, *Sakubun kumitatehō* (Principles of arrangement in composition), a piece also included in *Tsūzoku bungaku zensho,* where he dealt with specific grammatical issues such as the *onbin* (euphonic changes) and verb conjugations. There, he affirmed that the difference between classical and vernacular styles could not be entirely reconciled but added that the gap between the two was, in his view, minimal and mostly a matter of ornamentation. The vernacular appealed more to the sense of hearing, whereas classical language appealed to the sense of sight. Since they had different purposes, there was no need to argue over which one was superior to the other. While this view seemed to concede equal prestige to colloquial styles, it also implied that they were not fully appropriate for writing because of their lack of refinement.[40]

Rhetoric's inability, at this time, to formulate a solid theoretical framework for the employment of the vernacular in literature should not come as a surprise. The *bundan* of the 1890s was itself characterized by a resurgence of traditional literary modes and by a general atmosphere of skepticism with respect to the feasibility of a *genbun itchi* style. From this point of view, rhetoric just mirrored the state of affairs during those years. Shōyō was among the first to take notice of this backward trend.[41] He indicated that a revived interest in past literary practices had recently swept the literary world as if to counterbalance the persistent call for a simplified literary language that in the previous years had accompanied Japan's opening to the West and Western literature. These new developments led to the revival of Edo writer Ihara Saikaku, whose *gazoku setchū* (mixed elegant and colloquial) prose style was largely emulated by literary giants Ozaki Kōyō and Kōda Rohan, and the rise of the *shin kokubun* (new Japanese prose style) movement, which through the leadership of Ochiai Naobumi called for a return to the classics and the establishment of a literary style based on that tradition. The 1890s saw then the publication of a number of celebrated novels by such authors as Kōyō, Rohan, Mori Ōgai, and Higuchi Ichiyō, who all shared in those years a manifest preference for classically based literary styles over the employment of the vernacular in writing. It was only at the end of the third decade of the Meiji period, at the turn of the century, that the debate over the feasibility of a *genbun itchi* style began to dominate academic and literary circles again.[42]

The last major work of rhetoric of the decade was Takeshima Hagoromo's *Shūjigaku* (Rhetoric), published in 1898. Like Fuzanbō's *Bunshō soshikihō, Shūji-*

gaku was strongly indebted to Genung's *The Practical Elements of Rhetoric*. It was divided into two parts, the first addressing problems of style such as the purity and accuracy of language and the structure of writing (from the sentence to the paragraph on to the chapter), and the second discussing the procedure of "invention," which he defined as the collection of ideas, the discernment between appropriate and inappropriate materials, and their final arrangement. Here, Hagoromo discussed the various phases of this procedure in each of the four styles he had identified, that is, description, narration, exposition, and argumentation.

Among this work's most important contributions was the redefinition of rhetoric's scope and domain. Hagoromo addressed rhetoric's disciplinary transition in the Western world, noting that during its millenary history it had been perceived at times as the art of speech and at other times as a system of rules for literary embellishment; in his view, however, it was neither of these. According to him, rhetoric taught "how to communicate one's thoughts to others in an effective way, through the use of language."[43] Rhetoric's first concern was to teach the proper use of language, while its chief task was the effective expression of one's feelings and thoughts.

Hagoromo went on to indicate that at present rhetoric covered the realm of both prose and poetry. He maintained that among previous scholarship only one native work of rhetoric deserved to be mentioned, Takada Sanae's *Bijigaku*. As a result, rhetoric's terminology, including the term *"shūji"* itself, was not only far from being established, but was also not reflective of its original meaning in the West. Finally, Hagoromo acknowledged the work of several Western scholars, among them Genung, Bain, and Herbert Spencer.

He then provided a detailed treatment of rhetorical devices. He divided them into tropes and figures, one of the very few scholars in Japan to do so.[44] He then classified tropes into three groups, according to relationships of similarity, contiguity, and contrast. Figures of speech were also divided into three categories, based on relationships of contrast, repetition, and combination. The rhetorical process was again defined as a deviation from the ordinary usage of the linguistic material.[45] Unlike preceding works such as *Bunshō soshikihō*, Hagoromo cautioned against the indiscriminate use of rhetorical figures. This, he said, could result in undesired affectation. Thus he created the premise for a redefinition of the rhetorical figure that would differentiate between effective rhetorical devices and mere embellishments. This significant statement, however, did not change the overall character of his work, which failed to address the *genbun itchi* movement and discussed only classical literary pieces.

Despite some evident overlap with previous works, Hagoromo's *Shūjigaku* was, however, able to change the view scholars had of rhetoric. Hagoromo significantly broadened the perspective scholars held of the discipline, seeing rhetoric not so much as a field of study concerned with elegance, whether in the oral or written realm, but rather as a science that governed the universal principles of communication itself. Communication was now the goal of the rhetorical process, and its study would be one of the objectives of the rhetorical investigations of the following decade.[46]

The last decade of the nineteenth century was thus a period of productive scholarship for rhetoric, characterized by a continuing change and evolution in the goals and objects of the investigation. First introduced as the art of speech in the early years of the Meiji era, rhetoric developed to include composition and literary criticism, which subsequently became the primary concern of the discipline, to the detriment of public speaking. Takada Sanae, in particular, delineated a watershed between the phase when rhetoric was mostly perceived as the art of speech and when it came to be understood as a discipline concerned with literature and composition. Native works published thereafter relied heavily on his treatise, both in content and terminology, and they all contributed to the establishment of the discipline as a legitimate field of study and a part of the scholastic curricula of several institutions in the years to come.

The works of Bain and Quackenbos were widely read.[47] Spencer's *Philosophy of Style* was also, reportedly, well liked.[48] Needless to say, eighteenth- and nineteenth-century English and American treatises played a key role in the development of studies of rhetoric in Japan. Japanese scholars borrowed heavily from these sources, discussing the definitions and scope of rhetoric and describing the various parts it comprised. However, their scholarship soon came to acquire a uniquely Japanese character as it sought to address linguistic and literary issues that were peculiar to Japan. The problem of language was among the most prominent of these issues. Unfortunately, at least until the end of the century, Japanese research on rhetoric was often characterized by a conservative view that did not easily support significant changes toward a more simplified literary style. The major works of the time either maintained the superiority of classical styles or completely disregarded the possibility of employing contemporary linguistic features in writing. This disregard contributed to the endorsement of the literary status quo, a fact that gave rise to a climate of antirhetorical sentiment among the younger generation of writers. These developments resulted in conflicting views over the role of rhetoric in the modernization of literature.

On the basis of these considerations, one may conclude that rhetoric did not play a relevant part in the modernization of the literary language. At the beginning of the new century, rhetoric found itself at an impasse, unable to justify its own raison d'etre and theoretically in conflict with the emerging forces in the *bundan*. However, the scholarly production of the first two decades of the twentieth century sought to divest rhetoric of its conservative character and to give it a new identity and a role in the quest for a modern literary language.

In the midst of this crisis, two scholars in particular, Shimamura Hōgetsu and Igarashi Chikara, were able to perceive the changing times and propose a new rhetorical theory better suited to the needs of the Japanese literary world. The following chapters discuss their works and clarify how they contributed to charting a new course within the discipline, thus making the end of the Meiji period a major turning point in the history of rhetoric in Japan.

5
A New Course in Rhetorical Inquiry

At the turn of the century, the conservative character of scholarship in the field of rhetoric caused the discipline to be perceived by many intellectuals and authors as anachronistic and incapable of reconciling its taxonomic nature with the notion of artistic freedom in writing. Rhetoric became subject to strong criticism from the literary coterie that supported the idea of an independent and self-serving literature and of a plain and concise mode of literary expression, based on the vernacular and therefore free from archaic literary constrictions. In particular, the rise of realism and naturalism dealt a great blow to the popularity of studies of rhetoric, which, at least on the surface, was the antithesis of their call for plain, "true," and concise literary writing.

However, as has been noted, rhetoric was by no means exclusively associated with archaic precepts and literary dogma. In fact, at the time of its introduction as the art of speaking in public, rhetoric was hailed as a champion of progress and democracy and was often identified with liberty and freedom of speech. Even later, as a field of study with close ties to literature, rhetoric continued to appeal to a large number of young scholars and intellectuals who were able to discern its importance not only as a means of communication, but also as the repository of centuries of Western knowledge. A symbol at the same time of both innovation and tradition, rhetoric contained the seeds of a latent ambivalence and thus epitomized the conflict between old and new that strongly characterized the Meiji years. Shimamura Hōgetsu's *Shin bijigaku* (New rhetoric) was published at the peak of this ideological conflict and as such constituted an important landmark in the evolution of rhetorical theory in Japan.

Shimamura Hōgetsu's *Shin Bijigaku*:
Rhetoric as Part of a General Theory of Aesthetics

Hōgetsu (1871–1918), a graduate of Waseda University, was a key figure of the Meiji *bundan*. His scholarly activity can generally be divided into three phases: the early part of his career through his trip to Europe, which took place between 1902 and 1905; the years when Hōgetsu, now back in Japan, distinguished himself for his writings on naturalism; and his withdrawal from the forefront of literary debate and progressive engagement in theater. Hōgetsu is thus widely known both for his activity as literary critic of naturalism and his contribution to the modernization of Japanese theater. He is also known for his writings on aesthetics, a subject he studied under the guidance of philosopher Ōnishi Hajime (1864–1901). However, he is almost never remembered for his *Shin bijigaku,* a treatise of rhetoric that ironically became the only work he ever completed.[1]

Written immediately before his departure for Europe, *Shin bijigaku* is important for at least two reasons: first, it represented the final product of Hōgetsu's early work in the field of aesthetics and rhetoric under the influence of Tsubouchi Shōyō and Ōnishi Hajime; and second, as will be discussed later, in terminating the tradition of *bijigaku* studies at Waseda University, this treatise also created the premise for the initiation of a new course for the study of rhetoric in Japan.

Published in 1902, *Shin bijigaku* was divided into three sections, namely "General Theory," "Theory of Figures," and "Aesthetics." The introduction comprised three chapters in which Hōgetsu defined rhetoric and set the stage for the following discussion of his rhetorical theory. Before defining rhetoric, however, Hōgetsu commented on his choice of the term *"bijigaku."* The term had already been employed by Takada Sanae and Tsubouchi Shōyō, who preferred it to the term *"shūjigaku,"* more widely used outside the Waseda circle.[2] Hōgetsu pointed out that the two terms were essentially synonyms, but he opted for the former on the grounds that it better exemplified rhetoric's close ties to aesthetics. In fact, according to him, rhetoric was "the science of writing that explained the principles through which the (modifying of) words generated beauty."[3] Writing was a form of art, and rhetoric, as a discipline that explained its principles, was part of a theory of art. The purpose of his treatise was then "to study the beauty in writing through rhetoric, within an aesthetic framework."[4] Having so postulated, Hōgetsu observed that rhetoric's scope had been originally limited to public speaking, but that its present major concern was now writing, thereby endorsing the disciplinary transition that had taken place in the second half of the Meiji period. Hōgetsu clarified the object of his study: it was beauty that most concerned him, and, particularly, the aesthetic experience generated by a rhetorical use of language.

The question of beauty had been a central theme in Hōgetsu's early scholarly endeavors. In 1894 he published a revised edition of his graduation thesis in the journal *Waseda bungaku* and had already expressed his strong determination to work as a scholar in the field of aesthetics.[5] Later in life, he often recalled his desire to "stand at the crossroads between philosophy and literature," reiterating the centrality of beauty in his thought.[6] This search for beauty is, then, at the core of Hōgetsu's entire scholarly production and constitutes an essential premise for the content and understanding of his rhetorical theory. It also defines his *Shin biji-gaku*, distinguishing it from preceding scholarship, which, with the partial exception of Takada and Shōyō, addressed rhetoric without giving much consideration to the aesthetics of literary production.[7]

Having thus elected beauty as the main focus of his rhetorical investigation, in the second chapter of the introduction Hōgetsu defined rhetoric. During the 1890s, most scholars had generally defined it as a science that taught how to write well. But for him, rhetoric was instead "the science that studied the source of beauty in words." The object of rhetoric was the study of rhetorical phenomena, that is, the phenomena that occurred through the process of "extension of thoughts and emotions." In his view, rhetorical phenomena were outside the realm of ordinary language, which aimed only at plain communication and was not concerned with persuasion and the stimulation of emotion. The stimulation of emotion was, however, a crucial step and condition for the production of these phenomena, whose ultimate objective remained the creation of beauty and the re-alization of an aesthetic experience.[8] The scope of Hōgetsu's investigation clearly lay within the framework of an aesthetic approach to language and literature.[9]

The second section of the treatise was divided into three chapters: "Structure of a Theory of Rhetoric," "Figures," and "Style." Hōgetsu began by describing rhetorical phenomena as being composed of two planes, one of content and one of form, the former being "an extension of thought" and the latter "an extension of linguistic use." He compared the expressions *"kao ga kirei da"* (the face is beautiful) and *"kanbase hana no gotoshi"* (a face like a flower). The former example represented, in his view, zero degree of the linguistic expression, an expression that did not contain any rhetorical device per se but that at the same time constituted a necessary condition for further linguistic manipulation. He called this type of expression "plain" and the rhetorical attributes that governed it "passive." On the other hand, the latter expression represented an extension of thought and was, strictly speaking, a type of rhetorical phenomenon. He called this type of sen-tence "rhetorical" and the rhetorical attributes that governed it "active."[10]

Thus rhetorical phenomena were divided, according to Hōgetsu, into "pas-sive" and "active." Plain sentences were the realm of passive rhetorical attributes, namely those attributes traditionally described by syntax and stylistics, like the logical order and the balance of propositions and the purity and accuracy of words. By contrast, rhetorical sentences were the realm of active rhetorical attributes, those attributes such as figures that added beauty and elegance to the sentence. The passive plane was the domain of clarity of thought and appropriateness of language and constituted the minimum prerequisite for the development of the active plane, which was in turn concerned with connotative meanings, that is, "the extension of thought and the expressiveness of language."

Hōgetsu developed his theory of figures along this line of thought. He distinguished two groups of rhetorical devices. The first group, called *sōsai,* addressed the description of most types of figures, while the second group, called *gosai,* addressed the concepts of purity and accuracy. The domain of *sōsai* was the place of traditional rhetorical figures. Hōgetsu partially disregarded earlier classifications by Western rhetoricians, dismissing, for example, the differentiation between tropes and figures that had also been accepted by Takeshima Hagoromo. He divided figures into four groups according to the mental processes of comparison, arrangement, transformation, and exposition. He discussed a total of twenty-nine figures, the most in any treatise ever written in modern Japan until then. In fact, Takada Sanae had stopped at twenty, Ōwada Takeki at thirteen, and Takeshima Hagoromo at twenty-three, while Shōyō had not discussed them at all. The number of pages required by this section totaled more than 40 percent of the whole treatise, which illustrates the high priority given by Hōgetsu to the discussion of these devices.

After his treatment of rhetorical figures, Hōgetsu discussed the types and properties of style. While the discussion of style could be found in earlier works of rhetoric such as Takada's *Bijigaku* or Hagoromo's *Shūjigaku,* Hōgetsu's discussion of the relationship between elegant and vulgar language was new and particularly poignant, since this conflicting relationship had been one of the causes of the multiplicity of written styles still extant during the Meiji period. To be precise, Hōgetsu had already touched on the *genbun itchi* issue in the second chapter of the introduction, the first to do so in almost a decade.[11] In that chapter, he advocated the importance of rhetorical devices in the sentence, thus reasserting the basic view held by rhetoricians on the centrality of rhetoric in a theory of composition. At the same time, however, he endorsed the possibility of creating a style based entirely on the vernacular. That position was, in a way, contradictory and new, if one considers that the dichotomy of "rhetorical devices versus vernacular" had been one of the main arguments in the theoretical conflict between classical and contemporary vernacular styles. But according to Hōgetsu, the acceptance of a literary style entirely based on the vernacular implied the commitment to "the creation of rhetorical devices particular only to the spoken language."[12]

On the basis of these earlier deliberations, Hōgetsu reconsidered the relationship between vulgar and elegant styles, reiterating that the difference between the two was not one of "quality" or "prestige," but rather one between spoken and written language. He acknowledged the vernacular as an independent language system that had its own mechanisms and rules and that, as such, was neither superior nor inferior to classical language. It was simply necessary, in his view, to refine it and turn it into an appropriate tool for literary production.

The section on aesthetics completed the treatise. This third part is said to have been hastily written because of Hōgetsu's upcoming departure to Europe.[13] Here, Hōgetsu once again dismissed the notion of rhetoric as being part of logic or ethics and reiterated its place within a general theory of aesthetics.

The significance of this point has not been addressed and deserves special attention. As discussed earlier, Hōgetsu inherited a rhetorical system at the turn of the century that could hardly justify its role in an age of growing dissent toward rules and literary precepts. In fact, although the 1890s had been a period of remarkable achievements in the field of rhetorical investigation, those same years had ironically contributed to the characterization of the discipline as an obsolete system of rules. To those who at the time strongly emphasized the independence of literature as a form of artistic achievement, a discipline such as rhetoric, so inevitably confined within the boundaries of its pragmatic goal of persuading the audience or appealing to the reader's emotions, seemed to have no intrinsic value. Its own heteronomous nature prevented rhetoric from coexisting with the common idealistic and romantic sentiment that saw literature as an absolute artistic expression beyond time and social conventions.[14] Hōgetsu's inclusion of rhetoric within a theory of aesthetics was his effort to reclaim its autonomy and sanction its pertinence to the major literary debates of the period. This convergence within a theory of art assured rhetoric of an artistic dimension that justified its reason for being and proposed it as a partner for a dialectical exchange with other disciplines on a variety of linguistic and literary issues.

In short, Hōgetsu developed a rhetorical theory capable of reconciling the extremes of the debate over the creation of a new literary language while bringing forth an acceptable compromise between the notions of elegance and truth in writing. He did so at a crucial juncture for modern Japanese literature, at a time when the publication of such works as Kosugi Tengai's *Hatsusugata* (New Year's finery, 1900) and *Hayari uta* (Popular song, 1902) signaled the rise of a realistic trend in literature that seriously questioned the role of sophistication in writing. In view of these new developments, of which he was well aware, Hōgetsu restated the importance of rhetorical signification. He viewed rhetoric as related to aesthetics and defined the domain of the rhetorical experience around the concept of beauty, bringing rhetoric within the boundaries of a theory of art. His theory of figures revealed itself to be quite elaborate when compared to those of his predecessors. Unfortunately, his extensive treatment of these contributed to making the discipline intimidating to the nonscholar, turning it into a corpus of notions difficult to apply to problems of ordinary writing. His rhetoric was, in a few words, coherent in a scholarly sense but still removed from the needs of the popular literary and pedagogical worlds. Yet it contained the seeds for a future theoretical compromise, a compromise that was reached just a few years later.

Igarashi Chikara's *Shin bunshō kōwa:* From Beautiful to Accomplished Writing

The years following Hōgetsu's *Shin bijigaku* were crucial for modern Japanese literature. Despite a period of decline at the end of the nineteenth century, the *genbun itchi* movement made a successful and decisive comeback in the first decade of the twentieth century. Individuals such as Yamada Bimyō had contributed significantly to the reappraisal of the vernacular, laying the foundation for the development of a new literary language. Concurrently, important literary figures such as Masaoka Shiki and Takahama Kyoshi reiterated the need for a plain and direct language in literature, thus postulating the existence of a crucial theoretical link between a realistic style and the use of the vernacular. Later, writer and literary critic Tayama Katai was among those who further sustained the drive toward a naturalistic approach to literature.

At Waseda University, scholars such as Igarashi Chikara (1874–1947) continued to be engaged in studies of rhetoric. Igarashi entered Tōkyō Senmon Gakkō in 1892 and studied mostly under Shōyō and Ōnishi, as had Hōgetsu, who was Igarashi's senior by one year. Igarashi graduated in 1895, and after working among the staff of the journal *Waseda bungaku,* he was appointed lecturer at his alma mater in 1901. He was in close contact with Hōgetsu, having shared the same teachers, friends, and club activities; their close relationship is evidenced not only by the epigraph he wrote on Hōgetsu's tombstone at the time of his death, but also by many other instances in which he played a key role in matters important to Hōgetsu's private life.[15]

Despite this close interaction and exposure to the same teachers and ideas, however, Igarashi eventually developed a rhetorical theory quite different from that of Hōgetsu, one that changed the course of rhetorical investigation in Japan for years to come. Igarashi rejected the aesthetic aspect of Hōgetsu's theory and brought forward a "simplified" rhetorical theory that addressed the crucial issue of how to write at a time when stylistic chaos ruled the *bundan*.

While Igarashi wrote extensively on rhetoric, he is certainly best remembered for his *Shin bunshō kōwa* (New lectures on writing), a study published in 1909 and regarded by many scholars as one of the greatest achievements of Japanese scholarship on rhetoric in modern times.[16] *Shin bunshō kōwa* was the revised version of an earlier work, *Bunshō kōwa* (Lectures on composition), a book that had been published in 1905, only three years after the publication of Hōgetsu's *Shin bijigaku*. *Shin bunshō kōwa* could be partially considered an outgrowth of *Bunshō kōwa,* with which it certainly shares important methodological premises and objects, such as a distinctively psychological approach to rhetoric, inherited from the British tradition, or the attempt to establish rhetoric within the framework of studies of national literature. However, *Shin bunshō kōwa* also boasts significant differences that helped distinguish it from Igarashi's earlier work and make it the most important study among Igarashi's overall scholarly production on the subject.

Divided into seven sections, *Shin bunshō kōwa* began, first of all, with a far-reaching statement: "our written language and more generally all the fields of art and literature have been experiencing a great revolution."[17] This observation was followed by a discussion of some of the major disputes of the Meiji period, such as the relationship between art and truth, form and content, and expression and thought. It was the first true acknowledgment in a rhetorical treatise of the profound changes the literary world was facing in those years. A "rhetoric of silence" had in fact been the common trait of earlier scholarship in the field, which hardly ever discussed the significance of the new current of thought among younger writers and scholars who called for a radical simplification of literary style. Breaking with this tradition of reticence, Igarashi finally addressed the issue, noting a new trend in writing that shunned embellishment and favored a plain and direct style, without ornamentation or exaggeration. In his view, this new style was realistic in nature and, as such, refused the authority and prestige of old classical conventions in favor of a colloquial usage of language that best conveyed the subtleties of modern life. Examples from leading contemporary authors such as Futabatei Shimei, Natsume Sōseki, and Tayama Katai illustrated the potential of this new style and with it the new status of the vernacular, which had now gained ground not only in the dialogical but also in the discursive portions of the literary text.

Igarashi openly supported the establishment of this new form of expression but also sought to correct the crucial misunderstanding that had characterized the debate on the creation of a modern literary style.

Because writing without affectation has become the password of the new written style, having misunderstood its meaning, many are now advocating that rhetorical devices are unnecessary, but this is a groundless theory. Writing without affectation means abolition of unnatural ornaments and classical conventions, it does not mean that all elaborate devices should be considered as unnecessary in writing.[18]

Naturalist writers were especially adamant about this notion, he noted, but examples from such writers as Shimazaki Tōson and Tayama Katai indicated that those very authors also made extensive use of rhetorical devices, as was reasonable to expect. Igarashi's argument was that the difference between the old and new styles did not lie in the presence or absence of rhetorical devices, but in the very nature of those devices.[19] After all, Igarashi pointed out, writing without rhetorical devices was itself an extreme rhetorical artifice.[20]

Thus in the opening statement of his book, Igarashi provided an essential description of the developments that had recently taken place in the literary arena, thereby creating for the first time a link between rhetoric as a field of study and the changing world of Japanese literature. In fact, except for Hōgetsu's *Shin bijigaku,* none of the treatises published previously had been able to create this link, and they thus contributed to the depiction of rhetoric as "foreign" and not applicable to issues of native language and literature.

Having laid the groundwork for a new dialogue between rhetoricians and writers, Igarashi went on to define writing. The purpose of writing was first to communicate and second to appeal to the reader's emotions. This definition was simple and unpretentious; more important, it deemphasized the notion of "beautiful writing," adamantly brought forward by Hōgetsu, in favor of a more general concept of "accomplished writing."[21] Here lay the major difference between Igarashi's work and that of his predecessors at Waseda. The primary object of rhetoric was no longer the production of beauty in writing, but rather that of skillful composition. Rhetoric was no longer an abstract entity, having complicated links to aesthetics, logic, and philosophy, but simply a corpus of practical rules that could lead to the achievement of effective writing. Igarashi's new vision limited the study of rhetoric to the understanding of basic standards and principles that could help improve one's writing skills.

To fully understand the magnitude of this statement it is necessary to consider not only the naturalistic trend sweeping the *bundan* in those years, but also the relationship that bound this work to the earlier *Bunshō kōwa.* There, Igarashi had maintained that "the ideal writing [was] beautiful writing."[22] That is to say, beauty appeared in Igarashi's definition of writing as if to indicate the continuity between his approach and that offered by Takada, Shōyō, and Hōgetsu before him. *Bunshō kōwa* was evidently still conceived within that framework insofar as the examples given were from premodern literature and inevitably written in a classically based literary style, this being a feature common to all the works of rhetoric published to this point. By contrast, *Shin bunshō kōwa* included a large number of works written in *genbun itchi,* including works by such authors as Futabatei Shimei, Kunikida Doppo, and Natsume Sōseki.

This transition was also reflected in the fact that *Shin bunshō kōwa* did not contain a complex definition of rhetoric, as had been the case in some of the preceding works. On the contrary, the only definition provided related to "writing," and thus the work's main concern seemed to lie more in the explanation and assimilation of useful rules for composition. Given the chaotic status of the Japanese written language at the time, such a change of direction was likely most appealing to reformers, teachers, and experts on language policy. In fact, as discussed earlier, Hōgetsu had succeeded in creating the premise for a compromise, opening new possibilities for a solution to the conflict between new and classical modes of literary expression. The complexity of his rhetorical theory, however, had at the same time deepened the gap between the discipline and the fast-changing needs of the Japanese literary world. Igarashi now faced the difficult task of proposing a new rhetoric, a rhetoric not confined to or dominated by the ideals of beauty, prestige, and authority, but with the clear goal of achieving efficient communication.

As a rhetorician, Igarashi understood that the partial criticism of "rules" and "precepts" was a next necessary step in promoting a climate of acceptance for rhetoric. Rules had been the cause of the conflict between rhetoric as a preordered system of values and the rise of new ideas modeled after the concept of free artistic expression. Now more than ever, rules represented a direct attack on the freedom of the writer who strove to go beyond the boundaries of the linguistic form, to achieve what centuries of Japanese literary tradition had not allegedly been able to achieve: the expression of the inner self. Thus Igarashi openly refuted the notion that rules could transform anyone into a gifted writer. This very argument revealed itself to be a successful strategic move in that it struck at the heart of the criticism of the discipline that had been coming from the younger generation of writers. Once rhetoricians became willing to acknowledge writing as an art independent from any form of categorization or classification, the ideological conflict came to assume completely different characteristics.

Having thus concluded his introduction, Igarashi went on to discuss rhetorical figures.[23] Figures were "the embellishment of words, a change in the way things are expressed, that is to say, a form of expressing one's thoughts in a way different from the ordinary, in order to appeal to people's emotions."[24] This definition was not very different from that of earlier works, which mostly emphasized the notion of a creative "deviation" from a certain norm. Igarashi went on to divide rhetorical figures according to eight different principles that, in his view, reflected the mental process of interpreting reality. He discussed a total of fifty-three figures, providing the most detailed treatment in this area in the history of modern Japanese rhetoric.

Paradoxically, Igarashi's elaborate treatment of figures seemed to contradict the ideas set forth in the opening pages of the book. In fact, the initial chapters constituting the introduction of *Shin bunshō kōwa* had represented and supported a major change in the perception of rhetoric, promoting its acceptance as a simple and straightforward assemblage of rules for composition. The elaborate discussion of rhetorical figures that followed seemed to be in disagreement with this original purpose, especially given the high technicality of its content. But perhaps it was precisely because of the new framework in which rhetoric was being discussed that a relatively detailed and taxonomic approach to rhetoric continued to be accepted. While *Shin bunshō kōwa* remains unsurpassed in its detailed explanation of figures, several works that followed similarly gave considerable space to the treatment of these devices.[25]

In conclusion, after Igarashi Chikara's *Shin bunshō kōwa,* rhetoric was no longer the antiquated and rigid discipline that had bloomed in the first half of the Meiji era, but rather a changing field of study that lent itself to assimilation and compromise. As Italian scholar Luciano Anceschi once put it, rhetoric once again proved to be a variable historical disposition that now and then seeks to codify, through norms and principles, the causes and reasons of the literary and artistic movements arising at different ages and times. Thus there is a rhetoric of Romanticism, a rhetoric of realism, and so forth.[26]

Hōgetsu and Igarashi were instrumental in changing the course of rhetoric at the beginning of the twentieth century. Both scholars were aware that the new developments in the literary world would inevitably sanction the end of the discipline as it had been perceived in the 1890s. Both sought, therefore, to provide the necessary theoretical latitude to guarantee its survival among the next generation of writers. Hōgetsu characterized rhetoric as a discipline concerned with the aesthetics of literary production, thus reasserting its utility as a tool of literary investigation. He did so by reclaiming its place within a general theory of aesthetics. But his contribution did not end there; he conceived a new relationship between rhetoric and modern literary language, opening a new range of possibilities for the employment of the vernacular in literature.

Igarashi, on the other hand, remained faithful to his training as a rhetorician, refining, in his work, what had now become a twenty-year-old tradition of scholarly achievements in the field of rhetoric at his home institution. His most representative treatise, *Shin bunshō kōwa,* contained the fruits of those achievements and further consolidated Waseda University's leadership in the field. However, it also broke from tradition, reconciling the taxonomic nature of the discipline with the antirhetorical sentiment that pervaded much of the *bundan.* Devoid of the archaic character that had characterized it at the time of its introduction, rhetoric was now ready to meet the new challenges brought about by the literary events of the following era.

6
The Taishō Years

After the publication of Igarashi Chikara's *Shin bunshō kōwa,* rhetoric entered the fourth and final phase of the fifty-year progression that characterized its history as a field of study in modern Japan. This last phase, which spanned the Taishō years, has been largely dismissed in the past as merely one of decline for the discipline. Nishio Mitsuo was among the first to observe the existence of a crucial gap between rhetoric's formalized approach to writing and the call for a literary style free from archaic constrictions that by the mid- to late Meiji era had taken root among writers. These writers rejected the notion of writing as something that could be described or taught through a preordered system of rules. As Akutagawa Ryūnosuke once put it, Japanese authors were so pressed by the challenging task of creating a viable tool for literary expression that they hardly had room for digressions on the nature of rhetorical language.[1] This decline of interest in rhetorical studies was furthermore reflected, Nishio noted, in the modest number of works published in the field; the scholarly production of the period was essentially limited to Sassa Masakazu's *Shūjihō kōwa* (Lectures on rhetoric) and Watanabe Yoshiharu's *Gendai shūjihōyō* (Essentials of modern rhetoric), while only a handful of writers authored works that dealt with writing or composition.[2]

While it is true that publications including the term "rhetoric" in their title decreased considerably following the end of the Meiji era, the Taishō years witnessed the appearance of a large number of works that drew from the Western rhetorical tradition. The importance of rhetorical inquiry during these later years should not, therefore, be minimized. In terms of popular interest, the mid-Meiji years certainly represented the apex of rhetoric's popularity in Japan: from the publication of Takada Sanae's *Bijigaku* to that of Igarashi Chikara's *Shin bunshō kōwa,* Meiji rhetoricians rode the wave of an increased interest in issues of native prose style and literary criticism, which contributed to the remarkable growth of interest in the field. By contrast, the Taishō years were characterized by a decline in the number of rhetorical treatises, which inevitably set this era apart from the splendors of the preceding age. Such a decline was actually a reflection of a process of adaptation to the changes that had been taking place both in the literary world and the social life of the nation. Taishō scholarship mirrored these changes.

Among the developments that were most significant for Taishō rhetoric was the definitive establishment of a modern form of written language. By the end of Meiji, the *genbun itchi* style had become the predominant form used in novels. On the one hand, this undermined rhetoric's position, given its past role as advocate of classically based literary styles. On the other, it cleared the way for a dialogue with neighboring fields such as *kokugogaku* (studies of national language) and *kokubungaku* (studies of national literature). With the establishment of *genbun itchi* and a partial solution to the conflict between elegant and vulgar styles, rhetoric was no longer stereotypically associated with classical modes of expression, but came to be simply perceived as a science, or art, that explained the principles of communication. In these new terms, rhetoric was able to hope for a place in current and future scholarly efforts, tackling the linguistic issues that were crucial for the modern Japanese state.

Another important change taking place in the Taishō years was the renewed interest in the practice of public speaking. After its overwhelming popularity during the early Meiji period, interest in and opportunities for speech making considerably declined in the late 1880s and 1890s. However, the turn of the century saw a decisive comeback of speech making in Japanese political and cultural life. This revival had important ramifications for the history of rhetoric in the final phase of its progression.

As discussed in chapter 5, the publication of Igarashi Chikara's *Shin bunshō kōwa* sanctioned the end of *bijigaku* studies. Igarashi's call for a rhetoric that was concerned with accomplished, rather than elegant, writing opened the door to a reassessment of the object and purpose of the discipline along those lines. The works published thereafter shared the rejection of the aesthetic nature of rhetoric and advocated its employment as a system of rules for composition and proficient communication.

This approach could already be observed at the end of the Meiji era, when scholars Haga Yaichi (1867–1927) and Sugitani Torazō (1874–1915) published their *Sakubun kōwa oyobi bunpan* (Lectures on writing with model compositions). Written in *genbun itchi* style, a rare occurrence among preceding works, this book was a practical guide of composition intended for the use of teachers and students. In the preface, the authors denounced the lack of an adequate pedagogy for the instruction of composition, which was in their view essential in an age of transition such as the Meiji era, when colloquial and classical styles were often used indiscriminately, causing confusion and grammatical inconsistencies. Haga and Sugitani called for the unification of the numerous literary styles, encouraged people to avoid the constraints of classical conventions, and maintained that modern literature had to be based on the vernacular. In doing so, they separated earlier notions of rhetoric that were concerned only with the aesthetic aspect of literary production from the more practical view that, beginning with Igarashi's *Shin bunshō kōwa,* had begun to break from the earlier tradition of rhetorical studies. Accordingly, the object of their work was the treatment of writing in general and not literary production per se; communication rather than beauty was the final goal of their investigation.

Sakubun kōwa oyobi bunpan showed that the new ideas spread by Igarashi had also found some sort of continuity among scholars outside the Waseda University circle. Haga and Sugitani acknowledged the basic differences between elegant and plain writing, but rejected the idea of beauty as the primary goal of writing at the expense of effective communication. They contributed to the idea of divesting rhetoric of its authority over styles of writing and instead proposing it as a valid system of rules for composition. Rhetoric had thus relinquished the aesthetic motives that had characterized its development during much of the Meiji period.

Several Taishō scholars and authors shared this new view of rhetoric. Utsumi Kōzō (1872–1935), for example, a graduate of Waseda University, embraced a notion of writing that was also far from that brought forth by earlier generations of rhetoricians. His *Bunshō jikkō* (Ten lectures on writing), published in 1910, was, according to the preface, his response to a growing concern for students' generally poor composition skills. The work was concerned exclusively with the practical aspect of writing. Divided, as the title itself indicates, into ten lectures, *Bunshō jikkō* dealt with rhetoric only in a very marginal fashion, confirming the trend at the end of the Meiji era to downplay the importance of the discipline in the elaboration of an effective methodology for the teaching of composition. In particular, Utsumi denounced the inappropriate use of rhetorical figures and criticized rhetoricians' claim of rhetoric as being absolutely indispensable to writing.[3]

Author Mizuno Yōshū (1883–1947) was also extremely critical of the discipline. Discussing the various trends that had characterized the debate on writing in the preceding years, Yōshū criticized rhetoric for being a field of study of no practical use and accused rhetoricians of having totally misunderstood the essence of the writing process.[4] Critic Kayahara Kazan (1870–1952) echoed this sentiment, stating that Meiji rhetoricians had indeed put too much stress on the formal and aesthetic aspects of writing. In doing so, he said, rhetoricians had overlooked the fundamental fact that writing ought to have as a priority a fusion of content and form rather than emphasize the purely external aspect of literary production. Kazan acknowledged the importance of rhetoric but reiterated that it was far from being an indispensable tool for writing.[5] Others joined him in dismissing the relevance of the discipline as it had been defined over the preceding decades.[6]

The two major works of rhetoric of the time, Sassa's *Shūjihō kōwa* and Watanabe's *Gendai shūjihōyō,* essentially ratified this viewpoint. Sassa indicated that rhetoric was no longer concerned with the discernment of beauty in writing or with the criticism of literary works, but rather with the practical knowledge necessary to write proficiently. Rhetoric's goal, he stated, was the attainment of fine writing, a statement that strongly resembled Igarashi's earlier definition of the discipline.[7] Similarly, Watanabe essentially refuted the separation between "elegant" and "ordinary" styles, arguing that the scope of rhetoric was to be found in writing in general and not only in literature.[8]

As was reasonable to expect, this continued attack on rhetoric, and in particular the criticism of rhetoricians' propensity toward taxonomy and dogmatism, resulted in a rejection of the very canon that best exemplified rhetoric's taxonomic character: elocution. The treatment of figures, a recurrent feature of Meiji rhetoric, declined among Taishō scholarship, totally disappearing in more than a few cases.[9] This does not mean, however, that rhetoric was completely ousted from the debates taking place within academic circles with respect to writing and composition. Several works acknowledged the importance of rhetoric's precepts, and some even strove to articulate convincing arguments in favor of figures and their employment in writing.[10] Such a partially positive assessment of rhetoric might seem incompatible with the somewhat antirhetorical climate that resided at the time among scholars, intellectuals, and educators, but it was not. On the contrary, it reflected the current ambivalence of rhetoric's reputation—praised on the one hand for the universal validity of its principles, but criticized on the other for being obsolete and lacking in methodological flexibility.[11] Moreover, such an antirhetorical climate was very different from the one that two decades earlier had opposed rhetoric in favor of the new trends of realism and naturalism. The antirhetorical sentiment of those years had been more extreme, to the extent that rhetoric was often perceived as antithetical to any attempt toward literary modernization—be it with respect to language, themes, or ideology. By contrast, Taishō scholars accepted the relevance of the discipline to the endeavors of writing and communication, providing a conclusion to the endless debate over the definition and function of refinement in literature. The manuals of composition and the few works of rhetoric of the period reflected the resolution of this debate, acknowledging, albeit not unconditionally, the importance of rhetorical refinement as a necessary aspect of the newly born literary language. The question was no longer whether to use rhetorical devices, but which devices to use. This left rhetoric enough latitude to negotiate a role in the literary experimentations that followed in those years.

This partial acceptance of rhetoric was also facilitated by the widespread effort to incorporate the discipline into the studies of national language.[12] The afore-mentioned *Sakubun kōwa oyobi bunpan* and *Bunshō jikkō* were representative of this endeavor. The former work showed clear ties to Meiji rhetorical inquiry. From the discussion of figures to the treatment of style and the discussion of the four tra-ditional forms of discourse, the extensive coverage of typically rhetorical topics is evidence that Haga and Sugitani regarded rhetoric as an essential premise to the treatment of the linguistic and literary issues that followed in the appendix—the correct use of *kana* characters, verb conjugations, particles, and so forth. These and other works contributed to the creation of an important link between rhetoric and those studies that sought to address questions of language and literature through the theoretical framework of Western scholarship.[13]

Sassa's treatise also reflected this trend. Sassa had already published *Shūjihō* (Rhetoric), a translation of Hill's *The Principles of Rhetoric,* in 1901. Now, sixteen years later, as an established scholar of rhetoric with over twenty years of experi-ence teaching students composition, he had decided to undertake the compila-tion of his own manual. The book was divided into two parts and an appendix. Part 1, "General Theory of Rhetoric," covered a variety of topics, from the definition of rhetoric to language and the elements of good writing. Part 2 dealt with the various styles of discourse. As for the appendix, it contained a treatment of "Epistolary Style" and "Composition." The section on composition provided an informative picture of the state of the field during the mid-Taishō years. Sassa observed that the Japanese had downplayed the importance of composition over the centuries, particularly after the Heian period. It was true that a number of Edo scholars such as Ogyū Sorai, Itō Jinsai, Kamo no Mabuchi, and Motoori Nori-naga had discussed the topic in some fashion in their works, but these amounted more to sporadic treatments rather than an established pedagogical tradition. Composition grew into an accepted area of study only after the Meiji Restora-tion. As Sassa eloquently put it, the overlapping of classical and contemporary language in writing represented one of the greatest obstacles to the formulation of a successful methodology for composition. His analysis showed, for example, how auxiliary verbs and particles were often mistakenly used and indicated the steps to follow in order to correct students.

Watanabe's *Gendai shūjihōyō* also reflected the new developments seen with respect to the rise of a new literary language. In a treatise that symbolically con-densed much of Meiji rhetorical tradition into an accessible manual written for the students attending his lectures, Watanabe, a scholar of aesthetics, became one of the first to show, within the context of a rhetorical treatise, the new character of the relationship between rhetoric and writing. Since rhetoric was concerned, in his view, with the actual rules needed in order to write effectively, his analysis, he stated, could rely only on contemporary pieces, which incidentally all employed either the copula *"da"* or *"de aru."* Watanabe drew largely from literature, demonstrating that the modern literary language had evolved to the point that it provided sufficient material for rhetorical analysis. In his treatment of figures, in particular, he quoted extensively from authors such as Natsume Sōseki and Shimazaki Tōson, but also from philosophers such as Abe Jirō and Nishida Kitarō, providing evidence that their language, too, was replete with rhetorical devices. The vernacular had thus developed its own rhetorical features.

The rejection of the aesthetic nature of rhetoric followed by its gradual application to composition and writing in general and the awareness that a new, full-fledged literary language was born were not the only traits of Taishō rhetoric. Despite the shift of interest toward written communication that took place in the late 1880s, publications in the field of public speaking had continued to appear. Although rhetoric was then mainly identified with written rather than oral discourse, studies of oratory continued to enjoy a large readership, and it was not uncommon for some books to have multiple reprint editions.[14] Among the reasons for this lasting popularity was certainly the appeal that speech making continued to have to the Japanese public, an enduring fascination that was also at the foundation of the new wave of interest seen in the Taishō years. But the main reason probably lay in the fact that new, important developments abroad had affected the course of the discipline. The so-called elocutionary movement, which had separated the last canon of rhetoric (i.e., delivery) from the rest of the rhetorical apparatus, had spread its influence to Japan, contributing there, too, to the birth of an entirely autonomous area of study.[15] The separation of delivery from the remaining four canons facilitated oratory's survival as an independent field of investigation and practice at a time when oral discourse was being marginalized in the literary debates of the mid–Meiji years.

While the great majority of books on oratory published throughout the second half of the Meiji era were similar in content, repeatedly addressing topics such as gestures, sound, and posture, some of them were also surprisingly ahead of the more famous contemporary rhetorical treatises, particularly on issues of language policy. Increasingly written in *genbun itchi* style, these works became the arena of important debates that linked the study of public speaking to the formation of a modern literary language and the creation of language unity.[16] Even if the oral dimension of rhetoric was being downplayed by many mid- to late Meiji rhetoricians and writers, oratory still played a primary role in addressing linguistic issues that represented a major concern for the modern Japanese state.

Furthermore, some of these works also displayed a number of original characteristics. One of these studies was Nakajima Kisō's *Enzetsu kappō* (Effective methods of speech making). Published in 1903, *Enzetsu kappō* began with a general introduction describing the prerequisites needed by the ideal orator, such as erudition, sincerity, and dignity, and the principles involved in preparing and delivering a speech. It then continued with interviews of prominent contemporary orators of the day from various fields of speech making. Contributors included political figures such as Ōkuma Shigenobu, Shimada Saburō, and Ozaki Yukio; scholars such as Takada Sanae, Amano Tameyuki, and Abe Isoo; and religious leaders like Uchimura Kanzō, Uemura Masahisa, and Katō Totsudō. Addressing the problem of public speaking from their individual perspectives, the contributors offered insights on a variety of topics, among them the relationship between oratory and the written language and the use of language in speech making. All, regardless of the type of discourse they addressed, noted the need for a simple but effective spoken language. Takada identified the gap between the spoken and written language as a major hindrance to the delivery of an elegant and, at the same time, intelligible speech. Abe called for delivering speeches in the same style as the written vernacular advocated by many, while Totsudō emphasized the importance of maintaining a good balance between simple words and rhetorical features. Others denounced the priority given to proper use of language and grammar, stressing instead the importance of demeanor and posture; Uchimura, for example, recounted how he was able to engage American audiences, even when his English was not always perfect.

The interviews contained various anecdotal elements as well. Ozaki, for instance, told of his poor oratorical skills at the beginning of his political career, while Amano mentioned his practice of having his wife and children read the text of his speeches beforehand to ensure they would be intelligible to the audience. *Enzetsu kappō* thus offered valuable information about the people involved in the study and practice of public speaking in the 1880s and 1890s.

Seireishi's *Shakōjō no danwa to endanjō no yūben* (Social conversations and podium oratory) was also of some interest in this respect. Published in 1910, this work was divided into two sections, "Conversation" and "Oratory." "Conversation" was essentially concerned with private acts of communication and was, according to Seireishi, a subcategory of oratory, which was by contrast concerned with public communication and generally larger audiences. The central theme of the book was "how to acquire speaking skills"; for this purpose, the author identified five steps in each section that would facilitate the learning process of the aspiring orator.

In the concluding chapters, the book introduced the reader to several passages written by renowned personalities. Each passage focused on some aspect of speech making. Thus Shimada Saburō defined oratory as the act of expressing one's thoughts through language. Accurate language, logical coherence, and the ability to appeal to the audience were, in his opinion, the three prerequisites for the effective use of this art. Religious leader Ebina Danjō saw the refinement of language as the discriminating factor in the delivery of a good speech. Ebina maintained that a speech should be first drafted in everyday language and then embellished in order to appeal to the listeners: from this point of view, he stated, speech making did not differ much from writing. Other crucial characteristics he highlighted were sound, intonation, demeanor, and physical and ethical integrity. Scholar of Japanese literature Haga Yaichi followed up by emphasizing the importance of creating an emotional stir within the audience, while literary critic Anesaki Masaharu and educator Tanimoto Tomeri reiterated that diction and the use of language were the most fundamental aspects of public speaking.

Another valuable work deserving attention is Komuro Shigehiro's *Jikken yūbengaku* (Experimental oratory). This book, published in 1903, consisted of twenty-six chapters covering topics typically addressed in works of oratory. Written in *genbun itchi* style, not because he had intended to do so but because, Komuro stressed, this was the natural outcome of the stenographic transcription of his lectures, *Jikken yūbengaku* offered a picturesque description of the speech meetings that were in vogue at the time. These meetings, Komuro observed, featured the participation of at least ten orators, and sometimes even twenty or thirty. The gatherings would start with introductory remarks by the main organizers and then continue with the delivery of speeches by each orator, who spoke in turn according to a ranking order that went from the least to the most famous. Unfortunately, Komuro noted, by the time several unknown orators had finished their speeches, the audience had already begun to show visible signs of exhaustion. People would gradually leave the site, content with simply having laid eyes on the famous orators, who would then be left to address a much smaller crowd than they had expected. Komuro pointed out that from an educational point of view, these speech meetings were useless and only served the purpose of political propaganda.[17]

The publication of several works on public speaking thus seen throughout the second half of the Meiji period facilitated the transition for later scholarly efforts to further elucidate the principles of oratory to the public. Taishō orators and educators continued to author books on the subject, riding a wave of interest in public speaking that matched the enthusiasm of the early Meiji years. With the exception of a few works, however, most of these books were mere repetitions of earlier ones. Notable among these exceptions was *Tsūzoku kōwa oyobi riron oyobi hōhō* (Theory and methods of public lecturing) published by Katō Totsudō in

1912.[18] In this treatise Totsudō sought to define popular lecturing, a form of instruction that was being strongly supported by the government at the time as a model of alternative education to the formal learning provided in schools. Totsudō included popular lecturing within the domain of oratory. Its main purpose was to spread knowledge and nurture interest and ethical behavior. He cautioned that no one had yet sought to define the boundaries of this new field, even though it claimed a long ancestry in Japan and had important antecedents in the lectures of Shingaku preacher Ishida Baigan. Totsudō stressed the public nature of this form of communication, including the diverse social and educational background of its audience, which called for careful preparation and adaptation skills.

A few years later Sanseibō Dōjin's *Dai Nihon yūbenshi* (A history of oratory in Japan) and Endō Takanojō's *Yūben to bunshō: Saishin kenkyū* (Oratory and composition: The latest research) appeared. *Dai Nihon yūbenshi* was an ambitious work that was, according to the author, the first attempt to provide a systematic account of the history of oratory in Japan. While the work failed somewhat to meet the high expectations set forth in its preface, it did succeed in identifying the major precursors to the sweeping popularity of speech making witnessed during the modern era, as displayed in the Buddhist homiletic tradition and the storytelling of the premodern years. Likewise, *Yūben to bunshō* was also an ambitious work. As the title itself eloquently put it, the author, a graduate of Waseda University, sought to reconcile the schism between oral and written discourse that had taken place in the early years of rhetoric's introduction to Japan. The principles of rhetoric, he stated, could be applied both to spoken and written communication, an argument that had crucial implications in that it struck at the heart of the opposition between written and spoken language asserted by many, even well into the Meiji era. Endō's statement suggested the essential proximity of the spoken and written language and therefore the possibility of creating a literary language that was closer to the vernacular.[19]

The years spanning the end of Meiji through the Taishō era were thus marked by intense negotiations aimed at redefining the role and scope of rhetoric in light of the new developments seen in the literary world. Japanese rhetoricians became engaged in a sort of rescue operation that would enable rhetoric to survive the demise of interest observed following the downfall of *bijigaku* studies. Several of the educators and writers that apparently challenged rhetoric's authority de facto supported this operation by conceding the importance of the treatment of such areas as figures, language, and style that were clearly part of rhetoric's domain. In doing so, they granted the discipline a place of continued relevance in the pedagogical and literary debates of the time. Concurrently, the Taishō period was also characterized by a renewed interest in public speaking as reflected in the countless books of oratory published in those years and in the strong participation of students and the general public in speech meetings around the country. Hence contrary to what has been thought thus far, the history of rhetoric in Japan was not a phenomenon limited to the Meiji period, but was instead something that extended into the following era, causing important ramifications to a number of issues of a linguistic, literary, and also sociopolitical nature.

Notwithstanding, the decline of the discipline proceeded inexorably. Treatises of rhetoric virtually disappeared after the end of the Taishō era. As Nishio Mitsuo also noted in his *Kindai bunshōron kenkyū,* almost no work of rhetoric was published in the early Shōwa (1926–1989) years.[20] As for oratory, these years were also gloomy. New political developments affected freedom of speech drastically, and in the late 1930s philosopher Miki Kiyoshi (1897–1945) became one of the first notable figures to denounce the decline of the art. In his "Yūbenjutsu no fukkō" (The revival of the art of speech), Miki embraced a theme that had been dear to early Meiji political activists, which was the centrality of freedom of speech in the political and social life of the nation. Oratory, he claimed, was essential for a political viewpoint that took into account the will of the people.[21]

Thus, as had already occurred in the West, rhetoric finally approached its twilight; however, new developments were already discernable on the horizon. In 1934, a then young Hatano Kanji predicted the rebirth of the discipline following the rise of a new interest in the linguistic mechanisms that characterized style and individual linguistic production.[22] In the same year, Tanizaki Jun'ichirō addressed the problem of writing in his *Bunsho tokuhon* (Composition reader), thus initiating a new genre that would later be perpetuated by such authors as Kawabata Yasunari and Mishima Yukio. And a decade later, Kobayashi Hideo's *Buntairon no kensetsu* (The foundations of stylistics) laid the theoretical foundation of stylistics in Japan. These and other developments reflected a latent interest in rhetorical investigation, an interest that would continue to grow during the mid- to late Shōwa years, when new advances in the field of linguistic and literary investigation placed renewed emphasis on rhetorical figures and the mechanisms of rhetorical communication. The arrival of Western rhetoric had thus left an indelible footprint on the vast landscape of Japanese literature and culture, fostering, among other things, the spread of public speaking and the development of literary criticism. But it was in regard to the formation of a modern written language that its influence was most felt.

PART 3

*Quest for
a New
Written
Language*

7
Rhetoric and the Genbun Itchi *Movement*

> They have but one language and it is the best, the most elegant and the
> most copious tongue in the known world; it is more abundant than Latin
> and expresses concepts better. . . . The written and spoken languages are
> very different, and men and women also differ in their way of speaking.
> There is no less diversity in their way of writing; they write their letters,
> for example, in one style but their books in another. Finally, it takes a long
> time to learn the language because it is so elegant and copious. To speak
> or write in a way other than their accustomed manner is impolite and
> invites ridicule, just as if we were to speak Latin backwards and with
> many solecisms.
> —Alessandro Valignano, *Historia del Principio*

The development of the *genbun itchi* movement (the movement for the
unification of the spoken and written language) was a major feature of Meiji culture and literature, a catalyst for the synergies that, generated by exposure to the
West, contributed to the creation of not only modern Japanese literature, but also
of the modern Japanese nation.

The realization of *genbun itchi* was by no means easy. The written language
of early Meiji was characterized by a multiplicity of styles, and long and strenuous debates within academic and literary circles accompanied the creation of a
modern mode of expression.[1] Transcending the boundaries of purely linguistic
and literary issues, the *genbun itchi* movement also came to embrace questions of
a social and political nature.[2] The bearing of the movement on the latter sort of

problem is, however, beyond the scope of this book, which focuses, in fact, on the theoretical process that led to the creation of an acceptable compromise between classical and vernacular literary modes.

In the field of literature, Futabatei Shimei was one of the most instrumental in the development of a new literary style. Futabatei published his well-known *Ukigumo* between 1887 and 1889. Considered by many to be Japan's first modern novel, *Ukigumo* made extensive use of authentic colloquial speech. It was of course not the first time that the vernacular appeared in novels. Many works of the Edo period employed colloquial language, but its use was mostly limited to the dialogical part of the novel, which was otherwise written in a style suffering "from a seemingly deliberate vagueness of expression which renders it unsuitable for precise description."[3] Futabatei faced, then, the task of creating a new literary language that would be suitable to the faithful description of reality. Shōyō is said to have played a crucial role in Futabatei's undertaking. He suggested, for example, the use of the upper-class Tokyo speech employed by raconteur Sanyūtei Enchō (1839–1900) in Enchō's stories. Following the advice of his mentor, Futabatei published *Aibiki* in 1888, which won wide acclaim, and completed his *Ukigumo* the following year, succeeding in developing a colloquial narrative mode that Tayama Katai would describe as "a marvelous new style."[4]

Creating a new literary language that was based on contemporary speech had not been a simple affair. Futabatei admittedly struggled in his search for an appropriate form, particularly with respect to the question of refinement.

> At the time, Tsubouchi advised me to make my writing a little more elegant, but I had no wish to do so. Indeed, it might be closer to the mark to say that I did my utmost to keep elegance out of my work, endeavouring instead to polish commonplace words.[5]

Ukigumo reflected Futabatei's interior struggle with the issue of rhetorical sophistication. The opening section of the novel was in fact still replete with conventional wordplay that was strongly reminiscent of earlier, classically based literary styles. The problem of creating a new mode of expression that was not merely a rough reproduction of speech was then clearly at the core of the quest for a modern literary language since the early developments of the *genbun itchi* movement.

The *genbun itchi* style eventually emerged as the answer to the quest for a literary mode that would satisfy the prerequisites of intelligibility, versatility, and refinement. The new form of expression had to be a relatively simple linguistic medium understandable even by the less educated; at the same time, to triumph over traditional styles, regarded highly among scholars and intellectuals, it had to be aesthetically pleasing.

The task of transforming the predominant system of written communication inherited from the Edo period into a popular, intelligible tool for the acquisition of knowledge and exchange of information was undertaken at a time when the country was being inundated by waves of Western thought. The encounter with Western culture had the double effect of spurring nationalistic sentiments on the one hand and calling for Westernization on the other. Contact with the literatures and languages of Western countries also provided scholars and writers with new methodological tools for analyzing their native language and literary tradition.

As the product of the dialectical interaction between tradition and modernity, Eastern legacy, and Westernization, the *genbun itchi* movement was thus shaped by multiple internal and external factors. Despite quite extensive research on this subject, one aspect has been thus far largely overlooked: the place of studies of Western rhetoric in the evolution of a new form of written expression.[6] Most of those who have touched on the role of rhetoric in the shift from traditional literary conventions to a modern colloquial style have taken the relationship to be negative. They have assumed that the call for the elimination of rhetorical embellishments that figured in the search for a modern literary language was antithetical to rhetoric as such. This is also essentially the opinion of those who have downplayed the importance of rhetoric by relegating it to the periphery of Meiji linguistic and literary studies. A few researchers have suggested, on the contrary, that notions of rhetoric did indeed play a part in the vernacularization of the literary language, but they have not explored the nature of this contribution in any depth.[7]

Taking a different approach, this book seeks to disclose the existence of a debate that, starting soon after the Meiji Restoration, began to point to strong correlations between the development of studies on rhetoric and the evolution of the *genbun itchi* movement. Cast in the form of a theoretical dispute over the need for rhetorical refinement in the new mode of literary expression, this debate permeated the Meiji literary scene. To put the matter simply, in its quest for modern forms of expression, the Meiji literary world confronted a dilemma: should the new language be completely devoid of rhetorical elements, or were they indispensable for its creation?

Genbun Itchi versus Rhetoric?

The grounds for the view that the relationship between rhetoric and the *genbun itchi* movement was primarily antagonistic lies in the tension between the spoken and the written language that had characterized Japanese literary tradition long before the modern age. During the Edo period a number of fiction writers incorporated vernacular elements into their works. Authors of *gesaku* (popular fiction) depicting life in the pleasure quarters, in particular, made extensive use of colloquial expressions. Generally speaking, however, the vernacular continued to be considered inferior to traditional styles such as *wabun* or *kanbun,* and most writers of other forms of literature rejected the extensive employment of the vernacular in favor of established conventions typical of traditional literary modes. The use of the vernacular by some thus did not fill the gap between the spoken and written language, but instead heightened the sense of division between elegant expressions from the classical linguistic repertory and vulgar ones deriving from authentic colloquial speech.

The study of the classical works of the native tradition, which flourished during the Edo period, reinforced the hierarchical nature of this relationship: the language in which these works were written came to be seen as the true repository of centuries of literary tradition. It was regarded as sophisticated, fluid, and refined and thus capable of conveying rhetorical tones unattainable by the colloquial language, which might vividly capture the expressions of the moment but was vulgar and lacking in dignity. The classical language was perceived as permanent and changeless, as something that was regulated and that therefore could be described by a system of rules. The spoken tongue, on the contrary, was held to be mutable, ever changing, and devoid of refinement and regularity. These suppositions led to the belief that the traditional literary language was superior to the vernacular, that the latter did not constitute a linguistic system capable of being thoroughly described and understood, and that the elegant and "rhetorical" character of classical language was ipso facto antithetical to that of the vernacular (which was, in turn, "nonrhetorical").[8]

These perceptions may be illustrated by comparing two representative examples of the *gazoku setchū* style, which was used widely in *gesaku* literature and in which a varying degree of contemporaneous speech components were intermixed with Japanese and Chinese elements. The first is from Ihara Saikaku's *Kōshoku ichidai otoko* (The life of an amorous man, 1682) and the second from Jippensha Ikku's *Tōkai dōchū hizakurige* (Shanks' mare, 1802–1822). As pointed out by Nanette Twine in her analysis of premodern styles, while the two are both representative of *gazoku setchū* styles, the former is considered to exemplify an elegant, higher mode of expression and the latter a vulgar, lower one.

"Ima made shiranu koto nari. Samo arubeshi" to shibito o mireba waga tazunuru onna, "Kore wa" to shigamitsuki, "Kakaru ukime ni afu koto, ikanaru inguwa no mawarikeru zo. Sono toki tsurete nokazuba samonaki o, kore mina waga nasu waza" to, namida ni kurete mimodae suru. Fushigiya kono onna ryō no manako o mihiraki warahigao shite, mamonaku mata moto no gotoku narinu. "Nijūkyū made no ichigo, nani omohinokosaji" to jigai o suru o, futari no mono iroiro oshitodomete kaeru. Fumbetsudokoro nari.

"This is the first I have heard of it. It must be so," he said. When he saw the corpse, it was that of the woman he was seeking. "This!" he cried, clutching her tightly, "What fate has brought us together in such bitter circumstances! If I hadn't taken you with me this would not have happened. This is all my fault." Dissolving into tears, he writhed in anguish. Strangely, the woman opened her eyes, smiled, and then became again as she had been. "I have lived twenty-nine years—I have no regrets!" he cried. His two companions restrained him from killing himself, and took him home. In that they showed good sense.

Koko wa katagawa ni chaya noki o narabe izuremo zashiki nikai zukuri, rankan tsuki no rōka kakehashi nado watashite namiuchigiwa no keishoku itatte yoshi. Chaya no onna kado ni tatte "Oyasuminasaiyaase. Attakkana hiyameshi mo gozaiyaasu. Nitate no sakana no sameta no mo gozaiyaasu. Soba no futoi no o agariyaase. Udon no otsuki no mo gozaiyaasu. Oyasuminasaiyaase."

Here a one-sided street of teahouses, all of them two-storied and with balustraded flying galleries, commanded a fine view of the sea. Women stood at their gates, crying, "Come in and rest! We have warmed-up cold rice! Cooled hot fish! Try our thick *soba!* Our *udon* is the fattest! Come in and rest!"

Twine identifies in the first passage several elements of classical usage (e.g., the *nari* and *beshi* terminations, the emphatic particle *zo,* the combination of the negative *zu* with the connective *ba*). These in turn are held to endow Saikaku's style with the qualities of linguistic refinement and elegance, which locate his prose, despite its use of colloquial components, firmly within the traditional heritage of Japanese literature. The Ikku passage, by contrast, is marked by the homespun character of its dialogue, as well as much more extensive use of colloquial components (e.g, the verb *gozaiyaasu*) from contemporaneous speech.[9]

In the Meiji period Saikaku was held up as a model by prominent literary figures such as Ozaki Kōyō and Kōda Rohan and by those who opposed the radical vernacularization of the literary language. His style came to constitute an ideal of what might be termed "rhetorical" in that it was regarded as capable of conveying nuances of tone by virtue of its innate elegance and refinement. Ikku's style, on the other hand, appealed to more progressive writers who sought, among other things, to overcome the convention that had long kept the vernacular from being employed in the discursive as well as dialogical sections of literary works.

The assumption that "rhetorical" meant "an expression from the classical linguistic repertory" ultimately gave rise in the early Meiji period to a limiting notion of the term. "Rhetorical expression" became for many a synonym for archaic linguistic embellishment.

The term "rhetorical expression" is employed here with two different meanings. First, it indicates any element that, provided the necessary linguistic, pragmatic, and cognitive conditions are met, can convey a special effect by means of deviation from a generally accepted norm. As such, it incorporates those linguistic operations (transformations, permutations, substitutions, etc.) that were classified as *elocutio* in the Western rhetorical tradition (i.e., tropes and figures of speech). Second, it refers to elements that, although no longer able to produce such a special effect, still retain a certain degree of ornamentality and prestige within the linguistic (and cultural) code. This is the case with many established rhetorical expressions, some of which may have become catachreses. This twofold nature of the term "rhetorical expression" was a major source of confusion in the controversy over the level of refinement of the modern literary language. While the term thus incorporates a degree of ambiguity, its vagueness provides a measure of neutrality not afforded by more specific phrases such as "rhetorical artifice" or "rhetorical embellishment."[10]

The persistent call for a simpler literary style accompanying the *genbun itchi* movement led some to regard the elimination of unnecessary rhetorical expressions from the new written language as a sine qua non for the modernization of Japanese literature. Such sentiments spilled over into attitudes toward the newly introduced Western rhetoric; since it was a discipline that classified and explained the usage of rhetorical devices, it took on negative connotations in the eyes of some.

It is thus not surprising that rhetoric has been regarded as playing a negligible role in the quest for a more concise literary language. It should be noted, however, that the antirhetorical climate described above was a consequence of the tension between spoken and written mediums, rather than an aversion to rhetoric as a discipline concerned with effective composition. The tension between the two mediums reinforced the notion that there were two different levels of expression in language and literature: an elegant, polished, higher level and a vulgar, verbose, lower one. Rhetoric came to be seen as something pertaining exclusively to the former realm, that is, that of elegant writing; as such, it was perceived as an obstacle by those who sought to recuperate the popular, lower side of linguistic and literary signification. In that it denied by definition a more fluid and democratic vision of language and literature as a medium for social communication, the younger generation of writers took it to be a barrier to modernization. They also saw it as a hindrance to artistic creativity, something that, by enforcing the employment of old literary conventions, constrained the writer's ability in his formulation of suggestive images.

The early Meiji literary world thus developed a rather reductive notion of rhetoric as an obsolete and anachronistic discipline that taught the creation and usage of embellished expressions and that as such was in conflict with the basic principles of the *genbun itchi* movement. In the face of such assumptions, those engaged in the study of rhetoric struggled to rearticulate its boundaries. Rhetoric was presented at times as the art of speech, at times as the art of writing, and at times as a mere classification of figures of speech and tropes. And the issues taken up in this process of configuration simultaneously fed the debate over the creation of the new literary language.

The Controversy over the Refinement of the New Written Style

The argument advanced by some that the employment of rhetorical expressions was incompatible with *genbun itchi* generated a controversy over the innate character of the new form of literary expression. Well into the Meiji period the literary world remained divided into two factions in regard to the nature and prerequisites of a modern written language: on the one hand were those who supported the "vernacularization" of the written style, and on the other were those who insisted on the supremacy of the classical language sustained by centuries of literary tradition. The former faction based its advocacy of a simplified literary style and belief in the feasibility of this project on the conviction that in Western countries the written language was substantially the same as the spoken one. Most of those who wrote in favor of *genbun itchi* used this point as their chief argument against the difficulty and elitism of traditional written styles. As early as 1870, Nishi Amane had already claimed that in Western countries the spoken and the written language coincided. In his view, since the spoken tongue abided by the rules of grammar, any spoken interaction could become, in those countries, written communication and vice versa.[11] In 1874, Nishi reiterated this claim and affirmed that the difference between spoken and written language represented a major hindrance to the spread of learning.[12] In the following year scholar Watanabe Shūjirō (1855–1945) echoed Nishi's words and stated that Japan should take the West as a model, since there the written language was extremely close to the vernacular and as such was easy to understand.[13] The articles that appeared in *Kyōiku zasshi* (Journal of education) a decade later also construed much of their support for the *genbun itchi* around this argument. The author of "Nihon bun-shōron" (On Japanese writing) claimed that the superiority of English over Japanese was essentially determined by the fact that its written language was a reflection of speech. And in the same vein, the editorial "Danwa to bunshō to no itchi o yōsu" (The need for an agreement between spoken and written language) maintained that "in Western countries both the spoken and the written language have a grammar. Hence the spoken language is like the written and vice versa, and there is no separation between the two."[14] Thus the movement that averred the need for a simplification of the written medium was often characterized by the assumption that in Western countries the written and spoken languages were virtually identical, and this had contributed to their civilization and remarkable literary tradition.

Accompanying the call for the employment of a more colloquial mode of written expression, however, was another important premise: unification of the spoken with the written language could take place only by first eliminating superfluous rhetorical expressions. Journalist and essayist Fukuchi Gen'ichirō (1841–1906) was one of the earliest to argue in these terms for the colloquialization of the literary style. In a succession of articles he set forth the need to purge the written language of extraneous elements for the sake of clarity and simplicity. Already in 1875, he hinted at the necessity of doing away with linguistic embellishments, observing in an editorial that "the charm of writing lies not in the imaginary but in factuality."[15] In a subsequent article he went on to claim that the written style had to be as close as possible to the spoken language; later, in 1887, on the eve of the first literary achievements of the *genbun itchi* movement, he challenged the conventional view in literary circles that the classical language was superior to the vernacular.[16] By attacking the notion of the superiority of the classical language over the vernacular, Fukuchi significantly contributed at an early stage of the debate to a call for the simplification of the written language, a call that characterized much of Meiji literary criticism and was central to any debate on the question of writing. Others joined Fukuchi in this call. Scholar and bureaucrat Kanda Kōhei (1830–1898), for example, wrote in 1885 that "if we wish to unite the spoken and written language that they may coincide, we must have a written language that can be immediately understood when rendered orally. For that to happen, we must use the language of everyday speech. To write in such a style means to write in *genbun itchi*."[17] Mozume Takami's *Genbun itchi,* published in 1886, also contained implications of this type. Mozume claimed the inferiority of written Japanese to speech and argued that Japanese should abandon the employment of archaic styles and use instead the vernacular.[18]

Shōyō's *Shōsetsu shinzui,* which appeared at the same time, also echoed this position, albeit in different terms. As is known, in the second section of his treatise Shōyō discussed the issue of style at length. He identified three main styles, the classical, the colloquial, and a third style that was meant to be a fusion of the first two. He praised the first style for its elegance but criticized it for its lack of vitality. He then praised the second style for its energy but rejected it as verbose and vulgar. Next, he turned to the third style, which he indicated was a viable candidate for the novel. This "third style" *(gazoku setchū)* was, as also pointed out by Dennis Washburn, Shōyō's idea of *genbun itchi*.[19] Shōyō generally opposed the indiscriminate use of the vernacular in the novel but acknowledged its advantages in the dialogical parts of the text, leaving space for possible future developments.

> My readers are very much mistaken if they think that I have been surreptitiously denigrating the spoken language by saying that it lacks euphony and is full of linguistic corruptions. Language is spirit; style is form. Emotions are expressed with complete frankness in speech, whereas in writing they are overlaid with a veneer which to a certain extent camouflages reality. . . . Dialogue is one area where a colloquial style does have advantages. Unfortunately, though, there is no getting around its defects. Perhaps one of my clever friends will discover a means of doing so. I shall wait impatiently for the day when a new version of the colloquial style appears.[20]

In addition to acknowledging the potential of the vernacular, Shōyō called for a realistic approach to literature. This call for a faithful reproduction of reality, without the subjective intrusion of the writer, was at the same time an argument for a plain, straightforward language that could describe the subtleties of human life without exaggeration or ornamentation. Shōyō confirmed this viewpoint in his "Bunshō shinron" of the following year, where, despite being still opposed to a radical vernacularization of the literary language, he called for the elimination of elegant expressions typical of classical styles. The theoretical backing that Shōyō provided for a simplified written medium spurred experimentation toward a new literary language. Poet and critic Masaoka Shiki (1867–1902), for example, strove to create a more objective and descriptive mode of expression in his *shaseibun* (literary sketches from life or nature). His essay "Jojibun" (Descriptive writing) of 1900 was particularly important for its argument against any form of elaborate expression that might compromise truthfulness and the verisimilitude of facts and events. In Shiki's own words, *"jojibun"* meant to depict facts and things the way they had been heard or seen, without exaggeration or embellishment.[21] A few months after the publication of "Jojibun," poet and novelist Takahama Kyoshi

(1874–1959) postulated that the *genbun itchi* style was the most appropriate for writing in a realistic manner. He thereby contributed to a firm alliance between two originally separate notions. It came to be taken for granted that a faithful approach to reality in literature could be guaranteed only by the employment of a plain form of expression. Others reiterated this position in the following years.[22] Reflecting this assumption, *genbun itchi* became the dominant style for literary works published after the turn of the century.

The gradual shift from realism to naturalism that took place in the first decade of the twentieth century further strengthened this alliance. Writers of these schools repeatedly called for the abolishment of affectation in writing and the necessity of depicting things and people in a faithful and concise manner. For example, in the preface to his novel *Hatsusugata,* published in 1900, Kosugi Tengai (1865–1952) strongly rejected the aesthetic values of traditional literature, advocating a type of objective realism that did not seek to please the reader but was self-serving. This same stance appeared even more forcefully in the preface to his work *Hayari uta,* published two years later, where Tengai argued that the writer "should describe exactly what he observed, and not attempt to please his readers by beautifying his materials."[23]

In the following years many leading figures of the *bundan* gave further impetus to this trend toward an objective interpretation of literature. Tayama Katai addressed the issue of "artistry" in his "Rokotsu naru byōsha" (Plain description), where he strongly criticized any writing that sought to compensate for the lack of content with stylistic embellishment.[24] He reiterated this call in his essay "*Sei* ni okeru kokoromi" (The experiment in *Sei*), where he urged writers to describe things the way they are seen and heard, in an unadorned and unaffected manner.[25] Others such as critic Hasegawa Tenkei (1876–1940) called for an unembellished art that was capable of depicting truth in life. Tenkei denounced traditional art as unable to capture reality and concurrently called for an art without ornaments and embellishments.[26] Several articles that appeared in the journal *Bunshō sekai* (The world of writing) likewise supported this call for a language devoid of unnecessary ornament. For example, critic and historian Miyake Setsurei (1860–1945) observed that the literary world was now prioritizing content over form and affirmed that "writing is not artistry but rather the faithful presentation of thought."[27] Critic Katakami Tengen (1884–1928) wrote that the age when one wrote just for the sake of writing and when form was just for the sake of form was over; writing now aimed at the free and bold expression of the self through the use of a free language.[28] The demand for truth in content was thus presented as a demand for a truthful form, in other words, one from which all artificial elements of embellishment had been eliminated.

This trend was opposed by those who favored a more elaborate and sophisticated written style. In 1886 Yano Fumio was among the first to oppose the *genbun itchi* as not feasible. He indicated four points as the cause for his disapproval, namely the verbosity of the colloquial, the large presence of honorifics, dialectical differences, and the allegedly false argument that the spoken and written languages of Western nations were identical.[29] In 1889 poet and scholar Ochiai Naobumi (1861–1903), one of the most notable supporters of the *futsūbun* movement, denounced the colloquial as being too vulgar and strongly criticized the grammatical errors and inconsistencies that appeared in journals and magazines of the time.[30] Scholar of Japanese language Mozume Takami, who had previously been one of the strongest supporters of the *genbun itchi,* changed his mind and pronounced himself against the movement.[31] Others reiterated their opposition toward the *genbun itchi,* totally rejecting the feasibility of a vernacularized written style.[32]

Ozaki Kōyō (1867–1903) did not think highly of it either; in particular, the popularity enjoyed by his literary coterie, the Ken'yūsha (The Society of Friends of the Inkstone), much of which took inspiration from the works of premodern authors such as Ihara Saikaku, contributed to a revival of classical language, themes, and literary conventions, posing a great obstacle to the establishment of the vernacular as a literary language.[33] Thus the anti-*genbun itchi* movement was characterized by a strong criticism of the vernacular, a criticism that ranged from outright rejection to more moderate disagreement. At the same time it was also characterized by the belief that the written language and spoken tongue were essentially separate and could hardly be reconciled. This recurrent notion, also detectable in several works of rhetoric of the time, elucidates the tension between spoken and written communication that swept the *bundan* in those years.

Accompanying the rejection of a more colloquial mode of expression was another premise: the idea that a lack of linguistic refinement was the major obstacle to the acceptance of the vernacular as a legitimate mode of literary expression. As discussed earlier in this chapter, Shōyō indicated the *gazoku setchū* style as the best interim solution to the conflict between the vernacular and the classical language, and a number of those who regarded *genbun itchi* as excessively colloquial and lacking in refinement championed *gazoku setchū* as an alternative. Shōyō himself described the last decade of the century as being characterized by a strong call for linguistic refinement, as if to counterbalance the steady progress toward vernacularization of the written language that had taken place in the years after the Restoration. In particular, his mention of Takada Sanae's *Bijigaku,* published that year (1889), illustrates how he saw the introduction of rhetoric as intimately linked not only to the problem of writing in general, but also to the general literary discourse of the period.[34]

The journal *Teikoku bungaku* (Imperial literature) was among those publishing articles in the 1890s that condemned *genbun itchi's* lack of refinement and rhetorical flavor. For example, in "Genbun itchi ni tsukite" (On *genbun itchi*), the *genbun itchi* style was again strongly criticized for its verbosity and rhetorical defects; in "Shōsetsu no buntai" (The style of the novel), its lack of rhetorical charm and beauty, which were instead said to be particular to the *gazoku setchū* style, were again strongly denounced.[35] A number of influential figures in the literary world also took this stance. Literary critic Takayama Chogyū (1871–1902) criticized the *genbun itchi* style for its lack of elegance; in his view it was lacking in rhetorical depth and melody, and the sentence endings that were so reflective of colloquial language added to the vulgarity of the style.[36] Takeshima Hagoromo also addressed the issue, discussing the merits and disadvantages of both styles and rejecting the claim that the *gazoku setchū* style was a kindred collection of unnecessary embellishments. If such were the case, he went on, the responsibility did not lie in the style itself but rather in the poor skills of the writer. Ultimately, he said, this style was superior in charm and prestige to the *genbun itchi*.[37]

Scholar Ōmachi Keigetsu (1869–1925) also spoke against *genbun itchi*. In particular, Keigetsu claimed that one of the problems with the *genbun itchi* style lay in the way the vernacular had evolved—or not evolved—in the premodern period. Because of the disregard for public speaking prior to the Restoration, he asserted, the spoken language had not developed a rhetorical repertory and was thus too plain and crude to be employed as literary language.[38] The lack of rhetorical flavor was thus among the most recurrent criticisms against the feasibility of the *genbun itchi* style.[39]

Japanese research on rhetoric did not concretely support the vernacular in the written language either, at least until the publication of Shimamura Hōgetsu's *Shin bijigaku*. As pointed out in chapter 4 of this book, Takada Sanae did not address the stylistic changes that had taken place at the end of the 1880s. His efforts to apply the precepts of Western rhetoric to native works were directed primarily at the classical tradition. In his discussion of problems of style, for instance, he often quoted from *Genji monogatari, Makura no sōshi* (The pillow book), and *Hōjōki* (An account of my hut). His successors likewise did not consider *genbun itchi* a valid object for analysis. They gave priority instead to the discussion of traditional styles like *kanbun* and *wakan konkōbun*. Hattori Motohiko asserted that "when we express thoughts and feelings using colloquial language, we cannot call this writing; the *genbun itchi* style now in fashion in novels is a clear example of that. From a rhetorical point of view, it should be called conversation notes rather than writing."[40] Hagino Yoshiyuki stated that "if writing were no more than expressing what one has heard or seen, it would be equivalent to having a conversation; *genbun itchi* is so verbose, vulgar and without literary taste that it would be better to use the classical rather than the spoken style."[41] Sassa Masakazu, while declaring that the object of his study was the standard written language of the time, held that *genbun itchi* did not provide an appropriate model in this regard.[42]

The limited importance that most of these writers on rhetoric attributed to the vernacularization of the written language is also evident from the examples they cite, which are taken almost entirely from classical works. Even Shimamura Hōgetsu, who defended *genbun itchi* and, as discussed below, contributed significantly to its eventual triumph as the dominant mode of expression, as late as 1902 still relied conspicuously on passages from Edo playwright Chikamatsu Monzaemon and novelist Ihara Saikaku. This heavy dependence on classical works attests that, for the rhetoricians of the time, the *genbun itchi* style was not mature enough to deserve analysis; in their view a manual for good composition or literary criticism should focus on literary masterpieces. Not until the end of the Meiji period would contemporaneous literary works become the object of rhetorical investigation. Thus most scholars of rhetoric believed in the supremacy of classical language and in the transience of the vernacular. This negative attitude toward the vernacular may be partially explained by the fact that the last decade of the century saw a revival of traditional cultural values, which in literature took the form of a return to the classics. Such a climate may have influenced rhetoric's position on the question of language, thus characterizing its metalinguistic discourse as conservative and possibly contributing to its image as an archaic and obsolete field of study. All the major works of rhetoric published between *Bijigaku* and the turn of the century employed a language that was strongly reminiscent of classical literary conventions, consistent with their conservative stand in matters of literary style.

> Yo wa zenpen ni oite mazu hito no shikō oyobi shikō no manzoku o kitasu beki sanshu no genso sunawachi suikō to yūbi to kashō to o ronji tsugi ni bunshō no shūshokuhō o nobe owari ni buntai to buntai ni kaku bekarazaru yōso no koto to o kōjitari kore mina bunshō zenpan ni watareru jikō narishi nari ima kono hen ni oite wa bunshō no shurui o shimeshi toku ni sono kaku no shurui ni kankei shitaru jikō o ronkyū sen to suru nari.

> In the previous volume I have discussed taste and the three elements that bring about the gratification of taste, namely "the sublime," "the beautiful," and "the ridiculous." Next, I discussed rhetorical figures and finally style and the indispensable attributes of style. These were the essential components of writing in general. In this volume, I shall indicate types of style and discuss the topics related to each of them.[43]

Shūjigaku wa bunshō o shūsei suru hōhō o oshieru gakka nari genbun itchi no kuni nite wa danwa no shūsei nimo mata kono gakka o tekiyō su. . . . Shūjigaku o ken-kyū shite eru tokoro no rieki wa yoku jiko no bunshō o shūsei shieru koto nomi ni tomarazu, yoku tanin no bunshō no zen'aku kōsetsu o shikibetsu subeki hyōjun mo sadamuru koto o erubeki nari.

Rhetoric is a science that teaches how to polish writing; this science is also applied to speaking in those countries where the spoken and the written language coincide. . . . The merits coming from the study of rhetoric are not limited to pol-ishing the elements of one's writing, but extend to the establishment of a standard for the appreciation of others' writing as well.[44]

Bunshō no sakan narazarishi jidai, shūjigaku ga tan ni yūbenhō no gi to serareshi wa kotowari no masa ni shikaru beki tokoro, saredomo, bunmei no zōshin suru ni shi-tagai, insatsu sono ta no shojutsu hirakete, bunshō no ōsei ni naru ni itari, sono han'i zanji ni kakuchō serarete tsui ni kyō no gotoku shika to iwazu, danron to iwazu, hihan to iwazu, subete no gengoteki hyōshō o fukumeru mono to [nari].

In an age when writing was not yet widespread, it was natural that rhetoric should be perceived simply as the art of speech. However, with the advancement of civili-zation, and the development of printing and other techniques, writing came to as-sume a major relevance. Its [rhetoric's] scope gradually widened so that today it is not limited to poetry, speech or criticism, but rather includes all possible linguistic forms of expressions.[45]

In 1902, Shimamura Hōgetsu's prose already employed several contempo-rary linguistic features, but classical elements continued to be present. *Shin biji-gaku*'s metalanguage was stylistically syncretic, which reflected Hōgetsu's theoretical position of compromise between colloquial and classical styles.

Kotai sunawachi bunshōtai o sutete, kontai sunawachi kōgotai ni ai su beki toki nari. Saredomo, sono gen ni kaeru wa, saishūten ni arazu shite, hossokuten naru koto o wasureru bekarazu. Gojin wa kore yori shite nijō no shinro o miidasu beshi. Ichi wa shūji no chikara ni yorite sara ni gen o hanare bun ni hairan koto nari. Shika mo sono bun wa mae no kobun naru bekarazaru ya ron nashi. Ni wa kotai no gohō, no shūjichū yori, aru mono o nukitomuru no hitsuyō aru koto nari.

It is necessary to abandon the old style, i.e., classical language, and conform to the present style, i.e., modern language. However, it must not be forgotten that going back to the spoken language should not be the final goal but rather a new point of departure. Here I see the following course of action. First, depart from the colloquial and move on toward written language through the employment of rhetorical features; it goes without saying that the written language meant here is not classical language. Second, retain some rhetorical features of the old grammar.[46]

The language used in the works of rhetoric of the last decade of the nineteenth century was thus rich in classical traits, consistent with its conservative stand in matters of literary style. This added to the already strong call for rhetorical refinement in writing, a call that constituted the major point of disagreement between advocates and opponents of the *genbun itchi* style.

The Idea of a Compromise

This controversy was not, however, a necessarily polarized debate between extremes. Several *genbun itchi* supporters—some adamant, others more moderate—also recognized the need to take the vernacular to a higher level of refinement. As Suzuki Sadami has recently pointed out, "the problem of *genbun itchi* in the Meiji novel was not an issue of whether a vernacular style could be established or not, but rather an issue of how to deal with the discursive part of the novel, that is, how to create an expression model for the novel."[47] In other words, even if some at the time possibly thought of the *genbun itchi* style as a mere replica of daily speech, many understood that it was more than that. The vernacular had already been largely employed in premodern literature. The main concern lay in the refinement of the so-called *ji no bun,* the discursive portion of the text. For example, already in 1888 the educator Miyake Yonekichi (1860–1929), while affirming use of the vernacular, denounced the lack of a colloquial rhetorical tradition and asserted the need to endow the new written language with appropriate rhetorical devices.[48] Linguist Ueda Mannen (1867–1937) also spoke in these terms and stated seven years later that refinement was a necessary prerequisite for a language in order for it to become the standard idiom of a nation. As he also reiterated in a different piece written in the same year, his idea of *genbun itchi* was not that of a reproduction of pure speech, but rather that of a language that contained an acceptable degree of sophistication.[49] *Gengogaku zasshi* (Journal of linguistics) took the same stance. Declaring that the contemporary Tokyo dialect was a language without refinement, the journal proposed that it nevertheless could serve as the basis for a new literary style, provided that more attention was paid to the development of elegant rhetorical features.[50] The same year, in an article advocating a more colloquial written style, the linguist Yasugi Sadatoshi (1876–1966) noted that "of course when we use the written language, since we not only pay attention to grammatical and logical mistakes but we also add rhetorical refinement, it is never just the same as speaking."[51] He, too, in this way hinted at the need for rhetorical nuances, which help to differentiate a sophisticated literary style from simple spoken language. Likewise, other individuals similarly argued for the necessity of applying rhetoric to the development of the colloquial.[52]

It is thus clear that in those same years, many writers, scholars, and intellectuals recognized the relevance of rhetoric to the new form of literary expression. In fact, as Twine points out,

> The major cause of dissension among opponents of the new style appears to have been their too-literal interpretation of the term *gembun itchi* itself. As their arguments show, many took this to mean that what was being proposed was that writing should be an exact reproduction of speech, and attacked this idea on the perfectly valid grounds that this would result in verbose, disjointed, vulgar prose, pointing out, quite rightly, that the written European languages which were being held as examples were not in fact mirror images of the spoken language of those countries. The concept of colloquial style *based on* but not a verbatim reproduction of contemporary speech had not yet taken firm enough hold to lure them from their devotion to the elegance of traditional literary rhetoric, resulting in a preference for *futsūbun* or some other similar blend of the best of classical elements from both east and west, or in impractical, hazy suggestions for "refining speech." It was thanks to the later labours of novelists in polishing and refining colloquial style and to the collections of model compositions by *gembun itchi* supporters that these twin ghosts of verbosity and vulgarity were eventually laid to rest and the advantages of colloquial style allowed to stand clear.[53]

The notion of a written language as a total reproduction of speech could not constitute a viable option for the final definition of a new literary language; in other words, as was reasonable to expect, a certain degree of refinement was essential.

The first step toward the creation of a simplified but refined written language was to establish the importance of the vernacular. The introduction and flourishing of public speaking had already contributed to an increasing awareness of the importance of the spoken tongue and the issue of a standard national language when the literary world was trying to define the role of the vernacular in literature.[54] In the 1890s, however, acceptance of the vernacular as the primary means of literary expression was by no means final. As indicated by the anti-*genbun itchi* trend that swept the literary world in the last decade of the nineteenth century, there was still substantial opposition to its use. The tension between studies of rhetoric and the development of a more colloquial form of written language made things even more complicated. But as the vernacular gradually gained in prestige as a form of social communication, rhetoric as a repository of theories of effective composition offered solutions to one of the major impediments to the creation of a generally accepted modern literary form: reservations about the lack of refinement of the new written language.

Theoretical Appraisal of the Vernacular: The Case of Yamada Bimyō

There were two fundamental prerequisites for the successful creation of a modern colloquial literary mode. One was the conferral of higher status on the vernacular and recognition of it as a legitimate form of literary expression. This required the vernacular to be established as equal to the classical language, defined as an independent linguistic entity with its own grammar and perceived as capable of developing its own rhetorical repertoire. The second prerequisite was the formulation of a notion of rhetorical expression, one that would go beyond the idea widely believed in literary circles that, for better or worse, "rhetorical expression" meant archaic literary embellishment. The fulfillment of the first of these prerequisites owes much to the novelist and scholar Yamada Bimyō (1868–1910).

One of Bimyō's earliest defenses of the colloquial was "Jijo," the preface to his unpublished novel "Nise daiamondo" (Fake diamond). There, Bimyō began by noting the criticism that was directed at the colloquial, namely that it was vulgar and lacking in charm. He then addressed the origin of the vernacular, discussing the development of Japanese and concluding that modern Japanese was simply the result of a natural process of selection. Next, by affirming that the contemporary Tokyo dialect was also based on a system of rules capable of being described, Bimyō rejected the notion from the previous era, which held that classical language had a grammar while contemporary language did not. He finally reiterated that there were no reasons why the colloquial should not be considered functionally and artistically equal to classical modes of expression.[55]

After this first strong pronouncement in favor of the vernacular, Bimyō wrote the following year that "among the supporters of the *genbun itchi* today there are two factions of scholars: on one hand those that want to bring the spoken word closer to the written language—about half of these scholars are supporters of the *futsūbun;* and on the other, those who want to bring the written language close to the spoken tongue—half of these are supporters of the *genbun itchi*."[56] He then acknowledged the criticism raised by *futsūbun* supporters, namely that the *genbun itchi* could not be understood throughout the nation, that it would become a dead language in the future, and that it had no grammar and was vulgar. Bimyō refuted all of the above allegations and, in reiterating that the vernacular had its own grammar, provided examples of verb tenses as evidence of his claim. He also again challenged the notion that the vernacular was vulgar and as such inferior to the classical language.

While Bimyō's early essays were thus mostly intended to enhance the status of the vernacular, several of his later ones contained strong references to rhetoric and its role in the development of a new literary language. "Omoitsukitaru koto sono ichi (genbun itchi)" (Reflections: Part 1—*Genbun itchi*) of 1888, for example, was a response to an editorial that had approved Bimyō's *genbun itchi* style but had at the same time criticized the use of certain colloquial expressions. Bimyō retorted that his ideal *genbun itchi* was far from being a total reproduction of speech. It was true, he noted, that everyday speech constituted the basis of such a style, but he pointed out that when used as a written style it displayed rhetorical color not necessarily present in everyday conversation. According to Bimyō, this style "followed the laws of rhetoric."[57] In "Genbun itchi kogoto" (A criticism of *genbun itchi*) the following year, Bimyō went a step further. In rejecting some of the criticisms made of the *genbun itchi* style, he addressed the notion according to which writing possessed a prestige that speech itself lacked. Bimyō pointed out that supporters of such a theory confused "tone" with "content" and added that a basic knowledge of the rules of rhetoric would enable even a middle-school student to understand that the arguments raised against colloquial forms were groundless. Bimyō probably meant that prestige in writing was determined by the quality of the content and not the gravity of the style.[58]

Yet Bimyō's greatest contribution to the debate over the level of refinement of the *genbun itchi* style probably came in his "Ware ware no genbun itchi tai" (Our *genbun itchi* style), an 1890 article responding to Mori Ōgai, who had praised his colloquial style but also asked for fuller use of elegant classical elements. "Is classical language elegant and modern language vulgar?" Bimyō asked in return. "I believe that we do not have the means to discern between the two. That is to say, elegance or vulgarity in language does not depend on when the language was created, nor on superficial characteristics of the style, but only on meaning and usage. If the meaning is elegant and so is the usage, the expression will also be elegant. If the meaning is vulgar and so is the usage, the expression will also be vulgar."[59]

In Bimyō's view, then, elegance and refinement were determined only by the way that language was used and not by adherence to archaic literary standards. This distinction hinted at the possibility of creating elegant expressions that were not necessarily from the classical language repertory, but rather the result of a skillful usage of the vernacular. As such, Bimyō's approach cleared the way for a notion of rhetorical expression that went beyond that of mere linguistic embellishment. Ultimately, Bimyō reiterated his own vision of *genbun itchi* in another essay appearing in 1890 as being not a pure reproduction of speech, as many seemed to believe, but a coherent language that was regulated by the laws of rhetoric and grammar.[60]

Bimyō's refutation of the assumption that the vernacular was inferior to the classical medium, lacking a grammar of its own and incapable of generating rhetorical meanings, helped to satisfy the first of the necessary conditions for the establishment of a new, modern literary language. He further demonstrated that to apply the notion of rhetorical expression to the *genbun itchi* style was not a theoretical contradiction in terms. To the contrary, as he presented it, a more systematic consideration of the rhetorical features of the vernacular style was the key to improving the written language. Although a strong supporter of the vernacular, Bimyō believed that rhetoric and rhetorical expressions were indispensable for the growth of the *genbun itchi*. He bestowed a different status to the vernacular by defining it as a living entity in constant evolution with its own particular grammatical and rhetorical features.

A New Notion of Rhetorical Expression:
The Case of Shimamura Hōgetsu

By the beginning of the twentieth century the vernacular had gained substantially in prestige. Proof of its heightened status may be found not only in the tangible increase in the employment of the *genbun itchi* style in novels and short stories, but also in the fact that rhetoricians now began to take it up in a more systematic manner.[61] The remaining element needed to resolve the controversy over the character of the modern literary language was a new notion of rhetorical expression.

As noted above, the assumption that "rhetorical expression" was a synonym for archaic linguistic embellishment was common at the time, especially among the new generation of writers. Those who had written on the subject of rhetoric were partially responsible for this state of affairs. Close examination of the definition of rhetorical expression found in the major works written in the decade after the publication of Takada Sanae's *Bijigaku* reveals that they, in line with centuries of Western literary traditions, emphasized the ornamental nature of the rhetorical process of signification. Rhetorical expressions were defined in *Bijigaku,* for example, as "a way to increase the effectiveness, power and beauty of language by replacing the ordinary expression with a special one."[62] The premise of an opposition between an ordinary and a special level of expression seen in this 1889 definition may well have reinforced the notion of the parallel existence of a higher, elegant code and a lower, vulgar one. To overcome such assumptions it was therefore necessary to provide an alternative perspective on the possible different connotations of the term "rhetorical expression."

A key role was played by Shimamura Hōgetsu, who distinguished himself both as a supporter of the *genbun itchi* style and as an advocate of rhetoric. His "Shōsetsu no buntai ni tsuite" (On the style of the novel), published in 1898, was the first of a series of articles that sought to answer the question of a modern and refined form of expression. In his article Hōgetsu first introduced the different views of writers Kosugi Tengai, Izumi Kyōka, and Gotō Chūgai, which had appeared three months earlier in the journal *Waseda bungaku*.[63] After upholding Tengai's theory, which incidentally rejected *gazoku setchū* as an impediment to the creativity of the writer, Hōgetsu discussed the reasons for his disapproval of this style. In his view, conventional expressions—that is, *kata*—were the cause of the friction existing between the classical and contemporary styles, which were otherwise very similar. He made an important distinction between such *kata* and *shūji*. *Kata* he described as those expressions that were reminiscent of classical language, such as, for example, the copula *"nari"* or the terminative *"keri."* While these words had been regarded as "rhetorical," he claimed, they were merely archaic linguistic conventions. Since they hindered the freedom of the writer, such elements should be eliminated from the contemporary written language. *Shūji,* by contrast, were defined as being "true" rhetorical expressions capable of generating connotative images on the basis of shared linguistic and extralinguistic knowledge. Hōgetsu indicated that the difference between the *genbun itchi* style and traditional styles rich in classical elements lay indeed in the presence or absence not of *shūji,* but of *kata*. While the latter could be discarded, *shūji* were indispensable to the creation of a new written language. Thus he emphasized two major points: no written style could ever be completely devoid of rhetorical features; and any call for the elimination of rhetorical elements from the sentence was merely the result of a misconception of the nature of rhetorical expressions.

The distinction between stereotyped and true rhetorical expressions was, then, the most crucial argument of this 1898 article. It is not easy to say what Hōgetsu meant by true rhetorical expression. He did not provide examples, and he developed his argument on a rather theoretical plane. The core of his concept of appropriate rhetorical devices would seem to lie in the notion of connotative meanings generated from a common social, linguistic, and cultural background. In the distinction he drew between *shūji* and *kata* he stressed the possibility of producing rhetorical effects through creative use of the vernacular, relying not on classical conventions but on effective utilization of the linguistic material available. It seems likely that he alluded here to such aspects of the rhetorical process

as the effect of surprise resulting from an unanticipated semiotic relationship between the parts of a linguistic message. Of course, Hōgetsu did not totally reject
elegance as an important dimension of the rhetorical message. However, by interpreting the process of rhetorical signification not necessarily as an act of substi-
tution (i.e., the employment of stereotyped literary conventions in place of
ordinary expressions) but as one of creation, he heralded the possibility for the
formulation of new rhetorical devices unique to the modern literary language.

Hōgetsu also expressed considerable criticism for an excessive colloquialization of the literary language. In his "Genbun itchi no genzai, mirai" (The present
state of the *genbun itchi* style and its future possibilities), he reiterated that the *genbun itchi* was to develop not as a unilateral reproduction of the spoken tongue, but
as a result of a balance between the spoken and written language of the time. He
therefore rejected a *genbun itchi* style that was a mere replica of speech. Indeed, the
absence of rhetorical traits was in his view the cause of the *genbun itchi's* erratic
success. He thus called for a more refined language, warning, however, that such
a refinement could not be achieved by using conventional classical expressions.
Albeit without further explanation, Hōgetsu hinted at the possibility of creating
rhetorical features that were particular only to the vernacular.[64]

In 1902, Hōgetsu continued his advocacy of the *genbun itchi,* reiterating that its
main problem was of a rhetorical nature. In "Genbun itchi no sannan" (The three
faults of *genbun itchi*) he addressed the three most often recurring criticisms made of
the style—that it was vulgar, verbose, and lacked rhetorical connotations.[65] According to Hōgetsu, vulgarity could not be avoided, since the vernacular was still
far from being established as a common all-purpose idiom, and furthermore, it had
never yet been used as a literary language, which contributed to its image as a tran-
sient and evanescent mode of expression. With time, however, even the vernacular would eventually achieve literary prestige. It was most important at this stage to
promote a process of rhetorical harmonization between the classical and the contemporary style. The second criticism of verbosity was proof, in his view, that the
genbun itchi was still lacking rhetorical sophistication. Especially in this case, it was
essential that new rhetorical features be added to give new distinction to the style.
Finally, the third criticism was due to the lack of any literary weight, a problem that
could be solved only through the development of rhetorical features.

The year 1902 also saw the publication of *Shin bijigaku,* in which Hōgetsu revealed his rhetorical theory and concurrently addressed the problem of creating a
new written language. Affirming the need to base the written language on what
was spoken, he declared that "going back to the spoken language should not be
the final goal, but rather a new starting point." For him the immediate problem
was "how to revise the modern language, how to adorn it, and how to create a

style with rhetorical features superior to the spoken language."[66] That is to say, Hōgetsu indicated that while the written mode of expression should be founded on the vernacular, it could not be identical to it. It was essential to develop rhetorical devices particular to the new written style.

Hōgetsu returned to this issue in an essay that was published four years later. Back from his trip to Europe, he took his argument in *Shin bijigaku* a step further. The difference between the classical language and the vernacular, he now suggested, was due not to the presence or absence of rhetorical features, but rather to a difference in the nature of those features. It was a mistake to think that the *genbun itchi* was devoid of rhetorical features, whereas the classical language was abundant with them. For Hōgetsu, the *genbun itchi* style was not a mere reproduction of speech, but an expression of a type of content, which according to a romantic model had revolted against the supremacy of a classical form. Of course, this new type of content was itself in need of a form, but such a form did not have any other function than to faithfully convey the content.[67]

Hōgetsu's "Shin bunshōron" (A new theory of writing) appeared in 1911 and witnessed the rise of the *genbun itchi* style as the predominant mode of literary expression in the literary world. In this essay Hōgetsu addressed the many developments that had taken place in the *bundan* since the Restoration. In his view, old styles had been dominated by the presence of *kata;* they had prioritized form over content, thereby constraining the freedom of the individual. By contrast, the new style prioritized content, rejecting dependence on any specific model, be it Ihara Saikaku, Western, or native classical literature. Most important, such a style was unadorned and against artistry—a stance that did not necessarily signify the complete elimination of rhetorical features, however. Indeed, the lack of ornament for the sake of a faithful reproduction of nature was not, as Hōgetsu put it, an indication that rhetorical devices had been discarded, but rather that they were so skillfully fused with the content that they had become an essential part of it. After all, he maintained, "true rhetorical devices do not have an independent object or strength; they are only a tool for the content."[68] It is then clear that Hōgetsu was able to address and successfully resolve within a solid theoretical framework the misconception that rhetoric was opposed to the formation of a modern literary style, by demonstrating both its necessity and its value to the newly developing written language.

Rhetoric versus Naturalism?

Hōgetsu strongly supported rhetoric and its role in the achievement of a modern, refined mode of literary expression. As one of the leading theoreticians of naturalism, however, he never abandoned the assumption that there should be a unity of content and form. His goal was the creation of a form of expression that would faithfully depict reality while maintaining the literary refinement necessary for artistic achievement. Until this point the naturalists had advocated the complete abolition of affectation for the sake of truth; now, as set forth by Hōgetsu, the goal was to express truth while pursuing beauty, both in content and form.

Interestingly, in his "Ima no bundan to shin shizenshugi" (Neonaturalism and the present literary world) of 1907, Hōgetsu proposed a theoretical compromise that reconciled the idea of refinement and truth in writing.[69] He identified the existence of two main trends in literature, one supporting artistry and the other rejecting it. He then identified naturalism as being antithetical to the former; naturalism, he argued, aimed at the reproduction of nature and truth and as such eschewed any form of embellishment or elaboration. Yet naturalism's ultimate goal was the production of beauty, and the representation of truth was only a necessary step toward the achievement of that goal. This concept was crucial to Hōgetsu's thought, and he strongly reiterated it in his "Shizenshugi no kachi" (The value of naturalism) the following year. He reaffirmed that "truth is nothing but an ingredient for the completion of beauty; the value of truth in art is determined by its ability to lead to beauty."[70]

The importance of this point cannot be overstated: naturalism and rhetoric were not necessarily antithetical, even if it is true that such a notion was widespread in the literary world. On the contrary, a close examination of essays by leading figures of the naturalist movement reveals the existence of a more softened stance, which may have been overlooked prior to this point. For example, Hasegawa Tenkei emphasized the importance of metaphor in literature, while Katakami Tengen wrote that writers of the naturalist school "were not trying to get rid of ornamentation, they were just trying to change it."[71] Kosugi Tengai likewise asserted that art could not be achieved without elaboration, showing that the rejection of affectation did not exactly mean total rejection of rhetorical devices.[72] Furthermore, this softened position can also be observed in the writings of Tayama Katai, who has often been regarded as one of the strongest advocates of plain and objective writing. As discussed earlier in this chapter, his essays "Rokotsu naru byōsha" and "*Sei* ni okeru kokoromi" epitomized the crusade against affectation that swept the *bundan* at the turn of the century. Scholars' claims to the effect that rhetoric declined because of the insurgence of naturalism probably find their root in these and other essays of the period. However, already in "Rokotsu naru byōsha," Katai specified that his criticism of artistry did not signify rejection of all types of elaboration; he supported the use of devices that promoted the harmony of content and form. Thus as Yoshida Seiichi also pointed out, Katai was in fact suggesting the development of new devices.[73] This new type of artistry, one capable of guaranteeing the cohesion of content and form and thus the elimination of futile elements from the sentence, very much resembled Hōgetsu's call for rhetorical devices particular to the vernacular and meant as tools for the effective conveyance of the content.

Other works by Katai were similarly oriented. In *Bibun sahō* (A manual for elegant prose, 1906), in heralding the ability to reproduce reality faithfully as one of the prerogatives of the *genbun itchi* style, Katai conceded that "it is not true that the *genbun itchi* style does not need aesthetic elements."[74] He thus left enough latitude for a position that recognized the potential for the development of a type of stylistic sophistication particular to the vernacular. Katai also recognized the need for the *genbun itchi* to resort to imagery and symbolism, to include elements that were not necessarily a reproduction of reality but were nonetheless a part of life. By doing so, he acknowledged the use of a linguistic artistry that existed not for its own sake but found legitimate justification in the necessity of the content it conveyed. Likewise, in *Shōsetsu sahō* (How to write a novel, 1909), Katai denied that naturalist literature meant by definition the employment of a form completely devoid of any kind of ornamentation. The naturalists, he claimed, had been advocating the need for a plain, simple form of expression only because it seemed the most suitable for expressing the feelings and thoughts of human beings within the context of their social environment. In other words, naturalism was merely trying to do away with affectation in writing.[75]

As Igarashi Chikara put it in the same year,

> Because writing without affectation has become the password of the new written style, having misunderstood its meaning, many are now advocating that rhetorical devices are unnecessary, but this is a groundless theory. Writing without affectation means abolition of unnatural ornaments and classical conventions, it does not mean that all elaborate devices should be considered as unnecessary in writing.[76]

8

From Old to New Artistry

Rhetorical Refinement as an Interpretive Paradigm

Hōgetsu developed a notion of true rhetorical expression that was not in conflict with the new needs of the literary world. His call for rhetorical features particular to the vernacular situated rhetoric squarely within the *genbun itchi* debate, contributing to a redefinition of its role within the controversy on the refinement of modern literary language. This did not mean, however, that total agreement had been reached on the viability of the vernacular as a literary medium. Scholars on both sides continued to argue in favor of one style over the other and often did so by emphasizing or dismissing the importance of rhetorical refinement in writing.

Among *genbun itchi* supporters, scholar of Japanese literature Haga Yaichi called for the elimination of unnecessary linguistic elements such as the rhetorical traits inherited from *kanbun*. These, in his view, considerably limited the creative freedom of the writer. Ueda Mannen refuted the claim that the vernacular was too verbose and confidently anticipated that it would eventually develop refined features of its own.[1]

In his support of *genbun itchi,* Shōyō opined that the style was not necessarily wordy or redundant, and he went on to distinguish four substyles. The first, which he dismissed as too crude, was modeled after the stenographic transcription of speeches. The second, he argued, still contained several classical elements, and although not as redundant as the previous one, was not appropriate as *genbun itchi*. The third, he held, was the closest to the spoken tongue and as such was easy to follow and understand. It was a style especially suited for popular lectures: he called it *zokubuntai* (or, he added, *kōgotai*) and praised it for its rhetorical purity. The fourth was the type of literary language widely used in novels at the time, a style he referred to as *bibuntai*. Shōyō maintained that the third of these four substyles was most likely to become the future written language and concluded that, as Ueda Mannen had already stated, the *genbun itchi* style had the potential to grow into an effective mode of written expression. A few concerns remained, however, such as the types of copula employed or the excessive use of deferential expressions typical of spoken language.[2]

On the other hand, there were still many detractors of the *genbun itchi*. Leading academic figures such as Ōmachi Keigetsu and Inoue Tetsujirō (1855–1944) opposed the vernacular for use as a literary language due to its lack of charm and rhetorical sophistication. Inoue, in particular, expressed his dissent on the *genbun itchi* question in an issue of the journal *Bunshō sekai,* where, during a time when use of the vernacular in novels was extremely popular, the editor asked whether or not the younger generation of writers should still devote time to the study of classically based literary styles. In Inoue's view, the answer was affirmative. The use of the *genbun itchi,* he stated, was legitimate only in a limited number of forms of communication. It could not be employed in public, legal, or military documents, and even the Ministry of Education did not see it as a subject fit for instruction, with the partial exception of elementary school. Private communications such as letters could hardly be written using this style, unless the parties, he maintained, were very familiar with one another. And even the *Yomiuri shinbun,* which had used the style temporarily in its editorials, later changed its policy and went back to classically based written modes. Inoue concluded that lack of distinction and prestige were serious obstacles to the employment of *genbun itchi* in all aspects of social communication.[3]

The debate continued throughout much of the Taishō period. In 1916, a special issue of the journal *Nihon oyobi Nihonjin* (Japan and the Japanese) addressed the problem of written language, asking scholars and intellectuals from a variety of fields whether they believed the unification of the multiple styles that were still extant at the time would ever become a reality. The question of refinement emerged again as a pivotal issue. Among the contributors, philosopher Kuwaki Gen'yoku (1874–1946) viewed the issue of rhetorical refinement as the ongoing cause of disagreement between factions. This was due, he argued, either to people's belief that writing in *genbun itchi* meant a total elimination of rhetorical features or to their assumption that the vernacular was not capable of conveying rhetorical distinctions. Kuwaki acknowledged that the stenographic transcriptions of speeches delivered by scholars and intellectuals could not be compared, in terms of artistic achievement, to the great literary works of the past. He contended, however, that rhetorical refinement was not a problem that could be solved by the employment of everyday language and the sporadic incorporation of classical literary conventions. Greater effort needed to be undertaken to achieve a refined mode of expression based on the vernacular. Indeed, he noted, the vernacular might not be appropriate in public and legal documents, but it was being largely employed in novels, many of which were already displaying significant new rhetorical traits.[4]

Others echoed this position and reiterated their support for the *genbun itchi* style, arguing that substantial progress had been made since the mid-Meiji years. The vernacular, it was stated by other writers, was used widely because it enabled the writer to express his thoughts and feelings freely. The only major problem was the lack of rhetorical charm.[5] Agreeing with this view, educator Yamamoto Ryōkichi (1871–1942), for example, while supporting the vernacular, lamented that investigation of its rhetorical aspects was still insufficient. Critic and novelist Uchida Roan (1868–1929) reiterated that the *genbun itchi* style was not intended to be a mere reproduction of speech but a refined version of the spoken language.[6]

As can be seen from this discussion, the question of refinement in writing was still a matter of concern and debate in the Taishō years. The terms of the discussion had, however, considerably changed. As an editorial that appeared in *Bunshō sekai* duly noted, 1906, in particular, had been an extremely important year for Japanese literature.[7] Writers had finally succeeded in developing a colloquial literary style that supposedly avoided embellishments by means of a direct and simple language that reflected the new reality of everyday life. The first tangible consequence of the transition from classical modes of expression to a literary language based on the vernacular was that almost all of the novels published two years later were written in the *genbun itchi* style. This crucial juncture in Japanese literary history was followed by the realization that the debate over the refinement of the new literary language had partially lost its reason for being. A new style had been created that was seemingly capable of appealing aesthetically to readers and of conveying efficiently the themes and ideas that were offspring of a new age. It was clear that such a new style had already developed rhetorical features of its own. The call for the abolition of rhetorical expressions that had characterized three decades of literary debates had lost much of its legitimacy and critical appeal.

Notwithstanding, the debate continued to unfold, but it did so centering on the rise of a new notion: *gikō* (artistry). As has been discussed throughout this chapter, the conceptual opposition between the literary trends of naturalism and "pre-naturalism" had often been posed as a distinction between unadorned and embellished writing. The characterization of naturalism as a movement that was, in matters of literary style, contrary to affectation, was an important strategic maneuver that facilitated the movement's self-identification process. By denouncing the "falsity" of traditional literary production, the movement was able to characterize itself (its themes and style) as true and thus was able to displace pre-modern literary production and its system of literary values. However, the same stylistic features of simplicity and clarity that had been one of the reasons for the movement's success gradually became an impediment to its own growth. Once the movement overpowered tradition, it suddenly lost an important referent in its battle for self-affirmation. It found itself confined within its "rhetoric" of truth and simplicity, imprisoned within the very stylistic prerogatives that had contributed to its affirmation.

The newly formed literary language had the potential to go beyond the canons of intelligibility and simplicity, and writers were fully aware of that. Thus under the motto of "new sake must be poured into a new cup," the critical discourse that beginning in early Meiji had addressed the feasibility of a modern literary style based on the vernacular soon evolved into one that addressed its future stylistic possibilities. Part of that discourse centered on the notion of *shin gikō* (new artistry). In this instance, the term came to indicate the literary production of writers who orbited the magazine *Shinshichō* (New tides of thought) such as Akutagawa Ryūnosuke (1892–1927), Kikuchi Kan (1888–1948), and Kume Masao (1891–1952). According to the *Nihon kindai bungaku daijiten* (Encyclopedia of modern Japanese literature), however, its exact origins are not clear, and thus far very few scholars have sought to clarify how the term was employed in the literary circles during those years.[8]

The use of the term "*shin gikō*" can be traced to at least the late Meiji era. In 1908, a special issue of *Bunshō sekai* questioned the meaning of the words "*shin gikō,*" which had recently come into vogue in literary circles. The editor noted that the term was being used as the antithesis of the term "*mugikō*" (artless art), which referred to the unadorned written style that had been advocated by many naturalist writers. What was the meaning of the new term, and to what did it refer? Novelist Shimazaki Tōson (1872–1943) opened the discussion by noting that the birth of the term was the result of a new interpretation of the concept of artistry. Fashion had incidentally contributed to its increased popularity, he held, causing it to include meanings not originally present. As far as he was concerned, *shin gikō* referred to an artistic activity that originated from a model, as in the tendency of early Meiji writers to emulate the style of premodern literary figures. The new generation of writers had opposed the emulation of this style and had broken away from tradition by seeking to create art not from art, but from nature. In their efforts to do so, they had followed the examples of European naturalist writers. In the process, however, they had created a type of art that did not reflect the inner self but was also, in a sense, the reproduction of a model. Tōson therefore cast a shadow of doubt on the artistic achievements of the Japanese naturalist school: the too-strict adherence to Western literary models had deprived native literature of its own character and originality. He thus urged authors and critics to reassess their interpretation of the term "artistry," a task far more fundamental than that of simply understanding the meaning of "new artistry."

For Takahama Kyoshi, the call for *shin gikō* was the natural outcome of the changes that had taken place in recent years. The rejection of old literary canons had led to the creation of a new form capable of sustaining itself independently from centuries of literary conventions. This new form, however, soon garnered the reputation of being too crude and unrefined. The call for *shin gikō* was then the realization that efforts should be made to give further shape to this new form. The writers of the *shaseibun* school, he contended, were already working toward that end.

Poet Kubota Utsubo (1877–1967) questioned the meaning of artistry. He underlined the ambiguity of the term, which could be taken to signify a number of different meanings: the emulation of past literary pieces, the talent to touch the heart of the reader, the ability to see life through different means of observation, or the skill to express one's thoughts and feelings without affectation or embellishment. Ultimately, he stated, he was not sure to which of these the designation applied, thus indicating the general sense of uncertainty and skepticism that lingered around the semantic value of the term.

Novelist Masamune Hakuchō (1879–1962) echoed this skepticism. Hakuchō stated that, personally, he refuted any kind of premeditation in writing. Writing was for him the result of an inner impulse that could not be controlled and needed to be satisfied. Hakuchō perceived artistry as an artificial process of artistic creativity that did not rely on emotion and inspiration but on careful, systematic, and thus almost unnatural, planning. He accepted, however, the possibility that his instinctive and unconstrained relationship with writing could itself amount to a type of artistry. Or perhaps, he continued, the term simply indicated the ability to draw the reader's attention.

Kosugi Tengai argued in favor of the presence of imagination in a work of art. Artistry was to him essential in giving a structure and shape to imagination. It was also necessary to appeal to the feelings of the reader. In his view, art and artistry were indissoluble. While neither an advocate nor an opponent of artistry, he stated, he believed that description was the ultimate goal of literature. To the extent that it served to facilitate description, artistry was an essential element of his writing.[9]

In sum, contributors shared doubts as to the exact meaning of the word, which became a vague signifier, fluctuating mainly between two diametrically opposed notions. In a pejorative sense, artistry indicated the unnecessary, conventional constraint to the freedom of the writer that came from centuries of literary conventions; in a complimentary sense it was nearly semantically equivalent to "effective rhetorical expression." In the former case, it was therefore almost a synonym for the notion of old rhetorical devices that had constituted a subject of debate for over three decades. In the latter case, it was closer to the notion of new rhetorical devices particular to the vernacular, elaborated by Hōgetsu in many of his essays. Between these two meanings, the pejorative was perhaps most prevalent at the time. In his "Rokotsu naru byōsha," Tayama Katai strongly condemned artistry as an impediment to the growth of Japanese literature, and Hōgetsu also rejected it as a form of interference in one of his essays appearing in 1909.[10]

Among rhetoricians, Igarashi Chikara embraced a concept of the term that included both of its meanings. In a 1911 essay, Igarashi acknowledged the birth of a new style that opposed affectation and old rhetorical artifices.[11] Such a new style, he argued, was natural, realistic, and devoid of those conventional traits that were by contrast characteristic of premodern literary modes. The term "artistry" indicated the indiscriminate employment of artificial rhetorical ornaments associated with classically based literary styles. An example of this was using ornamental words such as *shōkei* (short cut) and *tasogare* (dusk, twilight) in place of their synonyms *chikamichi* and *yūgata,* which were instead reflective of everyday language. The new style, on the contrary, made great use of such everyday language, which now appeared not only in the dialogical, but also in the discursive portions of the text. In Igarashi's exposition, the term "artistry" clearly carried with it a pejorative connotation. However, this was not the only acceptation of the term. To the extent that it sought to avoid stereotyped literary conventions, he argued, the new style itself became representative of a new type of artistry, the so-called *mugikō* that had been strongly advocated by many naturalists. Within this context, the term came to assume a positive connotation, coming to epitomize the core of naturalism's literary theory in matters of literary style: complete absence of affectation for the sake of truth in writing. Nonetheless, Igarashi stated, the choice of the term was not a fortunate one, in that artless art seemed to imply the complete rejection of rhetorical features, an argument that was unsustainable as long as one spoke about literature. In fact, he argued, representative works of this new trend such as Shimazaki Tōson's *Haru* (Spring, 1908), Tayama Katai's *Sei* (Life, 1908), and Masamune Hakuchō's *Doko e* (Whither, 1908) contained a substantial presence of tropes and figures, including metaphor, personification, and irony. The new unadorned style of the naturalist school was therefore not characterized by the absence of artistry, but rather by the rise of a new artistry, one that was different in nature from that of its predecessors.

Igarashi thus underlined the ambivalence of the term, which eventually often was employed to indicate the birth of new rhetorical features particular to the newly formed literary language. Interestingly, at this time Igarashi used the phrase *"shin gikō"* to indicate the *mugikō* of the naturalists, which was ironic, since the two designations soon came to be viewed as antithetical. In fact, in a publication that likely appeared in 1912 or 1913, Kobayashi Aisen referred to old artistry as the rhetorical trait of pre-naturalism literature and new artistry as those of post-naturalism literature.[12] In particular, *shin gikō* was, in his view, the outcome of a fusion between content and form. This fusion represented the last stage toward the birth of a literary language that was not created after the models of classical modes of expression but that contained the degree of refinement necessary to de-fuse the criticism of its fiercest detractors. Aisen urged writers to think of rhetorical features differently from the past; after all, he claimed, Katai himself had not ruled out their presence in writing. In fact, he had called for the birth of new devices. These new devices had no purpose other than to facilitate an effective delivery of the content, a position very much resembling that of Hōgetsu's a few years earlier.

As for the term "artistry," Aisen highlighted the existence of another major semantic ambivalence: did it refer exclusively to how language was used, or did it also refer to the overall structure of the literary work, including plot?[13] For him, the use of the term was limited to the former realm: his chief concern was the ef-fective and artistic use of language. Others also saw it as primarily linked to the no-tion of effective use of the linguistic material. For example, discussing the call for *mugikō* that characterized the *bundan* at the end of the Meiji period, writer Tokuda Shūsei (1871–1943) noted that this was nothing but an implicit reference to the writing skills of the author: it meant that writers no longer needed to possess extra-ordinary rhetorical techniques in order to compose literature.[14]

At about the same time, critic and author Kamitsukasa Shōken (1874–1947) employed the term *"shin gikō"* in a similar fashion. In a short review of the major works published during the year 1914, Shōken refuted the opinion advanced by some that the literary world was experiencing a period of stagnation. He argued that writers such as Chikamatsu Shūkō, Tanizaki Jun'ichirō, Masamune Haku-chō, and Iwano Hōmei had recently displayed stylistic traits that constituted significant new literary developments. These traits were very different from those seen prior to the rise of naturalism and were the product of a *shin gikō* he wel-comed.[15] Shōken did not provide any further explanation, and because of the brevity of the piece, his use of the term left a number of questions and interpreta-tions unresolved.

Critic Nakamura Seiko (1884–1974) was among the first to pose those questions in an essay that appeared in the *Yomiuri shinbun* in December.[16] Seiko wondered if with *shin gikō* Shōken perhaps wanted to refer to such writers as Mushanokōji Saneatsu, Toyoshima Yoshio, Nagayo Yoshirō, and Sōma Taizō, since these were, in his opinion, the authors who had emerged during that year. He also wondered if the term referred exclusively to skilled writing, as it seemed to, or also to something else. In any case, he argued, if any new element had appeared in recent literature, it was certainly not in the field of style, but perhaps in the way writing had evolved to include detailed psychological descriptions of the characters in a novel.

The terms "*gikō*" and "*shin gikō*" continued to figure in much of the literary discourse of the time. For example, Chiba Kameo (1878–1935) acknowledged the literary production of the year 1914 as one of innovation "in terms of artistry."[17] The above terms also recurred significantly in Akagi Kōhei's renowned articles on the Shirakaba writers and were associated by many with some members of that literary coterie, particularly Satomi Ton. They appeared with particular frequency among the contributors of the journal *Shinchō* (New tides) and also in essays published in other venues such as *Bunshō sekai* and *Waseda bungaku*. And, almost as if to confirm the semantic ambiguity that characterized them, they continued to be employed in some cases with exclusive regard to the effective use of language and in others with reference to the rhetorical devices that affected the structure of the literary work.

In 1917 the debate intensified. In an essay titled "Sōsakukai no genjō ni tai-suru utagai" (Doubts on the state of the world of literary production), Tanaka Jun (1890–1966) acknowledged the existence of such a wide variety of trends in the literature of those years that it was extremely difficult to employ a label with the name of a specific school or writer. In particular, this was true in respect to content. There no longer was, for example, a naturalist or humanist component so strong as to be considered predominant among authors. Tanaka observed that, contrary to the opinion of many, the major accomplishment of naturalist writers had not been the depth of content in their works, but rather the freshness of the expression they had been able to develop. Language, in his view, had been the discriminating factor between modern and premodern literary production. The new writers had continued to stress this very artistic aspect of writing to the extent that virtually every author—including Mushanokōji Saneatsu, who was criticized by some—could have been considered a skilled writer. As a result, Tanaka maintained, the literary world was putting too much emphasis on language and writing techniques, which in turn cast serious doubt on the future of literature in the coming years.[18]

Nakamura Seiko followed up Tanaka's article with a piece that appeared soon after in the journal *Waseda bungaku*. Seiko observed that some critics had recently used the phrase *"shin gikō"* to refer to post-naturalism writers. The phrase was employed in contrast to two others: *mugikō,* which referred to naturalist writers themselves, and *kyū gikō* (old artistry), which indicated the style of one faction of the Ken'yūsha's literary coterie. *Shin gikō,* Seiko noted, was not necessarily a term used to praise the works by new writers; indeed, at times it seemed to convey a sort of criticism mixed with scorn. Furthermore, he continued, it was not clear whether it referred only to form or also to content, which shows that the question he had posed three years earlier had not yet been answered. Then, after identifying Kamitsukasa Shōken as the first to have used the term in his short piece of 1914, Seiko rejected the interpretation of *shin gikō* as a synonym for artistic writing, which, in his view, had been brought forth by Tanaka Jun. The only new development worthy of being so named was, he reiterated, the new depth of the psychological descriptions that could now be observed in literary works. Finally, while criticizing Tanaka's interpretation, Seiko joined him in his concern for an excessive emphasis on the stylistic features of literary production.[19]

In the following issue of the same journal Seiko addressed the question further. A critic, he recounted, had suggested to him that the meaning of *shin gikō* possibly indicated the scientific and intellectual nature of the linguistic devices now employed in writing. He disagreed with this view, he said, since such a scientific approach to language had in fact been a prerogative of naturalism. He agreed that linguistic artistry should be considered an intellectual activity but did not see the necessity to characterize this process as "new."[20]

Nishinomiya Tōchō (1891–1970) joined the debate in an article that appeared in the journal *Bunshō sekai* the same month. Tōchō noted that the term *"shin gikō"* was being used by some to indicate the works of Mushanokōji Saneatsu and by others to include those by Toyoshima Yoshio, Nagayo Yoshirō, Sōma Taizō, and Satomi Ton. In both cases, he added, he was not sure of the meaning attributed to the term. Tōchō rightly observed that the meaning of the word should be determined in the first place by a comparison with the term *"gikō."* What was new compared to the way the term had been previously used? Nakamura Seiko's essay in the August issue of *Waseda bungaku* had been a valid attempt in this respect but had fallen short of providing a complete answer. Tōchō, however, conceded that providing an unequivocal definition of the word was a strenuous enterprise: it embraced a variety of issues of an aesthetic, psychological, and rhetorical nature and was therefore arduous and almost impossible.

According to Tōchō, the first half of the Meiji era had been characterized by the rise of writers who were deeply admired for their writing ability. In particular, authors such as Ozaki Kōyō had been well received because of the charm of their rhetorical skills. In comparison, he argued, the new writers were not competent in the rhetorical use of language, but this did not mean that they were not skilled writers. The problem was of a rhetorical nature; that is, the rhetorical mechanisms they employed were different from those of earlier authors. New writers put much more emphasis on the subjective character of literary production as the result of a change of the perception of art, which now placed more weight on individual creativity and consequently on individual artistic use of language. It was in the realm of individuality, in the expression of the self, that the question of *shin gikō* could possibly find a justification.[21] It then becomes evident that for Tōchō the notion of *shin gikō* went beyond the realm of effective linguistic communication to embrace the question of self-expression at the level of the literary text. Overall, in the same fashion that Akutagawa had rejected the label of a *shin gikō* school as too reductive at the end of his *Rashōmon,* Tōchō also did not believe that such a term could represent any particular school of writers of the time. Only to the extent that it indicated "individual artistic expression" could the term be accepted.

In an article appearing only two months later, Maeda Akira (1879–1961) joined Tōchō in rejecting the notion of *shin gikō* as representative of the *bundan* of the period. He argued that it was only natural to experience the rise of a new form following the birth of a new age and ideas. For this reason, he held, any attempt to consider the term *"shin gikō"* as a synonym for new rhetorical skills was nonsensical. It was, however, possible to talk about *shin gikō* when considering the works of such writers as Akutagawa. Maeda considered two pieces by this author, namely *Aru hi no Ōishi Kuranosuke* (One day in the life of Ōishi Kuranosuke) and *Katakoi* (Unreturned love). The former piece, as the title suggested, focused on one day of the protagonist's existence; the latter began and ended with two parenthetical propositions. According to Maeda, these devices were the result of a deliberate choice by Akutagawa and characterized his literature strongly, especially when compared to that of the naturalist school. Naturalist writers, Maeda observed, often engaged in confessional works that did not have a clear beginning or end. There was, in other words, no real resolution to the questions and dilemmas that unfolded in the naturalists' literary work. From this point of view, if their style was to be called *mugikō,* then Akutagawa's expression was denoted by a skillful manipulation of the linguistic and textual body. In other words, his techniques drew the attention of the reader in a way that had not been possible in the works of the naturalists.[22]

In 1918, a definition of *shin gikō* appeared in the journal *Bunshō kurabu* (The writing club), and precisely in the section dedicated to new literary terms. According to the journal, the naturalist school had advocated *mugikō,* that is, a technique of expression that did away with artistry and rhetorical flourishes. In contrast to this tendency, the literary world was now witnessing a renewed interest in artistry, which manifested itself in the language and structure of works recently published. Among these authors were, for example, Akutagawa, Shiga Naoya, Tanizaki Jun'ichirō, and Kume Masao, writers who, accordingly, shared a pronounced attitude in favor of free artistic creativity.[23] One month later, an article appearing in the same journal once again defined artistry and its school as referring to a rising generation of authors whose literary production contrasted with that of naturalist writers. The article cautioned that the term did not necessarily indicate rhetorical forms per se, but rather the ability to express one's individuality.[24] The definitions appearing in *Bunshō kurabu* became widely accepted and concluded a debate that had lasted for a decade.

As is evident from this discussion, the opposition of "old" and "new" artistry was a recurrent feature of Taishō literary criticism. Needless to say, the meaning of the two terms constantly fluctuated depending on context and user. Igarashi, for example, already employed the term *"shin gikō"* in the late Meiji years to signify the *mugikō* advocated by the naturalists against the pomposity of mid-Meiji literary production. Later critics, however, mostly adopted the same term in contrast to *mugikō* to signify a type of literary production that was almost antithetical to naturalism. No consensus was reached on the definition of these terms, and their employment was often accompanied by a latent semantic ambiguity that on the one hand generated skepticism and on the other contributed to the intensification of the debate. It is true, however, that the word *"gikō,"* especially when preceded by the word *"shin,"* eventually conquered many of the negative connotations associated with it at the end of the Meiji era and became a crucial signifier of the changes that were taking place at different levels in the literary works of the period. Bolstered by the same type of semantic ambivalence that had affected the acceptance of rhetoric and the definition of rhetorical expressions in the previous decades, the debate on artistry raged unabated throughout the first part of the Taishō era. Was artistry something positive and essential to writing, or was it a notion to dismiss, to exile from the lexicon of literary production? Profiting from this perennial dilemma and from the inevitable misconceptions and misinterpretations that followed it, the debate unfolded, posing again, albeit under a different disguise, the question of the role of refinement in writing.

Consequently, artistry often simply meant the effective use of linguistic material in writing. Of course, it is important to highlight here that this was not the *only* acceptation of the term. Indeed, as this discussion has shown, the term *"shin gikō"* went beyond mere form to embrace all those rhetorical mechanisms that affect and regulate the whole structure and organization of a literary text. This was perhaps the most significant development of the Taishō years in terms of rhetorical awareness: the conquering of a restricted vision of rhetorical signification so that it was no longer an activity limited to the creation of effective tropes and figures, but became applicable to the overall process of creating a literary text.

Nonetheless, the emphasis on form and expression continued to be a matter of active interest for authors and critics. In fact, the debate on artistry often overlapped with the one on the role of rhetorical sophistication in writing. Once critics and authors recognized that the realm of rhetorical refinement was not necessarily limited to embellishments that were artificial, they began to move the focus of their inquiry from whether or not rhetorical devices were essential to the new literary language to what types of such devices were particular to it. But why did the debate on artistry collide with the one on rhetorical expressions, and why did this debate continue to put such emphasis on the problem of form? By the end of the Meiji era most leading figures of the literary world had already agreed that the new literary language needed to develop rhetorical features of its own; the importance of rhetorical refinement in writing was no longer questioned the way it had been in previous decades.

The reason for continued focus on the question of form probably lay in the dynamics that had characterized the relationship between low *(zoku)* and high *(ga)* literature. The canonization of classical language that took place over the centuries had displaced the vernacular, relegating it to the peripheral areas of literary signification. Form ruled, and as such often put serious limitations on the generation of new content. In the late Meiji years, however, inheriting a literary tradition that emphasized the separation of form and content to the detriment of the latter, naturalists (and others) strove to create a form that would be acceptable to a literary milieu now prioritizing content over expression. Content, or more precisely *naturalistic* content, reigned supreme, becoming itself, paradoxically, rigidly formularized so as to resemble those very literary conventions the movement had sought to abolish in the first place. If it was true that until the early Meiji years content had been sacrificed for form, by the hand of the naturalists, form was now being sacrificed for content. Put in these terms, the relationship between naturalism and *genbun itchi* appears to have been one of exploitation, which it was not. It was more a de facto alliance that enabled both entities to achieve their common goal of self-affirmation. However, it is perhaps true that for some the content of naturalist literature existed before its form; in this sense, the new form of expression was molded according to the needs of the new content. The search for a new form of expression in these terms reinforced the separation of form and content in the consciousness of authors and intellectuals. Even if a compromise was reached, it was under the assumption that the two dimensions were separate and distinct.

The Taishō years brought with them a new perspective on the relationship between literature and self-expression. An article by Katakami Tengen (1878–1946), appearing in *Bunshō sekai* in 1913, epitomized the rise of this new viewpoint. Literary language was becoming concrete and personal. Writers finally expressed themselves with their own words and avoided borrowing from the models of the past. Having one's own distinctive way of communication served to express one's soul and thoughts.[25] Form was now therefore the product of the author's deliberate choice. It was the product of an individual act of creation; form reflected the individual. Albeit bound to content by a relationship of mutual dependence, in the early Taishō years form began to regain a central role in the process of artistic signification. As Tokuda Shūsei put it, "there is no art without expression . . . there is no content without form, form is content."[26] The characterization of the relationship between form and content as one between equals paradoxically gave form a renewed importance and centrality in the literary discourse of the period.

The formulation during the Meiji period of a refined written language based on the vernacular and the debate during the Taishō period on the meaning of *shin gikō* were thus crucially linked. The latter was in many ways the extension of the former; it was, in other words, the final stage of the search for a modern written language. The writers of early Taishō were challenged by a new task: to conquer the thematic borders of naturalism and prove that the new language had the prerequisites to act as a medium for *any* type of content. The Taishō years provided fertile theoretical ground for this final undertaking. The dichotomy of vulgar versus elegant language had been diminished by many, and the notion that rhetorical refinement did not necessarily require the use of classically based literary styles was widely accepted. Authors strove to create a form that did not have to meet any rigid thematic requirement; on the contrary, it had to be fluid, independent, and reflective of the individual's perception of reality.

Given its continued relevance following the peak of naturalism and the affirmation of the vernacular in novels, the question of rhetorical refinement in writing is shown by the evidence providing us with a key reading paradigm of Meiji and Taishō literature. This question constituted a pivotal issue in the literary criticism of those years. The adherence to or rejection of a specific rhetorical model often characterized the nature of literary works and the theoretical premises of their authors, epitomized trends and schools of thought, and defined literature and its process of literary signification. The question of rhetorical refinement provided the poles between which the debate on language and style unfolded. Whether it was on a conscious or unconscious level, whether it was openly clarified or only implied, critics, authors, and intellectuals discussed the problem of language in literature in terms that reflected their individual conception of such categories as form and content, elegance and sophistication, and rhetoric. The question of rhetorical refinement was ultimately a metaliterary operation that sought to establish an aesthetic canon for the writing of the time, through a redefinition of the role of form in the process of literary signification. Form, and the search for a form, served to ultimately guide the development of the literary changes that took place during the Meiji and Taishō eras.

9

The Revival of Oratory in Late Meiji Japan

As discussed in chapter 3, during the first years of the Meiji period various factors lent rhetoric an immediate relevance and shaped the process whereby scholars and intellectuals tried to understand its boundaries and envision its possible application to the needs of the Japanese linguistic and literary worlds. The absence of an established rhetorical tradition for the study of native prose on the one hand and the growing political awareness that accompanied the call for freedom of speech and social rights on the other resulted in a strong emphasis on the oral dimension of rhetoric in the early stages of its introduction. In its original connotation of the art of speech, rhetoric became an important medium for voicing the demand for democratic rights. Studies of oratory flourished, and the practice of public speaking became one of the most important forms of social discourse of early Meiji social life.

In the second half of the Meiji era, studies of rhetoric took on a more literary orientation. Defined as a discipline concerned with "public speaking, composition and literary criticism,"[1] rhetoric figured in the major debates of the time regarding the formulation of a new written style. Increasingly, however, it came to be perceived as something exclusively concerned with classical literary conventions and, as such, antithetical to the development of a modern form of literary expression based on the vernacular. Scholars also began to disregard its oral dimension. The reason for this disregard lay in the assumption that, as one work put it, rhetoric was viewed as pertinent to the realm of both oral and written communication only in "those countries where the spoken and the written language are quite close."[2] Awareness of a substantial gap between spoken and written Japanese led many scholars to eliminate oratory from the scope of rhetorical investigation.

Despite this increased emphasis on written communication, the interest in public speaking never declined. In fact, the study of oratory continued throughout the Taishō period, bearing crucial links to the establishment of a standard national language and the creation of a modern form of literary expression.

Student Oratory

After a time of increased political awakening as reflected in the activities and accomplishments of the Freedom and Popular Rights Movement, the political scene was characterized by the beginning of a new phase that saw the consolidation of the Meiji state. In the years following the promulgation of the Constitution and opening of the Diet, the government exerted tighter control over political associations, and the opportunity for speaking in public considerably declined. There was as well an effort to reinstate Confucian-based ethics in various areas of social life. As Carol Gluck points out, in the 1880s the impending changes in the domestic political system raised new concerns, among them that of national unity. "From 1887 to 1890 intellectuals, journalists, and civic-minded members of the local elite called for the establishment of a 'sense of a nation' among the people, and as they did, they also emphasized indigenous customs, national culture, and *kokutai*."[3] Attempts were also made to reformulate the content and methods of national education in ways consistent with the goals and priorities of the state. One step in this direction was the promulgation in 1890 of the Imperial Rescript on Education (Kyōiku Chokugo), an ideological measure that attested to the "gathering emphasis on moral education in Confucian, pedagogical, and general social comment in the 1880s."[4]

Such was the background at the end of the century that caused the decrease in speech making. According to Ōkuma Shigenobu, oratory and the practice of public speaking went into decline after the outbreak of the Sino-Japanese War.[5] Ozaki Yukio, who shared this view, argued that the rise of militarism suppressed freedom of speech for years to come.[6] Noma Seiji, founder, as discussed below, of the Great Japanese Oratorical Society (Dai Nihon Yūbenkai), which later became the Kōdansha publishing house, also commented on the decline of oratory in the years between the Sino- and Russo-Japanese Wars.[7] Other sources likewise refer to the years after the establishment of the National Diet as the grimmest in the history of public speaking in modern Japan.[8]

These circumstances help explain the tendency among researchers thus far to associate the popularity of public speaking exclusively with the heyday of the Freedom and Popular Rights Movement of early Meiji. Interest in oratory, however, was not confined to that period. In fact, the new century brought social and political developments that would foster a continued role for public speaking in the Taishō era. Among these, the Hibiya Riots of 1905, a mass demonstration of popular discontent regarding the terms of the peace treaty following the Russo-Japanese War, marked the beginning of a new age, characterized by renewed political awareness and the appearance of new political forces. It is hard to say "whether the disturbances were inspired predominantly by simple nationalistic chauvinism or whether they reflected to a significant extent the growth of a new kind of anti-authoritarian sentiment."[9] Yet it is beyond doubt, as Richard Sims has observed, that "[they] represented the greatest challenge to governmental authority for at least a quarter of a century. They signified in a dramatic fashion that the phase of modern Japanese history in which politics were confined almost wholly to the Diet and to the electoral process might not last much longer."[10]

The Taishō political crisis of the early 1910s, in which the Katsura cabinet was overthrown by the first Movement to Protect Constitutional Government (Kensei Yōgo Undō), was also a major political turning point. The mass meetings and riots that occurred in conjunction with this movement, as Gluck points out, were "of dual ancestry." They can be considered descendants of both "the speech meetings of the elite 'men of influence' of the eighties and nineties and also of the urban, often violent, mass protest that characterized the strikes and demonstrations of the last Meiji decade."[11] Together, such events attested to a broadening of public involvement in political affairs during these years.

It is not coincidental that the 1910s of Taishō witnessed a new wave of interest in public speaking. The groups at the forefront of this development, however, were of a rather different nature from those active in promoting speech making in early Meiji. At the beginning of the Meiji period, oratory became popular first among scholars and intellectuals, whose speeches were mostly of an academic nature, and subsequently among politicians and popular rights advocates, who employed public speaking to achieve their political goals. By contrast, the distinctive feature of the world of public speaking during the Taishō era was the prominent part played by students.[12] As Peter Duus points out, "there had always been an incipient tradition of student protest in Japan, but until the Taishō period it had been limited by and large to the private universities, particularly Waseda, where the example and early ideas of Ōkuma exercised considerable influence on the students and atmosphere of the university."[13] The first decade of the twentieth century brought wider student participation in political activities, marking "the emergence of student protest as a familiar phenomenon in national politics."[14] Simultaneously, students turned to speech making as a major vehicle for expressing their views and concerns.

As Duus suggests, students at Waseda were at the forefront of this trend. A tradition of public speaking had existed at the university since 1883, when the student association Dōkōkai was founded. The practice of public speaking was one of its main activities. Members initially presented speeches on campus twice a week. Eventually forbidden to use university space, they conducted their meetings in the halls of the dormitory and outside the buildings. The difficulties encountered in those years of growing opposition to speech making failed, however, to discourage students and teachers from the study of oratory; indeed, not a few students chose Waseda because of its strength in this field.[15] Building on this base, on December 3, 1902, a formal society for the practice of oratory, the Waseda University Oratorical Society (Waseda Daigaku Yūbenkai), was established with the backing of Ōkuma Shigenobu. Among its leading members were Takada Sanae and the Christian educator Abe Isoo.[16]

Elsewhere, other individuals were also promoting student oratory. One of the most instrumental was Noma Seiji (1878–1938), who had already developed an interest in public speaking by the time he entered the Prefectural Normal School in the city of Maebashi in 1896.[17] Noma later recollected that in the final years of the Meiji period a craze for speech making swept through Japan's student population. In many colleges, debating societies were founded, and they contended for the championship title at intercollegiate competitions. Interest in oratory spread beyond student circles, and young men's associations everywhere established debating societies.[18] By contrast, Tokyo Imperial University seemed reluctant to promote the practice of oratory within its confines, but when Noma took a position within the administrative division of the College of Law, with the support of several professors he persuaded university officials to allow an oratorical session within Midorikai, an already existing non-scholastic campus society. From November 1909, sessions for practicing oratory were held at Noma's house in Dangozaka, Tokyo, under the name of the Great Japanese Oratorical Society.[19]

The establishment of the society was, accordingly, a landmark in Noma's career. As he recalled, "it was not only the culmination of long and painstaking preparation on my part, but it was the starting point of a literary project which was chiefly my own—the publishing of a monthly magazine embodying the speeches of University professors and students, a sort of semi-official organ of the Debating Society—a magazine of model speeches to be read and studied by all the student world."[20] Having obtained the financial support of the Nippon Tosho Publishing Company, in February 1910 Noma put out the inaugural issue of this journal, titled *Yūben* (Oratory). The preface read as follows.

In the new Japanese nation of the Meiji era, there existed oratory. Well, there certainly was an age during which oratory tried to establish itself. However, it was suppressed before it had the chance to grow. . . . Japan has shown remarkable progress in the past twenty years, but from the viewpoint of oratory, it has regrettably suffered a relapse. . . . Yet, history repeats itself, and a new golden age for oratory is bound to come.[21]

Among those who contributed to the first issue were a number of young students who later made a name for themselves in various fields: Ōsawa Ichiroku (lawyer), Aoki Tokuzō (bureaucrat), Maeda Tamon (politician), Ashida Hitoshi (politician), and Tsurumi Yūsuke (social critic and writer). This first printing, having sold out in a few hours, was followed by a second and a third. A total of fourteen thousand copies were printed in just a few days.[22]

Yūben gained instant popularity among intellectuals, politicians, and university students. According to Yamamori Toshikazu, a politician of the time, it was read by virtually all members of the prefectural assemblies.[23] While the contributors to the first issue were mostly from Tokyo Imperial University, the following issues contained articles from a variety of institutions—public and private. Noma recollected with particular pride the encouragement the new venture received from Ōkuma Shigenobu, who told him, "I recognize the importance of our young men acquiring the ability to express themselves effectively in this era of growing democratic government."[24]

Yūben was not the first journal to reproduce famous speeches or introduce famous orators to the general public. Several magazines, primarily organs of the political associations active during the second decade of the Meiji period, had made a point of publishing excerpts and unabridged versions of speeches by prominent personalities.[25] *Yūben,* however, offered not only transcriptions of speeches, but also articles on the historical significance of oratory and its relevance to the country's modernization. As a result, it provided a crucial stimulus for a resurgence of interest in public speaking.[26]

The journal prospered, particularly in the first years of the Taishō period, becoming the center of a theoretical debate on the importance of public speaking and an active promoter of speech making within the community. Beginning in 1914, the publishers of *Yūben* undertook the organization and sponsorship of speech meetings and competitions. On September 1 such a meeting was held in Hibiya, Tokyo; the guest speaker was Ozaki Yukio, and admittance was set at one yen and twenty sen. A few months later, on January 19, 1915, *Yūben* sponsored a general oratorical contest in Osaka (Kansai rengō daienzetsukai [The great speech meeting of the Kansai league]), and on February 27–28, 1915, it held a nationwide student debate meet in Tokyo (Kantō Kansai gakusei rengō daienzetsukai [The great speech meeting of the Kantō and Kansai student league]). On the latter occasion, approximately thirty orators, mostly students, delivered speeches. After these first events, the journal "sponsored speech meets almost on a daily basis."[27]

Reflecting these developments, many scholars began to view oratory as a necessary component of a student's education. Already in 1895 linguist Ueda Mannen had called for the incorporation of oratory in the school curriculum; now, fifteen years later, economist and educator Tanaka Hozumi suggested that its study be made mandatory.[28] The writer and translator Ashikawa Tadao lamented that while clubs for the practice of oratory existed in many schools throughout the country, the study of public speaking had not been incorporated into the curriculum anywhere as a compulsory subject, to the inconvenience of the large number of young students increasingly interested in practicing the art of speech.[29] Miyake Yūjirō and Sassa Masakazu also strongly affirmed the central role of oratory in the education of the individual.[30] Reflecting this new emphasis on oratory as part of a proper general education, a number of manuals were published for students approaching the study of public speaking for the first time.[31]

The effective establishment of a modern literary language in this same general period had meanwhile served to reduce the perceived gap between written and spoken mediums. The vernacular, now accepted as a legitimate form of literary expression, had gained considerably in prestige, and scholars began to take an interest in speech making as something relevant to the study and development of a modern written as well as spoken language.

The Contribution of Oratory to the Development of a Modern Written Language

The creation of a modern form of written expression that was relatively simple but at the same time aesthetically pleasing was made possible by, among other things, a theoretical reappraisal of the vernacular. The first step toward the creation of a simplified but refined written language was to establish the importance of the vernacular. As noted in chapter 7, the popular fiction of the Edo period had already incorporated colloquial elements, and in his *Shōsetsu shinzui,* Shōyō affirmed the use of such elements in literature. For the vernacular to be accepted as an alternative to other written styles, however, it was necessary to overcome the common view that the spoken language was stylistically inferior to the written. Rhetoric provided an effective platform for carrying out a theoretical reappraisal of the vernacular along those lines.

The introduction and proliferation of public speaking during the early Meiji years promoted a new awareness of the nature of language: its power to appeal to people and their emotions meant that language, if rightly employed, could become an exceptional device for persuasion. This was not a discovery of the power of language as such; theories of the "spirit of words" *(kotodama)* and the like, current in national learning circles in the previous centuries, had already identified language as something endowed with a special force intimately linked to the sacred. Rather, what was new was a realization of the possibilities of manipulating language as an instrument of communication. This was perhaps one of the greatest changes in language awareness brought about by the spread of public speaking in the late nineteenth century.

The sense that language could be structured to serve a specific purpose stirred interest in the mechanisms that regulated it. It was recognized that to accomplish the aim of communication, the language of the orator had to be plain, concise, refined, and, as Ozaki Yukio indicated in 1877, correct. But a further requirement was paramount: a common language. In the second decade of the Meiji period, Matsumura Misao's *Enzetsu kinshin,* Kuroiwa Dai's *Yūben bijihō,* and Baba Tatsui's *Yūbenhō* were among those works that, within the framework of public speaking, had already paid considerable attention to the problem of language and related issues. Along the same lines, writing in the 1880s, political activist Shiroyama Seiichi pointed out that "there are no fixed rules in our national language today, which makes giving a speech a difficult matter."[32] Concurring, orator and Buddhist educator Itō Yōjirō held that to practice public speaking, one first needed to study language.[33] As an example of the lack of linguistic unity, in 1903 the politician and Diet representative Komuro Shigehiro recounted that "one day a member of the Diet from a remote area of the country gave a speech at the House of Representatives; I could not understand a third of what he said, and even the stenographer was at a loss."[34] In the 1920s linguist Hoshina Kōichi similarly pointed to dialectical differences as the cause for a historically poor tradition of public speaking. Dialects were not appropriate for speech making, he argued, in that they caused laughter and miscommunication. Dialecticisms could become an effective tool in the hand of the orator only if used parsimoniously. Thus the first goal of the study of oratory was "the correction of dialects," which could be achieved by encouraging children to practice speech making from a young age.[35]

Studies of oratory throughout the Meiji and Taishō periods agreed that the elimination of regional differences, foreign words, and archaisms was a prerequisite to the effective delivery of a speech.[36] To this end, some writers argued, it was necessary to promote research not on classical language, but the "language spoken by ordinary citizens."[37] Writing in 1917, Haga Yaichi noted that in spite of increased awareness of the importance of the vernacular, many orators still tended to employ archaisms and classical linguistic expressions, which made it difficult for the audience to understand the content of their speeches. In an age that no longer exclusively relied on written communication but recognized the importance of the spoken word, it was crucial, he held, to foster the development of a national language that would be accessible even to the less educated. He thus encouraged the practice of speech making, which he viewed as essential for the development of both a standard national language and a national literature.[38] Other scholars called for the adoption of the Tokyo dialect as a standard national mode of speech.[39] Such concerns led several researchers to argue that oratory should be brought within the scope of scholarly studies of the national language and that efforts should be made to formulate a coherent policy for its improvement.[40]

On the other hand, many shared the view that the principles regulating the preparation, arrangement, and delivery of a speech should apply by extension to written communication. Writing in the late Meiji period, scholars such as Ōmachi Keigetsu and Nishimura Shigeki maintained that the main cause for the conflict between the spoken and the written language and for the difficulties in realizing a colloquial but refined written style lay in the lack of an oratorical tradition.[41] A different stance toward the study of oratory, they held, might lead to a resolution of this conflict and facilitate an acceptable compromise between classical and vulgar styles.

The adoption of stenography, which was introduced to Japan in 1882 by Takusari Kōki, made it possible to publish faithful transcriptions of actual speeches, a development that contributed to a gradual familiarization with a written style that obviously employed several colloquial features.[42] It also provided scholars and intellectuals concerned about issues of language with concrete contemporaneous materials for considering the options available for the establishment of a modern written language. In 1909, Uchida Roan acknowledged the crucial role played by stenography and the transcription of the popular storyteller Sanyūtei Enchō's *Kaidan botan dōrō* (The strange story of the peony lantern) in the development of a *genbun itchi* style; and a few years later, the philosopher Inoue Tetsujirō reiterated that the introduction of stenography had been instrumental to the formation of modern written Japanese.[43]

In more recent years, researchers have pursued the specific connections between stenographic transcriptions of speeches and the development of a written vernacular. In a 1962 study, for example, Kanda Sumiko examined eighteen stenographic transcriptions of speeches included in a compilation published by Hayashi Shigeatsu in 1886. The adjectives and verbs employed in the speeches, she noted, largely follow the grammatical rules of the vernacular.[44] Shiozawa Kazuko similarly examined five stenographic transcriptions of speeches published in *Tōyō gakugei zasshi* (Journal of Eastern arts and science) between 1885 and 1892. The particles, auxiliary verbs, verbs, and adjectives used in the speeches were consistent, she found, with the standard features of modern Japanese later adopted by *Kōgohō* (A grammar of spoken language) and *Kōgohō bekki* (A grammar of spoken language: A supplement), official grammars published by the National Language Research Council in 1916 and 1917.[45]

Comparison of speeches published before and after the introduction of stenography confirms that speeches transcribed by this method served as a textual precursor of what later came to be accepted as standard linguistic forms. Collections of speeches published prior to the introduction of stenography, such as Miyake Torata's *Nihon enzetsu kihan* (Models of speech making in Japan, 1881) and Kitaki Seirui's *Nihon enzetsu tōron hōhō* (A manual for speech and debate in Japan, 1882) seem to have been uniformly rearranged in a more classical written style.

> Yo ga chōshū shokun ni mukatte iken o chinjutsu sen to hossuru tokoro no rondai wa kiwamete jūdai naru jikō ni shite iyashikumo Nihon jinmin taru mono wa kore ga tame ni kushin shōryo sezaru bekarazaru yōken *nari*.

> The topic I wish to discuss today is an extremely important one. It is also something that those who are Japanese should especially ponder and carefully consider. (Baba Tatsui, "Gaikōron")

> Kyō wa Tōkyō dai ichi chūgaku sunawachi koko ni oite hajimete enzetsukai o moyōsare beki mune nite ware wa sono kyōin yori manekare nanzo isseki no wasetsu o nasu beki yoshi o shoku seraretari. . . . Oyoso ronzetsu to iu mono wa shisō yori hassuru mono *nari*.

> We are here today at Tokyo First Middle School to hold a public speech meeting for the first time. I have been invited by the teachers of this school and have been asked to deliver a speech. . . . Generally speaking, an argument is something that originates from thought. (Nakamura Masanao, "Enzetsu no shugi o ronzu")

> Yoron no imi o kantan ni toki akaseba kokumin no tasū no iken yori seiritsu suru giron to iu koto *nari*. Konnichi waga kokumin wa sanzen gohyakumannin no ōki ni noboreri. Shikareba hinpu o wakatazu kengu o ronzezu sanzen gohyakumannin no dōi o etaru mono o sashite yoron to iu ka. . . . Yo wa yoron no kanarazu kono gotoki mono ni arazaru o shiru *nari*. Shikareba kokumin ga kahansū ijō no dōi o etaru toki ni oite . . . yoron no na o motte subeki ka. Kore mata kanarazushimo shikarazaru *nari*. Shikareba jūnin ijō hyakunin ijō hata bannin ijō no dōi o etaru wa yoron to iu beki ka. Kore mata kanarazushimo shikarazaru *nari*.

> If one were to explain the meaning of "public opinion" in a simple fashion, it would be "the arguments that are formed through the opinions of the majority of the population." Today the population of our nation has reached thirty-five million. Can we call it "public opinion" when the entire population, regardless of

whether they are poor or rich, wise or foolish, agrees upon something? I believe public opinion is not necessarily something of this sort. Can we call it public opinion when the majority of the population agrees? . . . This is also not necessarily so. If more than ten, a hundred people, or all agree? Again, it may still not be the case. (Suehiro Shigeyasu, "Yoron no imi")[46]

These examples consistently use the classical *nari* for the copula. Other instances of classical written usage include the attributive forms *naru* and *taru* of the copulas *nari* and *tari,* perfective verb forms *(seraretari, noboreri),* and use of the case particle *ga* instead of *no* before *tame.*

By contrast, speeches published in Sawada Masatake's *Enzetsu bijihō* (A manual of rhetoric and speech making, 1894) and Nakajima Kisō's *Enzetsu kappō* (Effective methods of speech making, 1903), both of which appeared after the introduction of stenography, made no use of classical forms. As the following examples indicate, in Sawada's work, *de arimasu* was the predominant form of copula, followed closely by *de aru,* while in Nakajima's compilation *de aru* was by far the most widely used, followed by *de arimasu.* Other verb forms, too, as well as euphonic changes follow colloquial rather than classical patterns.[47]

Mazu dai ichi ni koko ni kakageta shippei hokenhō ga naze konnichi hitsuyō ni natte kita ka to iu koto o mōshiagenakereba naranu. Meiji nijūichi nen ni watakushi ga shokugyō eiseihō o ronjita toki wa somo somo dō iu toki *de aru* ka to iu koto o kangaete mireba, ichiban hayaku wakaru. Kono toki wa sunawachi Takashima tankō no mondai no okotta toki *de aru*. Takashima tankō no mondai wa nan *de aru* ka. Sunawachi rodō shakai ga shippei hoken, sono hoka shokugyō eiseihō no hitsuyō o kanki shita toki *de aru*.

First of all I must talk about why health insurance has become necessary. One can understand immediately by thinking of what happened in the twenty-first year of the Meiji era, when I talked about a law for a healthful working environment. This was the year of the Takashima coal mine incident. And what was the Takashima coal mine incident all about? It was when the working society realized the necessity of health insurance and a law for a healthful workplace. (Gotō Shinpei, "Shippei no hokenhō")

Yōsuru ni kono gakkō mo kōtō naru jitsugyōka o tsukuru gakkō *de aru*. Shuwan aru riji nari tōdori nari shachō nari o tsukuru mokuteki o motte taterarete iru gakkō *de aru*. Tada sono shudan ga ta no gakkō to wa chigau. Ta no gakkō wa gakkō kyōiku ni oite riji ni nari, shachō ni naru koto o sanjū gurai made ni gakkō ni oite oshieyō to iu no *de aru ga*, kochira wa hatachi gurai made hitotōri no koto o oshi-

ete, ato wa shakai kyōiku de rippa na ningen o tsukutte ikō to iu no *de atte,* mokuteki wa onaji de mo hōhō ga chigau.

In other words, this is also a school that produces high-level entrepreneurs. It is a
school that was founded with the purpose of creating skilled directors, managers,
and presidents. However, the methodology is different from that of other schools.
While other institutions seek to teach the student until the age of thirty how to become a director or a president, this school provides students with a general education until the age of twenty and then entrusts society with the further development
of the individual. The goal is the same, but the method is different. (Amano Tameyuki, "Waseda jitsugyō gakkō kyōiku hōshin")[48]

The speech transcriptions in these later works seem to reflect more closely
the actual language used by orators, which was probably reproduced for the most
part unaltered. The extensive employment of *de aru* at a time when as yet few authors used this form of the copula in writing indicates that speeches can be considered true forerunners of the modern written language. The predominance of
the copula *de aru* is even more significant when one considers that the social context of speech making, a type of discourse that calls to some extent for expressions
of deference, might have dictated the use of the more polite *de arimasu.*

As the above examples indicate, stenographic transcriptions of speeches
helped naturalize certain vernacular modes of expression as written forms. Those
who wrote about speech making contributed in other ways to the development
of a modern written language. Sensitive to the *genbun itchi* issue, scholars in this
area strove from an early stage to write in a manner that would be intelligible to
as large an audience as possible. Matsumura Misao's *Enzetsu kinshin* and Baba
Tatsui's *Yūbenhō* were representative of this effort. Although these works, published in the early 1880s, retained some classical conventions, they showed a clear
disposition toward a more simplified form of written expression. By the beginning
of the 1890s, the genre of public-speaking manuals offered promising examples of
genbun itchi.[49] In comparison, treatises on composition published in the 1890s still
employed a more conservative written style.

As the written language came to gradually employ a larger number of colloquial linguistic traits, scholars began to realize the possibility of discussing oral and
written communication simultaneously. This new awareness was epitomized by
works such as Endō Takanojō's *Yūben to bunshō: Saishin kenkyū* (Oratory and composition: The latest research, 1917). With a preface by Takada Sanae and Haga
Yaichi, this book was, according to the author, the first attempt in Japan to address
the problem of oratory and composition concurrently and in a balanced fashion; as
such it was a "response to the needs of a new age."[50] Of course, scholars still con-

fronted some basic differences between colloquial language and those conventional literary expressions that had survived the simplification process carried out under the name of *genbun itchi*. Abe Isoo, for example, still questioned in 1906 whether a speech could ever be regarded as a "piece of literature"; in his opinion, the differences between spoken and written Japanese were such that the gap between the two could hardly be reconciled.[51] Abe could not completely overcome the same dilemma that in the late 1880s and 1890s had prompted scholars such as Takada Sanae to exclude oratory from the scope of rhetorical investigation.

Others were also aware of the seemingly perpetual gap separating spoken and written Japanese; however, they were not all so pessimistic. Haga Yaichi, for example, insisted that oratory should be brought within the scope of literature and hoped for a day when orators would create refined literary pieces.[52] "Studying public speaking," another researcher maintained in the 1920s, "leads toward an improvement of writing."[53]

The major issue in the debate over the creation of a new written style was whether the vernacular could ever rise to take the place of literary conventions that had been highly regarded for centuries and assume the rank of literary language. Developments in oratory that paralleled this debate contributed to its ultimate resolution in favor of the acceptance of a written vernacular.

The reproduction of speeches was a significant factor in this process in that it made it possible to see the modes of expression used in such speeches as more than merely oral forms of communication and thereby led to a growing recognition of the correlation between public speaking and writing. In seeking to assess the impact of Western rhetoric on late nineteenth-century Japan, one should thus take into account its role not only as a discipline concerned with matters of style, but also as a branch of learning that, by disclosing the secrets of speaking in public, concurrently shaped modern written Japanese.

Epilogue
Rhetoric and Modern Japanese Literature

This book has sought to explore the contribution of the large number of works of rhetoric produced throughout the Meiji and Taishō eras in shaping the modern Japanese cultural and literary world. In this volume it has become clear that such works, hitherto largely overlooked by researchers, played a significant role in the developments that took place during the period.

One question often posed by the few scholars who have thus far addressed some aspects of Japanese rhetoric was whether Japan did or did not have a tradition of rhetorical inquiry prior to the Meiji era. A synopsis of representative works of classical Japanese literature has shown the existence of a strong awareness, among the literati of that age, of the potential of rhetorical signification. The poetics developed by the critics and poets of the classical period represent concrete proof of a mature interest in the rhetorical use of language—an interest reflected in the achievement of an unrivaled poetic sensitivity now universally recognized as characteristic of that age.

This book has confirmed that pre-Meiji interest in rhetorical practices was not limited to written discourse but also extended to the domain of oral communication. The Buddhist homiletic tradition and its derived forms of itinerant preaching, storytelling, and popular lecturing are clear evidence that the Japanese have been exposed, at different stages in their cultural history, to the fascination exerted by the power of the spoken word. This book has thus provided an affirmative answer to the question of whether Japan had a native history of rhetorical inquiry prior to Western influence. It has attached to it, however, an important provision: Meiji scholars and intellectuals downplayed such history and considered the Meiji period the true beginning of rhetorical investigation in Japan.

The dismissal of the premodern rhetorical heritage has affected the modalities of Western rhetoric's introduction and development in Japan. The growth of the discipline as a field of study took place virtually independently from the premodern tradition, on the assumption that no relevant heritage of rhetorical inquiry existed prior to the Meiji era. This volume has had to accept this notion, because it was the fundamental premise from which the inquiry of Meiji rhetoricians departed. This should not, however, be seen as equivalent to denying either the existence of a pre-Meiji native rhetorical tradition or the possibility that this very tradition may have facilitated the assimilation of Western rhetoric in Japan. After all, the ultimate goal for the poet was to please, through the creation of suggestive images, the aesthetic sense of those who read his poetry; and for the preacher, it was to convince the ordinary man, through sound arguments, that the faith he professed contained the truth necessary for enlightenment. In both of these cases, the continued search for an effective way to communicate feelings and ideas certainly contributed to the establishment of a native rhetorical tradition that cannot be dismissed.

With the Meiji Restoration and the opening to the West, Japanese scholars and intellectuals became exposed to social, philosophical, and literary theories and ideas that were either gaining ground in the West at that time or that were considered the foundation of Western thought. Rhetoric was one of these sciences, or arts, that were viewed as intimately connected to Western cultural and philosophical heritage. As such, it soon attracted the attention of many young scholars and intellectuals who saw in the mastering of this art a shortcut to the understanding of the West. Interestingly, almost all of those who left a mark on the history of the discipline were notably very young at the time of their most distinguished contribution. Ozaki Yukio, for example, was only nineteen years old when he published *Kōkai enzetsuhō*. Kikuchi Dairoku was twenty-four when his *Shūji oyobi kabun* appeared; Takada Sanae was twenty-eight at the time of his *Bijigaku,* and Takeshima Hagoromo and Shimamura Hōgetsu were, respectively, twenty-seven and thirty-one when their *Shūjigaku* and *Shin bijigaku* were published. Rhetoric found, therefore, a fertile ground among this younger generation of rising scholars, who became instrumental in promoting its study after its introduction.

It was as the art of speech that Western rhetoric made its first decisive impact. Public speaking had been until the beginning of the Meiji period a prerogative of preachers and teachers, mainly a sort of one-way form of communication that often placed the speaker in a position of superiority in respect to his audience. The arrival of oratory from the West changed the dynamics of this relationship. The orator was now required to carefully consider a variety of factors if he was to be successful: the psychology of the audience, the rigor of his arguments, the effectiveness of his language, the dignity of his demeanor, and, of course, the social and political circumstances of the time. Not that these elements had never been given consideration prior to the modern age; as already mentioned, classical Japanese literature on the one hand and the Buddhist homiletic tradition on the other already provide evidence of an established native rhetorical tradition. However, this time the premise was different. The concept of persuasion revolutionized the hierarchical configuration that had characterized most public address in Japan until then. The authority of the speaker was now no longer taken for granted; the orator had to win the confidence of his audience and persuade them of the veracity of his arguments. Furthermore, the issue of freedom of speech accompanying the arrival of rhetoric bestowed a completely different character on speech making, creating political and social expectations that went beyond the original enlightenment goal of pure exchange of knowledge.

Although the art of speech first found application among scholars and their academic debates, in the early post-Restoration years, times were ripe in Japan for decisive changes that expanded oratory's area of suitability. Social and political leaders were in need of an effective and direct tool that allowed them to communicate with as many people as possible. In an age that saw fierce governmental censorship of other important forms of discourse such as the press, rhetoric offered a practical and revolutionary model of communication. It provided a framework through which ideas and information were exchanged. In its most original connotation as the art of speech and in the form of public speaking, it brought with it a thirst for reform and change that was motivated and carried out according to the models of Western civilization. It thus embodied themes and beliefs that, to an extent, clashed with the preexisting order of values and, as such, encouraged the process of transformation and cultural reconfiguration that eventually became a major feature of the Meiji era itself.

The popularity of oratory was not, however, an exclusively Meiji phenomenon, as has been often thought. Its practice flourished considerably also in the following era, albeit with traits and characteristics particular to that age. Students were the new factor in the Taishō revival of public speaking. Some of them, like Nagai Ryūtarō at Waseda University, helped to found oratory clubs that became the gathering point for hundreds of young Japanese interested in speech making. Others, like Tsurumi Yūsuke at the Great Japanese Oratorical Society Publishing Company, contributed to the editing of journals and magazines, which became the forum of much of the political and social discourse during the Taishō era.

Despite the differences that separated Meiji and Taishō oratory, the popularity of public speaking in modern Japan was characterized throughout its history by a strong awareness among scholars and intellectuals of its crucial importance in the debates on language that were taking place at the turn of the century. Beginning in the mid–Meiji years, scholars saw in public speaking one of the most effective ways to eliminate dialectical differences and clear the way toward the creation of a standardized form of the Japanese language. In doing so, they also contributed to the reappraisal of the vernacular, establishing the premise for its employment as literary language.

Concrete evidence for this claim can be found in the text of speeches that were recorded in the mid–1880s and after. Comparison of speeches published before and after the introduction of stenography has shown that speeches transcribed by this method served as a textual precursor of what later came to be accepted as standard linguistic modes. The practice of public speaking therefore had important ramifications in the formation of a modern written language in that it helped naturalize certain vernacular modes of expression as written forms.

Ultimately, as the art of speech, rhetoric helped to enhance the prestige of the vernacular, which constituted a major step toward its acceptance as a valid medium for literary expression. At the same time, the new weight given public speaking as a major form of social discourse strengthened the relevance of Western rhetoric, thus giving birth to a relationship of mutual benefit that lasted for a period of over fifty years.

Western rhetoric also left an indelible mark on the realm of written discourse. As it came to be understood as a discipline concerned with composition, rhetoric was instrumental in compensating for the lack of a consistent native tradition in this area. The scholarship of the 1890s was the response to an increased interest both in writing and in literary criticism. Many denounced the lack of manuals of composition and strove to bring to order the chaotic state of written communication. The growing conflict between classical and vernacular styles and the rise of literary and pedagogical issues that were closely related to questions of a sociopolitical nature, such as the reduction or elimination of Chinese characters, constituted a remarkable challenge for even the most experienced scholars and government officials. Systematizing and synthesizing centuries of literary tradition under the pressing urgency of making writing more accessible to the masses was not an easy task. Rhetoric came to the rescue of those engaged in this undertaking by providing a platform for debate and offering a system of rules and precepts that could be applied to the Japanese case. These rules and precepts, by then already regarded as obsolete in much of the Western world, proved to be a useful source of reference as scholars and educators tackled the issue of literacy and, with it, literature.

There was, however, much more that concerned the question of writing. The problem was not only how to write, but also how to distinguish between good and bad writing, and, as some British rhetoricians had also put it, between "the beautiful" and the "non-beautiful." The search for an aesthetic standard intensified with the rising interest in literary criticism. This search was not necessarily a rhetorical issue; however, many of the works of rhetoric that were widely read in the first half of the Meiji era stressed the close link between rhetoric and the appreciation of literature. This likely led Shōyō and others to disregard the idea of rhetoric as a system of rules that taught composition. Instead, it prompted them to emphasize rhetoric's relevance to literary criticism, which consequently encouraged studies in this area, particularly at Waseda University.

Be it in the field of composition or of literary criticism, the blooming of rhetorical inquiry seen at the end of the nineteenth century was substantial evidence that the knowledge imported from Western rhetorical tradition was deemed helpful, if not critical, to the literary undertakings that were transpiring during those years. Among the issues that soon came to dominate literary circles was the search for a modern written language. Rhetoric remained for a long time detached from such debate; if anything, it was more supportive of traditional classical styles than *genbun itchi*. Rhetoric's metalanguage, in particular, became a constant reminder of classical language's alleged superiority over the vernacular: all the works of rhetoric that appeared between Takada Sanae's *Bijigaku* and the turn of the century were written in a language replete with classical characteristics, and virtually all of these works disregarded the possibility of using the vernacular in writing. Rhetoric's own metalanguage was thus among the causes of its characterization as an outmoded field of study that opposed a written language based on the vernacular.

The *genbun itchi* debate unfolded over a period of at least four decades, with the literary world essentially splitting into two factions, one supporting the vernacularization of the written style and the other insisting on the superiority of classically based modes of expression. Because much of the *genbun itchi* discourse centered on the elimination of superfluous rhetorical elements from the sentence, and because classical language was considered to be synonymous with elegance and refinement, rhetoric soon came to be associated with the traditionalist forces that opposed the excessive vernacularization of literary language. The conservative traits displayed in the scholarship of the 1890s added to this characterization. Rhetoric during this time was quickly labeled as antithetical to the more progressive trends of the *bundan* such as realism and naturalism, which had elected the vernacular as their medium of preference.

This period of conservatism and the somewhat negative characterization that accompanied rhetoric in these years began to take its toll. The call for a literary style devoid of rhetorical elements, which was gaining momentum at the turn of the century, exemplified this rejection of rhetoric and its precepts. The discipline, now even more severely removed from the ongoing debate regarding the creation of a modern written language, faced a theoretical collapse. However, at the beginning of the twentieth century, rhetoric took a new course. The transition to a conception of rhetoric that was more in line with the needs of the time occurred mainly through the contribution of scholars such as Yamada Bimyō, Shimamura Hōgetsu, and Igarashi Chikara, who situated the discipline squarely within the debate over the formation of a new literary language. Bimyō did not write any rhetorical treatise per se, but through many of his essays he contributed to a reassessment of the role of rhetoric in the creation of a new literary language. Bimyō refuted the common belief that the vernacular was inferior to classical language or that it was incapable of generating rhetorical meanings. As a supporter of *genbun itchi,* his call for rhetorical devices had major implications. It signified that the application of the principles of rhetoric to the *genbun itchi* style was not a theoretical contradiction in terms. To the contrary, Bimyō believed that the study of rhetoric could help authors and scholars refine the vernacular style and perhaps make it more acceptable to a broader range of writers.

Hōgetsu, was, however, the crucial figure in the debate that addressed the feasibility of a refined literary language based on the vernacular. He emphasized that the difference between the classical language and the vernacular was due not to the presence or absence of rhetorical features, but rather to a difference in the nature of those features. He declared that any call for the elimination of rhetorical elements from the sentence was obviously the result of a misconception of the nature of rhetorical signification. This represented a crucial realization. The search for a new form that was free from the constrictions of classical language did not mean rejection of refinement in writing, and naturalism, which made this search one of its priorities, was not and did not have to be necessarily antithetical to rhetoric. The failure to grasp this critical point has led over the years to a negative assessment of Western rhetoric's place in the history of modern Japanese literature and possibly to a misinterpretation of the dynamics that led to the formation of a modern literary language.

The idea of a compromise began to take shape as early as the very beginning of the twentieth century. Supporters of *genbun itchi* conceded the possibility of a role for rhetoric in the improvement of literary language, thus providing a new common ground for later discussions. Among rhetoricians, Igarashi Chikara was the first to follow up on Hōgetsu's realization. Familiar with the ideas of naturalist writers, many of whom had studied at Waseda, Igarashi dismissed the extreme naturalist position that advocated a literary style completely devoid of rhetorical devices. He pointed out that writing without affectation did not mean elimination of all rhetorical features. On the contrary, he stated, the elimination of all devices would itself amount to a complex rhetorical operation, which would be inconsistent with the claim that writing ought to be simple, direct, and spontaneous.

Igarashi's main contribution lay in the elaboration of a rhetorical theory that reconciled the search for a more refined form of expression with the renewed emphasis placed on content by the younger generation of writers. This reconciliation was accomplished by removing the aesthetic motives that had characterized the discipline of rhetoric during the blooming of *bijigaku* studies. This transfer of focus from the realm of literary criticism to that of effective writing and composition enabled the discipline to survive criticism at a point when naturalism had become the predominant current in the *bundan*.

In the late Meiji era and well into the Taishō period, rhetoric continued to be a valid interlocutor for those scholars who were concerned with writing, literature, language policy, and so forth. The rejection of the aesthetic nature of rhetoric was accompanied by the widespread effort to incorporate the discipline into the studies of national language, which granted rhetoric continued relevance in the scholarly debates of the time. Many of the works published in the Taishō years were in fact largely indebted to the scholarship of the previous era. Thus contrary to what has been thought so far, rhetoric did not completely disappear at the end of the Meiji period, but continued to play an important role in the following years, tackling questions and issues that were a product of that age.

Notwithstanding, it would be a misrepresentation to argue that studies of rhetoric did not show signs of decline during this time. Treatises of rhetoric certainly became rarer; however, the debate on literary language that had accompanied the discipline throughout four decades was still ongoing. The Taishō years brought the realization of a new, full-fledged literary style. Such a new style had clearly developed rhetorical features of its own, which weakened the Meiji argument against the use of rhetoric in writing. Writers and scholars revisited the problem of refinement, centering their discourse on "artistry," a term that seemed to thrive on its characteristic and intrinsic ambiguity.

The debate on the concept of (new) artistry characterized much of mid-Taishō literary criticism. The meaning of the term fluctuated between two diametrically opposite notions, a somewhat pejorative one of "mere embellishment" and a rather positive one of "effective rhetorical expression." Although no consensus was reached, the term became a crucial signifier of the changes that had taken place in the literary works of the period. Among such changes, the final establishment of a modern literary form was perhaps the most significant. Although by this time the supremacy of *genbun itchi* could have put an end to the debate on language, the question of form continued to be a matter of discussion for authors and critics. These, however, began to move the focus of their inquiry from whether rhetorical devices were essential or forbidden to what types of devices were most suitable for the new literary language. And in the process they employed the notion of artistry, a term that often overlapped with the notion of rhetorical sophistication.

The Taishō debate on artistry was a continuation of the Meiji debate on rhetorical refinement. Because the earlier deliberations had already provided the poles between which much of the debate on language and style unfolded throughout the Meiji era, the continued relevance of the issue of form in Taishō literary discourse leads to an important final determination: the concept of rhetorical refinement constitutes a cardinal point in the history of modern Japanese literature. The quest for a new form and its subsequent refinement represents a key reading paradigm of the literary developments of the Meiji and Taishō eras.

Within the span of only fifty years, rhetoric completed in Japan what had been a twenty-five-hundred-year disciplinary transition in the West. From its introduction as the art of speech to its establishment as the art of composition, from its engagement in literary criticism to its assimilation within the studies of national language, rhetoric played a prominent and vital role in modern Japan's cultural and literary history. It was a crucial interlocutor in the debate over the creation of a modern literary language, where it presented a necessary counterbalance to the extremism of the realist and naturalist calls for plain literary expression, and became the chief arbiter in the conflictive relationship between elegant and vulgar styles that had marked the history of Japanese literature for hundreds of years. Rhetoric guided and influenced the development of the Japanese written language in its modern evolution to become the literary medium that it is today.

The Question of Language and Modern Narrative

Given rhetoric's critical contribution to the creation of a modern literary language, it is possible to postulate the existence of crucial links between the discipline and the formation of modern narrative. Of course, generalizing about "modern" and "modernization" can be problematic. As several scholars have pointed out in recent years, the term "modernization" and the issue of what constitutes the modern pose a problem that puts at risk the understanding of Meiji and Taishō literature. For example, Masao Miyoshi has warned against forcing parallelism between certain literary forms such as the (Western) novel and the (Japanese) *shōsetsu*, characterizing postmodernist discourse as something that requires "retracing the meaning of the modern as the Japanese have confronted it since the fateful decision to transform society in the image of Western 'enlightened' wealth and power."[1] Echoing Miyoshi and others, Edward Fowler has more recently reiterated the need to strip terms such as "modern" of their specific cultural connotations. In his illuminating study on the *shishōsetsu* (I-novel) Fowler views the modern in the Japanese intellectual context as "the institution-alized process by which Japanese continue to apply traditional (and specifically non-western) modes of thinking to contemporary social, economic, and political issues."[2] Similarly, in his study on the subject in modern Japanese prose, James Fujii has cautioned against the risks of superimposing Western discourse in a criti-cal reading of modern Japanese literature, denouncing such common practices as considering it "an extended attempt to appropriate conventions of the nineteenth century European realist novel."[3]

Dennis Washburn has addressed the issue of what constitutes the modern in even more depth. For Washburn, modernity is "an irresolvable dilemma involv-ing two fundamentally opposed impulses. One is an adversarial effort to gain pri-ority for the present by creating discontinuity and thus the possibility for cultural renewal. The other is a conservative effort to preserve or recenter traditional values and forms." It is in this discontinuity between past and present values that Wash-burn identifies the predicament of the modern, which can be seen as a "universal process of change with its usage to indicate particular values arising at historical moments of discontinuity."[4]

While the question of what constitutes the modern, particularly in the Japa-nese context, has no easy solution and is open to further debate, the key role played by rhetoric in the cultural, literary, and sociolinguistic developments of the Meiji and Taishō periods should be sufficient proof of the importance of the disci-pline in recent Japanese literary history. In fact, the existence of crucial links to contemporary critical discourse is additional evidence of its importance. A com-mon denominator among the studies that have recently addressed Meiji and Taishō narrative is the recognition of the centrality of the question of language. Washburn is among those who have deemed the reformation of language as criti-cal to Meiji literary discourse.[5] Washburn has seen "the crisis of language—that is, the need to make literary language relevant to the new configurations of Meiji so-ciety through the creation of a realistic idiom"—as one of the primary concerns of the time.[6] Tomi Suzuki has also viewed the search for a new literary language as "inextricably related to the formation of the modern nation-state and the devel-opment of the modern Japanese *shōsetsu.*"[7] Suzuki maintains that new paradigms of reality emerged in and through the newly constructed vernacular literary lan-guage, and she views Meiji writers' preoccupation with the creation of a transparent language as a vital theme of Japanese modern literary discourse. Fujii has similarly situated the question of language squarely within the realm of Meiji literary discourse. Fujii has acknowledged writers' efforts to develop a written language adequate to the new reality as central to the process of subject expression in the Japanese novel. The issue of language, and, with it, of its assumed transparency, has also been an object of concern in Fowler's study on the *shishōsetsu*.

In recognizing the influence of a strong, realistic drive behind writers' aspirations for a modern literary language, scholars have also taken due notice of the antirhetorical sentiment that accompanied such aspirations. The shunning of sophistication and the espousal of an unadorned style free from literary constrictions was a fundamental trait of the search for a new literary medium. Discussing, for example, the case of Kunikida Doppo, Fowler identifies in his thought a "theory of writing that lays claim to its importance by deemphasizing the role of artifice" and that later exerted a strong influence on Tayama Katai and others. In 1908 Doppo wrote,

> I have never troubled myself over stylistic matters, as form is not my object in writing. I am simply concerned with how to express the thoughts that fill my breast.
> . . . To take up your pen out of a desire to produce fine writing is to ignore your own true feelings and make it impossible to move others. Only by putting down precisely what you feel and expressing your thoughts frankly and without deception or decoration, no matter how awkward the attempt, can you create a genuine and appealing work of literature.[8]

Doppo, who advocated a writing style devoid of aesthetic motives and rhetorical nuances, expressed this viewpoint in a piece that had appeared two years earlier.

> I have never thought about what kind of writing style was suited for describing nature. . . . One thing that we should consider is that those who write too well, that is to say, those who have read too many classical travel accounts and who can freely use Chinese characters, may be more susceptible to distorting nature as a result of being carried away by those writing styles. In order to see and describe nature, you have to write exactly as you see it and feel it. . . . The written styles of my nature sketches must be chaotic in terms of style. I do not intend to write well. I represent in unsophisticated language what I see and feel as faithfully as possible.[9]

Doppo's rejection of art for art's sake is representative of the tendency of the time to associate a realistic writing style with the absence of sophistication and rhetorical connotations. This association caused, as discussed in this book, the rejection of rhetoric, even if, paradoxically, Doppo's concern with "how to express the thoughts that fill my breast" was precisely an issue of a rhetorical nature. Thus "the so-called Naturalist writers . . . began to write *shōsetsu* in the belief that it was the ultimate medium for directly representing 'true reality' and out of a desire to realize a new language free from traditional rhetoric that could directly transcribe this true reality."[10] The *aru ga mama* (unadorned reality) ideology of a faithful description of feelings and reality, so cogently examined by Fujii in his analysis of Tokuda Shūsei's narrative, is yet another example of this eager flight from the traditional rhetorical fabric in search of a new mode of expression. The main consequence of this escape from tradition was the eschewal of rhetoric and the resultant triggering of a historical fallacy that has caused later presumptions about the nature of modern Japanese literature as well as a paucity of interest in Meiji rhetorical studies. This fallacy—that is, the assumption that the realization of a modern literary style could take place only by eliminating all rhetorical artifices—became deeply rooted in the minds of writers and intellectuals. Thus *genbun itchi* was perceived to be, to borrow Fredric Jameson's words, "a kind of scriptive aesthetic . . . or a Japanese version of that drive to break up rhetoric and to bring writing closer to popular speech and the vernacular."[11]

It is then evident that the creation of a modern literary language remains a pivotal issue in Meiji literary criticism. But not only that; insofar as the call for an unadorned writing style and the rejection of rhetorical sophistication are linked to the formation of modern narrative in general, rhetoric proves to share some significant convergences with recent critical discourse.

Central to the creation of a transparent literary language, faithful reproduction of reality was, as discussed in this book, the *genbun itchi* movement. Revisionist readings in recent years have provided a variety of new approaches that have further highlighted the formidable bearing the movement had on a number of problems, including the formation of a new cultural identity and the creation of the nation-state. Karatani Kōjin has defined *genbun itchi* as "first and foremost a new ideology of writing," and specifically a transformation of orthography motivated by the abolition of *kanji,* which eventually resulted in "the institutionalization of a phonocentric conception of language."[12] Others such as Komori Yōichi, for example, have seen the movement as a rearticulation of the distinction between self and other. *Genbun itchi* narrative reflects, in Komori's opinion, "a change in social structure from that based on *kyōdōtai* (cooperative system) to one requiring clearer means of articulating self-other distinctions."[13] Komori also suggests that much of modern Japanese literature "is best viewed as an effort to produce a written language that catered to a new set of social conditions," among them the changes in the writer-reader relationship.[14] Echoing Komori, Fujii cautions against the common practice of regarding the *genbun itchi* movement merely as a question of style. Such practice, in fact, would ignore "the politics of standardization that was perhaps the most important impetus be-hind the government's appropriation of the movement."[15]

While these and other approaches enrich the *genbun itchi* debate with a critical dimension that transcends the strictly linguistic and stylistic aspects of the problem, they also challenge the historicist view that language played a subordinate role in the literary discourse of the period. They defy the leading realistic discourse that in early twentieth-century literature predominantly favored content to the detriment of form. Fujii remarked that language (i.e., *genbun itchi*) "was viewed as the essen-tial handmaiden of western realism" and that "to the extent that *genbun itchi* could make the speaking subject less obtrusive, if not completely effaced (as could be done in Western prose), it was seen as effective in investing the novel employing it with claims of truth and reality."[16] These remarks signal the existence of a wide-spread notion of language in the *bundan* that viewed it as essentially subordinate to the dominating content-based realistic and naturalistic discourse of the time.

Karatani is among those who have approached the *genbun itchi* issue from a dif-ferent perspective. Karatani has attempted "to reverse the assumption that it was the needs of the inner self that gave rise to the *genbun itchi* movement and to pro-pose instead that it was the formation of the *genbun itchi* system that made possible the so-called 'discovery of the self.'"[17] In his view, *genbun itchi* was the driving force toward the development of the modern novel rather than the product of it. Thus when Washburn refers to the naturalist movement as "a direct outgrowth of this concern to find a language that gives an unmediated expression of reality," he also seems to posit the existence of a different relationship between language and the literature of those years.[18] Fujii's critique of the depiction of modern Japanese liter-ature as something that "has been overdetermined by a realist discourse that insists on the priority of the individuated self"[19] is similarly a symptom of a shared sense of discontent with this historicist view of language. And Suzuki's remark that the paradigms created by the naturalists were the result of a historical process in which an ideologically charged reality was constructed through language further suggests the possibility of a more critical role of language in the literary developments of the Meiji and Taishō years.[20] The idea that language was not just a mere construct of a dominant realist and naturalist ideology but rather something that contributed, in critical terms, to the construing of that ideology's discourse and, consequently, of modern narrative, is a fascinating one that deserves to be explored further.

The Rhetorical and the Modern

While departing from a different premise and concerned first and foremost with the subject of rhetoric, this book has readdressed the question of language, (temporarily) removing it from the sociopolitical implications that permeated it and recasting the issue of *genbun itchi* within the thematic confines of rhetorical refinement. The question of refinement, I have argued here, is so central to the literary developments of the time that it constitutes a key reading paradigm to such developments, if not the axis around which most of Meiji literary discourse revolved. As recent scholarship has acknowledged, with the coming of the modern era the native system of rhetorical conventions died out, leaving writers and intellectuals searching for a comparable system of literary conventions that would take its place. Writers then faced the daunting tasks of formulating a new poetics, creating a new critical idiom, redefining aesthetic hierarchies and criteria, and reconstituting the apparatus of "meaning." The proliferation of studies of rhetoric was a clear answer to the vacuum caused by the sudden separation from the past. As early as the 1870s, works such as Ozaki Yukio's *Kōkai enzetsuhō,* in the domain of oral communication, and Kikuchi Dairoku's *Shūji oyobi kabun,* in that of writing, began to outline the contours of a new field of study that promised to fill that vacuum authoritatively. Making up for the loss of meaning caused by the rejection of the old literary heritage, rhetoric favored a process of renewal that aimed at the reconstruction of that meaning.

This process of renewal and reconstruction took place while rhetoric continued to experience the dilemma of irreconcilable polarities that have characterized its development throughout history. Rejected in the West concurrently with the rise of positivist thinking, it was accepted in Japan as a result of that same philosophy. As a repository of the millenarian cultural heritage of the West, rhetoric appealed to a multitude of young scholars who yearned for Western knowledge, but at the same time it discouraged just as many young authors and intellectuals who saw it more as a replica of their native practices than as a driving force toward novelty and change. As a synecdoche for the West and its modernity, rhetoric promoted innovation and originality by rearticulating the boundaries of "the rhetorical" and codifying a series of new realities in the literary memory of writers and rhetoricians alike. As a synecdoche for the East and its traditions, however, it was a symbol of a fixed and rigid world that opposed novelty and transformation in an attempt to recreate canon and therefore authority.

Put in these terms, it becomes apparent that rhetoric exemplified Japan's predicament of modernity. The arrival of rhetoric gave further momentum to the ongoing process of separation from a primordial cultural identity, but, paradoxically, also provided the ideological premise for a reassessment of that very tradition, promoting a rediscovery, although not without resistance, of the native cultural and literary heritage. From this point of view, rhetoric was the locus of a theoretical and ideological conflict that was two dimensional in nature: on the one hand, rhetoric epitomized the spatial (and also cultural) opposition of East and West, an opposition driven by ambivalent, dichotomous forces favoring at times assimilation and at times resistance; on the other, it was the center stage of the metatemporal confrontation between past and present that caused Japan's predicament but also propelled it toward its own self-renewal. Writers, intellectuals, and rhetoricians found themselves at the junction of this two-dimensional quandary, engaged in the complex operation of recreating a literary and aesthetic canon according to the tenets of modernity. Their task was not only to recreate a canon, but also to reconfigure the rhetorical and redefine it in modern terms.

It is here that rhetoric and the modern intersected. They converged precisely in the common effort to redefine literary signification in an updated sense. The redefinition of what constitutes the rhetorical was an absolute condition for the affirmation of the modern. Redefining the rhetorical, in fact, also meant regeneration of canon and, with it, meaning. Yet this redefinition of the nature of the rhetorical message had a much greater implication that is important to recognize: it implied the existence of a system of signification that could support it. In fact, there can be no (rhetorical) deviation without an accepted norm, and the newly born literary language served the purpose of providing that system. Hence finalizing the reconfiguration of the boundaries of the rhetorical was equivalent to acknowledging the realization of a modern form of literary expression.

Paradoxically, the mid- to late Meiji call for an unadorned literary style was not a rejection of rhetoric per se, or at least it should not have been so. In fact, this call was not prompted by the "opacity" of classically based styles, but rather by the belief that the rhetorical resided in catachrestical expressions that were by now part of the classical repertoire. The realization of a modern literary language saw writers become increasingly aware of this misconception. Writers saw that the rhetorical could reside in the ordinary. They saw the possibility of complex associations of meaning in their own everyday life and ordinary language. They realized that the Meiji years had already provided them with a memory—a "new" memory containing an unlimited rhetorical potential to be explored, possibly in modern terms.

The resolution to the debate over rhetorical refinement, I have argued here, came about at the end of the Meiji era. The realization of a new literary medium was accompanied by writers' awareness that the importance of rhetorical refinement was no longer questioned. It was rather a matter of what type of refinement was needed. It is not by chance that the resolution of the debate coincided with the canonized beginning of the modern Japanese novel. It is in fact over these very years that Shimazaki Tōson's *Hakai* (The broken commandment) and Tayama Katai's *Futon* (The quilt) were published and that the I-novel tradition found its canonical roots. It is not by chance, either, that specific rhetorical strategies began to be affirmed at this time. As maintained in this book, the debate over the meaning of new artistry shifted the question of rhetorical refinement from the purely linguistic plane to the domain of textual narrative strategies. The rhetorical apparatus sustaining the myth of sincerity in the I-novel, for example, to which Fowler refers in his study, is but one of the results brought about by the overcoming of a restricted notion of rhetoric.

The identification of a crucial link between the Meiji debate on rhetorical refinement and the Taishō debate on the meaning of new artistry, discussed at length in this book, proves the existence of a totally different dynamic in the relationship between form and content. It shows the existence of a continuing dialectical process where form and content competed to alter the balance of the discourse to their own respective gain. It was an ongoing, osmotic process that fed perfectly into the form–content binarism that was often encountered in Meiji and Taishō critical discourse. Language emerged from this new relationship under a completely different light, not as a mere product, but rather as a "producer" of that discourse that has been so often said to have determined its fate.

Ultimately, from the point of view of rhetorical inquiry, the study of Meiji and Taishō rhetoric prompts a reconsideration of the meaning of rhetoric and the rhetorical in the pre-Meiji literary tradition. It is through contrast with the arrival of Western rhetoric that the existence of a complex native rhetorical system becomes apparent and the Japanese concern with rhetorical signification shows itself incontrovertibly. From a broader perspective, however, the study of Meiji and Taishō rhetoric also represents an extremely valuable metaliterary tool that guides us through the language and literature of the time. It is a tool that enables us to observe the "recreation of canon in the making." We are then reminded that the language from mid- to late and post-Meiji literature that we read today was not always so. We are reminded that this language was the product of its own discourse, the result of a long and painstaking effort to recreate an apparatus of meaning within a modern context. And we are reminded that, all things considered, Meiji and Taishō literature is in many ways the history of a quest for a single answer—the answer to Doppo's concern of "how to express the thoughts that fill my breast."

Notes

Introduction

1. Quackenbos, *Advanced Course of Composition and Rhetoric*, 151.
2. Keene, *Dawn to the West*, 220.

1. Western Rhetorical Tradition: A Synopsis

1. Plato, *Gorgias*, 269–271.
2. Ibid., 311–313.
3. Ricoeur, *The Rule of Metaphor*, 12.
4. Aristotle, *Rhetoric*, 345.
5. Ibid., 351.
6. Ibid., 353.
7. Ibid., 355.
8. Ibid., 359.
9. Ibid.
10. Barilli, *Rhetoric,* trans. Giuliana Menozzi, 26.
11. Cicero, *De inventione*, 3.
12. Ibid., 19–21.
13. Cicero, *De oratore*, 15.
14. Ibid., 105. According to Quintilian, "eloquence will never attain to its full development or robust health, unless it acquires strength by frequent practice in writing." See Book 10 of *Institutio oratoria*, 3. Other works of rhetoric by Cicero include *Brutus* and *Orator*.
15. Anonymous, *Rhetorica ad Herennium*, 269.
16. Ibid., 189.
17. Ibid., 205.
18. Quintilian, *Institutio oratoria*, 16–17.
19. Ibid., 9–11.
20. On this point see also Todorov, *Theories of the Symbol*, 65.
21. Kennedy, *A New History of Classical Rhetoric*, 271.
22. On the developments that took place in this period, see Murphy, *Rhetoric in the Middle Ages*.

23. Barilli, *Rhetoric*, trans. Giuliana Menozzi, 45.

24. See, e.g., Richard Sherry's *A Treatise of Schemes and Tropes,* published in 1550, and Henry Peacham's *Garden of Eloquence,* published in 1577.

25. Todorov, *Theories of the Symbol,* 84.

26. See Golden and Corbett, *The Rhetoric of Blair, Campbell, and Whateley.*

27. Ibid., 25. See also Michael G. Moran, *Eighteenth-Century British and American Rhetoricians,* 5.

28. Richard Whateley's 1828 *Elements of Rhetoric* was also among the works often cited by Japanese rhetoricians. For an overview of this work, see Golden and Corbett, *The Rhetoric of Blair, Campbell, and Whateley.*

29. For a discussion on the semantic problems deriving from the employment of this term, see Howell, *Eighteenth-Century British Logic and Rhetoric,* 147–151.

30. Lunsford, "Alexander Bain's Contributions to Discourse Theory," 290.

31. For a discussion on the origins of the four forms of discourse, see Lunsford, "Alexander Bain's Contributions to Discourse Theory," and D'Angelo, "Nineteenth-Century Forms/Modes of Discourse: A Critical Inquiry," 31–42.

32. Stewart, "The Nineteenth Century," 165.

33. D'Angelo, "Nineteenth-Century Forms/Modes of Discourse," 36.

34. For a discussion of this point, see Mulderig, "Nineteenth-Century Psychology and the Shaping of Alexander Bain's *English Composition and Rhetoric,*" 95–104.

35. Shearer, "Alexander Bain and the Teaching of Rhetoric," 37.

36. Stewart, "The Nineteenth Century," 165.

37. Reid, "The Boylston Professorship of Rhetoric and Oratory, 1806–1904," 253–254.

38. Stewart, "The Nineteenth Century," 165.

39. According to Paul Rodgers, "American textbooks reflected this shift as early as 1827." Rodgers notes that Samuel P. Newman's *Practical System of Rhetoric,* published that year, concerned itself almost exclusively with written composition. See Rodgers, "Alexander Bain and the Rise of the Organic Paragraph," 402. On Genung and his rhetorical theory, see Ettlich, "John Franklin Genung and the Nineteenth-Century Definition of Rhetoric," 283–288.

40. Kitzhaber, *Rhetoric in American Colleges, 1850–1900,* 59. The other two scholars included are Barrett Wendell and Fred Newton Scott.

41. The price was set at two yen and fifty sen. Among the catalogues that included this book, see, e.g., the appendix to Kyōeki kashihonsha, ed., *Kyōeki kashihonsha shoseki wakansho bunrui mokuroku,* 2. This catalogue also listed W. D. Cox's *The Principles of Rhetoric and English Composition for Japanese Students* and Alexander Bain's *English Composition and Rhetoric.*

42. Richards, *The Philosophy of Rhetoric,* 3.

43. Perelman and Olbrechts-Tyteca, *La Nouvelle Rhétorique: Traité de l'Argumentation.*

44. Group μ, *A General Rhetoric,* xiv.

45. See, e.g., Genette, "Rhetoric Restrained," 103–126.

46. See, e.g., Nakamura Akira, ed., *Nihongo no retorikku;* Seto Ken'ichi, *Retorikku no uchū* and *Retorikku no chi;* Amagasaki Akira, *Nihon no retorikku;* Nakamura Akira, *Nihongo retorikku no taikei;* and Nakamura Miharu, ed., *Kindai no retorikku.*

47. See Hayamizu Hiroshi, *Kindai Nihon shūjigakushi;* Hara Shirō, *Shūjigaku no shiteki kenkyū,* and Arisawa Shuntarō, *Meiji zenchūki ni okeru nihonteki retorikku no tenkai katei ni kansuru kenkyū.* None of these works seriously addresses the issue of rhetoric's possible contribution to the search for a modern literary language, except for *Shūjigaku no shiteki kenkyū,* where this possibility is openly postulated.

2. Japanese Rhetorical Tradition Prior to the Meiji Era

1. See Kennedy, *Comparative Rhetoric.* This work examines the non-Western rhetorical traditions such as the Indian and Chinese; it does not include, however, a discussion of Japan.

2. Day, *"Aimai no ronri:* The Logic of Ambiguity."

3. Ibid., 2. Other studies include Claiborne, *Japanese and American Rhetoric;* and Wolfe, "Towards a History of Classical Japanese Rhetorics and Their Recognition in American Composition Studies."

4. Morrison, "The Absence of a Rhetorical Tradition in Japanese Culture," 89.

5. See, e.g., Satō Nobuo, *Retorikku kankaku.* Other works by Satō include *Retorikku ninshiki* and *Retorikku no shōsoku.* Another scholar who has written in English on rhetoric is Okabe Rōichi. A few of his articles deal with Western rhetoric's introduction to Japan; see "Yukichi Fukuzawa: A Promulgator of Western Rhetoric in Japan," 186–195; "*Yūben* in the Early Twentieth Century," 1–12; "American Public Address in Japan," 37–51; and "The Impact of Western Rhetoric on the East," 371–388.

6. Shimamura Hōgetsu, *Shin bijigaku,* 200; Igarashi Chikara, *Shin bunshō kōwa,* 593; Sassa Masakazu, *Shūjihō kōwa,* 102.

7. Baba Tatsui, *Yūbenhō,* 109; Shiroyama Seiichi, *Yūben hiketsu: Enzetsuhō,* 3.

8. Komuro Shigehiro, *Jikken yūbengaku,* 1; Katō Totsudō, *Yūbenhō,* 7.

9. See, e.g., Nihon buntairon kyōkai, ed., *Buntairon nyūmon,* 129–146; Yoshitake Yoshinori, *Gendai buntairon,* 274–278; Suzuki Kazuhiko and Hayashi Ōki, eds., *Kenkyū shiryō Nihon bunpō.*

10. Chance, *Formless in Form,* 259.

11. Bodman, "Poetics and Prosody in Early Medieval China," 16.

12. Ibid., 15.

13. Ibid., 262–263.

14. Smits, *The Pursuit of Loneliness,* 72.

15. Ibid., 74.

16. On this and other works of the period, see Smits, *The Pursuit of Loneliness.*

17. Rabinovitch, "Wasp Waists and Monkey Tails," 471.

18. The English translation is by Rabinovitch; ibid., 526–527.

19. Ibid., 490–491.

20. Ibid., 530–540.

21. English translation in Rasplica Rodd and Henkenius, Kokinshū: *A Collection of*

Poems Ancient and Modern, 35–36. On the *Kokinshū,* see also Craig McCullough, *Brocade by Night,* and the translation by the same author, Kokin Wakashū: *The First Imperial Anthology of Japanese Poetry.*

22. The six terms employed here follow the translation provided by Rasplica Rodd and Henkenius.

23. Ibid., 47.

24. Ibid., 14.

25. See LaCure, *Rhetorical Devices of the* Kokinshū.

26. Brower and Miner, *Japanese Court Poetry,* 24. Quoted also in Rasplica Rodd and Henkenius, Kokinshū: *A Collection of Poems Ancient and Modern,* 14.

27. Fujiwara no Shunzei, *Korai fūteishō;* quoted in Brower and Miner, *Japanese Court Poetry,* 259.

28. Rasplica Rodd and Henkenius, Kokinshū: *A Collection of Poems Ancient and Modern,* 14.

29. Ibid.

30. Kamens, *Utamakura, Allusion, and Intertextuality in Traditional Japanese Poetry,* 78.

31. See Teele, "Rules for Poetic Elegance," 154.

32. Ibid., 157.

33. See Brower, "Fujiwara Teika's *Maigetushō,*" 399.

34. English translation in Brower and Miner, *Fujiwara Teika's Superior Poems of Our Time,* 41.

35. Ibid., 44.

36. Brower, "Fujiwara Teika's *Maigetsushō,*" 410.

37. Ibid., 414.

38. Ibid.

39. Ibid., 417.

40. Ibid., 419.

41. Brower, "The Foremost Style of Poetic Composition," 393–394.

42. English translation in ibid., 399.

43. Ibid., 419–426.

44. See, e.g., Levy, *Hitomaro and the Birth of Japanese Lyricism.*

45. Amagasaki Akira, *Nihon no retorikku,* 213–214.

46. On this point see Ichikawa Takashi, "Edo jidai no bunshōron," 34–35.

47. Suzuki Kazuhiko, "Tachibana Moribe no kokugo ishiki (2)," 23.

48. See Suzuki Kazuhiko, "Tachibana Moribe no kokugo ishiki (1)," 25–26; and Tanabe Masao, "*Bunshō senkaku* no buntaironteki igi," 61–67.

49. See Keene, *Essays in Idleness,* 3–4.

50. See Seki Hidesaburō, "Masashige no yūben," 77.

51. Seireishi, *Shakōjō no danwa to endanjō no yūben,* 14.

52. Sekiyama Kazuo, *Sekkyō no rekishiteki kenkyū,* 6.

53. Morioka and Sasaki, Rakugo: *The Popular Narrative Art of Japan,* 211–212. On *rakugo* see also Welch, "Discourse Strategies and the Humor of *Rakugo.*"

54. Satoshi Ishii, "Buddhist Preaching," 396.

55. Quoted in Jin'ichi Konishi, *A History of Japanese Literature,* 315.

56. Anderson Sawada, *Confucian Values and Popular Zen,* 1. "Heart learning" or "the learning of the mind," the Shingaku movement was originally founded by Ishida Baigan (1685–1744) and was primarily based on the Chu Hsi school of Confucianism. Anderson Sawada's study focuses mostly on one of Baigan's disciples, Teshima Toan (1718–1786).

57. Nosco, "Masuho Zankō (1655–1742)," 181.

58. Sawada, *Confucian Values and Popular Zen,* 141–143.

59. Ibid., 160.

60. See Joseph F. Moran, *The Japanese and the Jesuits,* 181.

61. Luis Frois, *Cartas* (1575). English translation in Cooper, ed., *They Came to Japan,* 347. In his commentary, Cooper notes that in another instance Frois described these preachers as "for the most part eloquent and apt to draw with their speech the minds of their hearers"; see *They Came to Japan,* 352.

62. Ibid., 373.

3. The Golden Age of Oratory

1. Nishi Amane, *Hyakugaku renkan* (1870), 91–92.

2. Nishi Amane, "Chisetsu," 451–466. English translation in Braisted, *Meiroku zasshi,* 308.

3. Sawada Akio, *Ronbun no kakikata,* 224.

4. Sawada Akio, *Ronbun no retorikku,* 279–281.

5. One of the most well known of these dictionaries, *Vocabvlario da Lingoa de Iapam* (1603), included Japanese words such as *benzetsusha* (an eloquent person) and *dangi* (sermon); see Doi Tadao, ed., *Vocabvlario da Lingoa de Iapam,* 41, 140. According to Sawada Akio, the presence of these words in the Japanese lexicon facilitated Japanese understanding of the basic nature of rhetoric; see *Ronbun no kakikata,* 225.

6. See Tōkyō teikoku daigaku, ed., *Tōkyō teikoku daigaku,* 453.

7. It should also be noted that at this time rhetoric found itself truncated by the disengagement of the last canon of delivery, which had then been mostly absorbed within the teachings of the elocutionary movement.

8. Fukuzawa Yukichi, *Kaigiben* (1874), 615. The English translation is from Oxford, *The Speeches of Fukuzawa,* 21–22 (slightly modified). Obata Tokujirō and Koizumi Nobukichi himself probably assisted Fukuzawa with the translation, as they are listed as coauthors. According to Suda Tatsujirō, a member of the Mita Oratorical Society, the title of the original work was (the unlikely) *American Debation;* quoted in Ishikawa Mikiaki, *Fukuzawa Yukichi den,* vol. 2, 201. Miyamura Haruo has suggested, however, that the following three texts may have been the original sources for Fukuzawa's translation: Reginald F. D. Palgrave's *The Chairman's Handbook: With an Introductory Letter Addressed to the Right Honourable The Speaker of the House of Commons;* Luther S. Cushing's *Manual of Parliamentary Practice: Rules of Proceeding and Debate in Deliberative Assemblies;* and Frederic Rowton's *The Debater: New Theory of Art of Speaking; Being a Series of Complete Debates, Outline of Debates,*

and Questions for Discussion. See Miyamura Haruo, "*Goseimon* to *Kaigiben* no aida: Ishin no seishin o megutte," 198–199. For a brief discussion in English of this work, see Oxford, *The Speeches of Fukuzawa,* 20–27; in Japanese, see Matsuzaki Kin'ichi, *Mita enzetsukai to Keiō gijukukei enzetsukai,* 2–15. It has also been suggested that a governmental publication, *Kaigibenpō* (A useful method for meetings), may have been published before Fukuzawa's *Kaigiben;* see Ishii Mitsuru, "Meiji shoki no enzetsu ni tsuite," 48; and Noji Junya, *Hanashi kotoba kyōikushi kenkyū,* 97–105.

9. Nishi Amane, "Enzetsukai no setsu" (1877), 288–291; see Ōkuma Shigenobu's preface to Nakajima Kisō, *Enzetsu kappō,* 1. Several other sources agree with this view; see, to cite only a few, Itō Chiyū, "Genron kin'atsu jidai no jitsu rekishi (2)," 170–176; Kawaoka Chōfū, "Meiji benron hattatsu shōshi," 45–62; Okano Takeo, *Meiji genronshi,* 72; and Haga Yasushi, *Genron hyakunen,* 5.

10. See Katō Totsudō, "Yūbenron," 89; Ishikawa Hanzan, "Nihonjin no enzetsu," 55; and Ōsawa Ichiroku, "Nihon yūbenjutsu," 82.

11. Fukuzawa Yukichi, *Fukuzawa zenshū shogen,* 58–59. For more information on this dispute, see also Kamata Eikichi, "Keiō gijuku daigaku ni okeru enzetsu no enkaku ni tsuite," 126–129. The English translation is from Oxford, *The Speeches of Fukuzawa,* 45.

12. For limited information on these forms of oratory in pre-Meiji Japan, see Baba Tatsui, *Yūbenhō,* 108–114; Katō Totsudō, *Tsūzoku kōwa oyobi riron oyobi hōhō,* 19–24; and Sanseibō Dōjin, *Dai Nihon yūbenshi.*

13. Public speaking was not initially contemplated in the constitution of the Meiji 6 Society; it was only after an amendment in May 1875 that regular meetings for this purpose were formally recognized. On this point, see Ōkubo Toshiaki, *Meirokusha kō,* 21. On the activities of the Mita Oratorical Society, see Fukuzawa Yukichi, "Mita enzetsu dai hyakkai no ki" (1874), 476–480; see also Matsuzaki Kin'ichi, *Mita enzetsukai to Keiō gijukukei enzetsukai.* The cost for the construction of the building, which remains a landmark in the history of public speaking in Japan, was over two thousand yen: see Ishikawa Mikiaki, *Fukuzawa Yukichi den,* vol. 2, 239.

14. Fukuzawa Yukichi, *Gakumon no susume.* English translation from Oxford, *The Speeches of Fukuzawa,* 42. A translation of this essay can also be found in Dilworth and Hirano, *Fukuzawa Yukichi's An Encouragement of Learning,* 75–79.

15. I.e., "*zetsu*" was written with the character for "tongue" instead of the one for "opinion, view, theory," which is commonly used today.

16. The records mentioned by Ishikawa told of a defendant who "gave an eloquent speech" *(tōtō mizu no nagaruru ga gotoku enzetsu shita);* see Ishikawa Hanzan, "Nihonjin no enzetsu," 55; and Saitō Tsuyoshi, *Meiji no kotoba,* 391–392. On the existence of the term in pre-Meiji Japan, see also Kawaoka Chōfū, "Meiji benron hattatsu shōshi," 45; Okano Takeo, *Meiji genronshi,* 72; and Takahashi Yasumitsu, *Kindai no yūben,* 5–7.

17. Miyatake Gaikotsu, *Meiji enzetsushi,* 7. English translation from Oxford, *The Speeches of Fukuzawa,* 24.

18. Bowen divides the movement into three parts: "the formative period" (from 1874 to 1878), "the period of promotion and organization" (from 1878 to 1881), and

"the period of activism" (from 1881 to 1884). See Bowen, *Rebellion and Democracy in Meiji Japan,* 107–125.

19. Duus, *Party Rivalry and Political Change in Taishō Japan,* 7.

20. For some information on these associations, see Itō Jintarō, "Genron kin'atsu jidai no katsu rekishi," 172–175; Kawaoka Chōfū, "Meiji benron hattatsu shōshi," 45.

21. See, respectively, the preface to the first issues of *Ōmei zasshi* (October 1879) and *Kokuyū zasshi* (August 1881); both reproduced in Matsumoto Sannosuke and Yamamuro Shin'ichi, *Genron to media,* 196, 209. The Kokuyūsha was founded in 1881 and had among its members Baba Tatsui, Taguchi Ukichi, and Suehiro Tetchō.

22. Kawaoka Chōfū, "Meiji benron hattatsu shōshi," 50; Haga Yasushi, *Genron hyakunen,* 9.

23. According to Itō, the father of this type of speech is Arakawa Takatoshi; see Itō Chiyū, "Genron kin'atsu jidai no jitsu rekishi (2)," 170. The differentiation between *"gakujutsu kōdan"* and *"seidan enzetsu"* seems to have originated from the Public Assembly Ordinance issued in 1880; see Nakajima Kisō, *Enzetsu kappō,* 93. Both *"gakujutsu"* and *"seidan"* were already recurrent in speeches of the early Meiji period; see Shiozawa Kazuko, "Enzetsu no goi," 157. As for *"kōdan,"* this term is generally thought to have replaced the word *"kōshaku"* during the Meiji period.

24. Ozaki Yukio, *The Autobiography of Ozaki Yukio,* 24.

25. Ibid., 23.

26. Ozaki Yukio, *Kōkai enzetsuhō* (1877), 1–29. Ozaki did not cite the source of his translation, not even in his original autobiography; see Ozaki Yukio, *Gakudō jiden,* 38. He later recalled translating a piece from a foreign magazine he had found at Maruzen bookstore; see Ozaki Yukio, "Yo ga hansei no yūben," 114. In 1879, however, Ozaki also published a revised edition of this work, *Zoku kōkai enzetsuhō,* where he acknowledged being indebted to Merritt Caldwell's *A Practical Manual of Elocution,* a treatise originally published in 1845. In 1903, Ozaki referred to his *Kōkai enzetsuhō* as a pioneering work in the field of public speaking; see Nakajima Kisō, *Enzetsu kappō,* 54.

27. Ozaki Yukio, *Kōkai enzetsuhō,* 2.

28. Ibid., 9.

29. Ozaki referred to rhetoric as *kabungaku;* see ibid., 22.

30. Ibid., 5.

31. For an interesting discussion on language and ideology, see Gluck, *Japan's Modern Myths,* 247–278.

32. Nishi Amane, "Enzetsukai no setsu" (1877), 288–291.

33. Nakamura Masanao, "Enzetsu no shugi o ronzu," *Dōjinsha bungaku zasshi* 31 (April 1879); reproduced in Matsumoto Sannosuke and Yamamuro Shin'ichi, *Genron to media,* 282–284. Suehiro Tetchō also spoke on the significance of speech making in the same year. See his "Shita no kōyō," in *Ōmei zasshi* 3–4 (1879); also in *Genron to media,* 284–288.

34. Numa Morikazu, "Bōchō shokun ni tsugu," in *Chōya shinbun,* May 14–16, 1879; reproduced in Okano Takeo, *Meiji genronshi,* 80–83.

35. Nakae Chōmin, "Genron no jiyū," in *Tōyō jiyū shinbun* 31 (1881); reproduced in Okano Takeo, *Meiji genronshi*, 69–71.

36. Ienaga Saburō, *Ueki Emori kenkyū*, 746.

37. Ibid., 133–134.

38. Ueki Emori, *Genron jiyū ron* (1880); reproduced in Matsumoto and Yamamuro, *Genron to media*, 44–60.

39. See Tanaka Sumiko, ed., *Josei kaihō no shisō to kōdō*, 53–61. On Ueki and his contribution to the women's cause, see Sotozaki Mitsuhiro, *Ueki Emori to onna tachi*.

40. For an interesting study on women's criticism during the Meiji period, see Sievers, *Flowers in Salt*.

41. Ibid., 25.

42. Tanaka Sumiko, ed., *Josei kaihō no shisō to kōdō*, 45.

43. See Sōma Kokkō, *Meiji shoki no san josei*, 42–47.

44. The text of this speech is reproduced, slightly modified, in Itoya Toshio, *Josei kaihō no senkushatachi*, 37–45.

45. Sōma Kokkō, *Meiji shoki no san josei*, 48.

46. Sievers, *Flowers in Salt*, 36.

47. "Hakoiri musume," in Itoya Toshio, *Josei kaihō no senkushatachi*, 38. Quoted and translated in Sievers, "Feminist Criticism in Japanese Politics in the 1880s," 608.

48. Sievers, *Flowers in Salt*, 35.

49. See Fukuda Hideko, *Warawa no hanshōgai*, 15.

50. Murata Shizuko, *Fukuda Hideko: Fujin kaihō undō no senkusha*, 22–23.

51. Ibid., 25.

52. Some manuals were written especially for women interested in the art of speech; see, e.g., Kagawa Rinzō, *Fujin enzetsu shinan*. For a brief discussion of the content of this work, see Takahashi Yasumitsu, *Kindai no yūben*, 251–252.

53. Several sources corroborate this view. For articles that appeared in the newspapers of the time, see Haga Yasushi, *Genron hyakunen*, 25. See also Maeda Tamon, "Enzetsu kanken," 77; and Kokubo Kishichi, "Yūbenron," 33.

54. Baba Tatsui, "The Political Condition of Japan," 54–55.

55. As Yamamoto Masahide pointed out, the *kanbun kundoku tai* (a style derived from classical Chinese) was the writing style predominantly used in magazines and newspapers of the first half of the Meiji period, making information still inaccessible to a large part of the population. See Yamamoto Masahide, *Genbun itchi no rekishi ronkō*, 14.

56. Several articles appeared that were against this ordinance; see "Kanpō kokuritsu," *Yūbin hōchi shinbun*, June 16, 1878; "Enzetsusha wa hongetsu jūninichi no fukoku o mite ikanaru kankaku o okoseshi ya," *Kinji hyōron*, 143, June 1878. See Okano, *Meiji genronshi*, 73.

57. Reproduced in Miyatake Gaikotsu, *Meiji enzetsushi*, 67–70. Against this ordinance, see "Shūkai jōrei wa bunmeigai ni oyobu mono ka," *Aikoku shinshi* 15 (November 1880). According to Matsumoto Sannosuke and Yamamuro Shin'ichi, the author of this article is Ueki Emori; see *Genron to media*, 379.

58. Matsumoto and Yamamuro, *Genron to media,* 527. See also Miyatake, *Meiji en-zetsushi,* 204–205.

59. For a comparison of the content of these translations to the original Western works, see Arisawa Shuntarō, *Meiji zenchūki ni okeru nihonteki retorikku no tenkai katei ni kansuru kenkyū,* 46–72, 73–101.

60. Matsumura Misao, *Enzetsu kinshin.* According to the preface, this treatise was based on a Western work titled *The American Elocutionist.* Further investigation has revealed that this was most likely Lyons' *The American Elocutionist and Dramatic Reader.*

61. Matsumura Misao, *Enzetsu kinshin,* 13.

62. Ibid., 7. This definition was likely indebted to "Aesthetic View of Elocution," i.e., the third section in Lyons' original work. See Lyons, *The American Elocutionist and Dramatic Reader,* 73–98.

63. Kuroiwa Dai, *Yūben bijihō,* 5.

64. Quackenbos had originally distinguished eleven types of style—dry, plain, neat, elegant, florid, simple, labored, concise, diffuse, nervous, and feeble—and identified six essential elements—purity, propriety, precision, clearness, strength, and unity.

65. Kikuchi Dairoku, *Shūji oyobi kabun.* See chap. 4 of this volume for a discussion of this work.

66. Kitaki Seirui, *Nihon enzetsu tōron hōhō.* Other works include Sannomiya Torae, *Nihon yūben biji kihan,* with speeches by Fukuzawa Yukichi and Numa Morikazu; and Uchiyama Kametarō, *Jitchi enzetsu hikki,* with speeches by Katō Hiroyuki and Naka-mura Masanao.

67. Yano Fumio, *Enzetsu bunshō kumitatehō,* 2.

68. See Endō Takanojō, *Yūben to bunshō.*

69. Baba Tatsui, *The Life of Tatsui Baba,* 157.

70. Quoted in Soviak, "The Case of Baba Tatsui," 202. Takada Sanae also commented on Baba's oratory skills; see Takada Sanae, "Hanpō mukashi banashi" (1927), 81.

71. Soviak, "An Early Meiji Intellectual in Politics," 164–165.

72. Baba Tatsui, *Yūbenhō,* 87.

73. Itō Yōjirō, *Jitsuyō enzetsuhō,* 8.

74. Ibid., 7.

75. See, e.g., ibid., 8–12; Chōutei Seisho, *Futsū enzetsuhō,* 65–66; and Komuro Shigehiro, *Yūben kappō,* 24.

4. The Supremacy of the Written Medium

1. Kikuchi Dairoku, "Shūji oyobi kabun" (1879), 1–38. For a study of the links between this and Bain's work, see Sugaya Hiromi, *"Shūji oyobi kabun" no kenkyū.*

2. Yoshitake Yoshinori has praised this work as a major achievement in the field of translation, even superior to that of Nishi Amane's "Chisetsu"; see Yoshitake Yoshinori, *Meiji Taishō no hon'yakushi,* 203.

3. Iwaki Juntarō, *Zōho Meiji bungakushi* (1909), 84.

4. Honma Hisao, *Meiji bungakushi: Jōkan* (1927), 281.

5. Takaichi Yoshio, "*Shūji oyobi kabun* kaidai," 2–3.

6. Yanagida Izumi, *Meiji shoki no bungaku shisō*, 136. For a comprehensive study on "Shūji oyobi kabun," see Sugaya Hiromi, *"Shūji oyobi kabun" no kenkyū*.

7. Tsubouchi Shōyō, "Kaioku mandan" (1925), 341–372. On the links between these works, see, e.g., Seki Ryōichi, *Shōyō, Ōgai: Kōshō to shiron*, 166–186; Yamamoto Masahide, *Kindai buntai hassei no shiteki kenkyū*, 458; and Sugaya Hiromi, "*Shōsetsu shinzui* to sono zaigen," 25–48.

8. Tsubouchi Shōyō, "Kaioku mandan."

9. See Oshima Kenji, "*Shōsetsu shinzui* to Bein no shūjisho," 22–33.

10. Kamei Hideo, *"Shōsetsu"ron: Shōsetsu shinzui to kindai*, 15–52. Yanagida Izumi has indicated that first-year students at Tokyo Kaisei Gakkō (later Tokyo Imperial University) studied rhetoric under the subject of "English" and that the manual adopted was E. O. Haven's *Rhetoric*; see Yanagida Izumi, *Wakaki Tsubouchi Shōyō*, 74. Haven's book would later be mentioned by Takada Sanae in the preface to his *Bijigaku*.

11. Keene, *Dawn to the West*, 100, 106.

12. Dennis C. Washburn, *The Dilemma of the Modern in Japanese Fiction*, 90.

13. Hara Shirō, *Shūjigaku no shiteki kenkyū*, 54.

14. "Shūji no gaku o sakan ni sezaru bekarazu," in *Yomiuri shinbun*, December 6, 1887. This piece was reprinted as "Bijigaku no hitsuyō o ronzu" in *Senmon gakkai zasshi* 1 (October 1888): 16–21.

15. This theme—the application of Western literary rules to Japanese literature— became a recurrent trait of scholarly production during the 1890s. See, e.g., Hattori Motohiko, *Shūjigaku;* Fuzanbō, ed., *Bunshō soshikihō;* and Ōwada Takeki, *Shūjigaku.*

16. Takada Sanae, *Bijigaku*, 19.

17. Ibid., 21.

18. Ibid., 22–23.

19. Takada distinguished four groups of figures based on relationships of similarity (simile, metaphor, etc.), contiguity (metonymy, synecdoche, etc.), contrast (antithesis, hyperbole, etc.), and "arrangement of words" (climax). He then added a fifth group, where he identified figures such as personification and exclamation, which, in his view, did not fall in any of the previous categories. This classification was extremely close to Bain's.

20. Futabatei released the first and second sections of his *Ukigumo* [Drifting clouds] in 1887 and 1888, while Bimyō published both his *Fūkin shirabe no hitofushi* [A melody played on the organ] and his *Natsu kodachi* [A summer grove] in 1888. For a general discussion of the *genbun itchi* movement in the various fields of education, politics, and literature, see Twine, *Language and the Modern State*. For a discussion of women writers' contribution to some aspects of the movement, see Copeland, *Lost Leaves*.

21. The leading rhetoricians of the time agreed in regarding this work as crucial to the scholarly developments that took place at the beginning of the third decade of the Meiji era. Takeshima Hagoromo viewed it as the only Japanese study of rhetoric worthy of any mention; see the preface to his *Shūjigaku*. Igarashi Chikara also praised it as one of the major achievements of Japanese research on rhetoric; see Igarashi Chikara, *Shin bunshō kōwa*, 595.

22. Tsukahara Tetsuo, "Bunshō kenkyūshi," 234; Namekawa Michio, *Nihon sakubun tsuzurikata kyōikushi,* 240.

23. Hara Shirō, *Shūjigaku no shiteki kenkyū,* 57.

24. Nishio Mitsuo, *Kindai bunshōron kenkyū,* 96.

25. Nakajima Kanji, *Bunshō kumitatehō.* It seems that Nakajima contributed in some fashion to Takada Sanae's *Bijigaku.* He is in fact acknowledged in the preface, together with novelist Aeba Kōson and historian Mikami Sanji.

26. Nakajima Kanji, *Bunshō kumitatehō,* 31.

27. Nishio Mitsuo, *Kindai bunshōron kenkyū,* 109–119.

28. Genung, *The Practical Elements of Rhetoric,* 85.

29. Hattori Motohiko, *Shūjigaku,* 39.

30. *Sakubunpō* was divided into six sections. The first two covered fundamental principles of composition, providing an interesting overview of the written styles still extant in the third decade of the Meiji era. None of the works published before then had concretely discussed these styles in detail, and this omission aided in giving rhetoric the negative characteristic of being unable to address problems peculiar to the Japanese language. While strictly speaking not a rhetorical treatise, Nishio states that this and other works of national literature were influenced considerably by Western rhetoric; see Nishio Mitsuo, *Kindai bunshōron kenkyū,* 108.

31. The *futsūbun* movement opposed the colloquial style: the term *"futsūbun"* indicated the style most commonly used in the Meiji era. "In the Meiji period, however, it came to designate the Classical Standard, the special style which came into use about 1887 in newspapers, magazines, textbooks, and government business"; see Twine, *Language and the Modern State,* 188. On the *futsūbun* style, see also Kenbō Gōki, "Meiji jidai no bungo-bun," 32–41.

32. Hagino Yoshiyuki, *Sakubunpō,* 30.

33. Tsubouchi Shōyō, "Bunshō shinron" (1886); reproduced in Yamamoto Masahide, *Kindai buntai keisei shiryō shūsei: Hassei hen,* 335–342. Shōyō also taught rhetoric at Waseda; see Waseda daigaku daigakushi henshūjo, ed., *Waseda daigaku hyakunenshi,* 676, 1037.

34. Quoted in Sugaya Hiromi, *"Shūji oyobi kabun" no kenkyū,* 377.

35. Kawatake Shigetoshi and Yanagida Izumi have pointed out that Shōyō's "Bungaku kanken," appearing in *Rikugō zasshi* of the same year, contained a treatment of the persuasive style. See Kawatake Shigetoshi and Yanagida Izumi, *Tsubouchi Shōyō,* 264.

36. Hara Shirō, *Shūjigaku no shiteki kenkyū,* 58.

37. Kawatake and Yanagida, *Tsubouchi Shōyō,* 264; Hayamizu Hiroshi, *Kindai Nihon shūjigakushi,* 118.

38. Kamei Hideo, *"Shōsetsu"ron: Shōsetsu shinzui to kindai,* 3.

39. "Bijironkō," 5–6, 8. For a discussion of this work, see also Ishida Tadahiko, *Tsubouchi Shōyō kenkyū,* 112–121.

40. Ōwada Takeki, *Sakubun kumitatehō,* 1–14.

41. See Tsubouchi Shōyō, "Meiji nijūninen bungakukai (omo ni shōsetsukai) no

fūchō," in *Yomiuri shinbun*, January 14–15, 1890. Reproduced in Yamamoto, *Kindai buntai keisei shiryō shūsei: Hassei hen*, 599–603.

42. For a cogent summary of the events that took place during this period, see Yamamoto Masahide, *Genbun itchi no rekishi ronkō*, 13–29.

43. Takeshima Hagoromo, *Shūjigaku*, 1.

44. Hayamizu Hiroshi, *Kindai Nihon shūjigakushi*, 140.

45. Takeshima Hagoromo, *Shūjigaku*, 44.

46. On the similarities between this work and the corresponding sections of Genung's and Hill's books, see Hayamizu Hiroshi, *Kindai Nihon shūjigakushi*, 149–154.

47. Both books widely circulated through book lenders; see, e.g., Kyōeki kashihonsha, ed., *Kyōeki kashihonsha shoseki wakansho bunrui mokuroku*, 2. Quackenbos' manual also appears, e.g., in the curriculum of Tōō Gijuku, a private school founded in 1872 by Kikuchi Kurō; see Sasamori Junzō, ed., *Tōō gijuku saikō jūnenshi*, 24.

48. On the popularity of Spencer's book, see Nishio Mitsuo, *Kindai bunshōron kenkyū*, 97; and Oshima Kenji, "*Shōsetsu shinzui* to Bein no shūjisho," 23. Educator Tanimoto Tomeri is among those who recalled reading this text; see his article, "Bunshō to wa nani ka," 51.

5. A New Course in Rhetorical Inquiry

1. For some information on Hōgetsu in English, see Keene, *Dawn to the West*, 531–545. See also Fowler, *The Rhetoric of Confession*, 93–102.

2. The term *"bijigaku"* eventually became a trademark of studies of rhetoric at Waseda University.

3. Shimamura Hōgetsu, *Shin bijigaku*, 1.

4. Ibid., 2.

5. See Sadoya Shigenobu, *Hōgetsu Shimamura Takitarō ron*, 189.

6. Shimamura Hōgetsu, "Saikō shita koro no *Waseda bungaku*."

7. For an overview of Hōgetsu's aesthetic thought, see Masao Yamamoto, "The Aesthetic Thought of Shimamura Hōgetsu," 107–113.

8. Shimamura Hōgetsu, *Shin bijigaku*, 126.

9. The section ended with a survey of the history of Western rhetoric, from its conception in ancient Greece to its further development in Rome and, through the centuries, to the more recent theories of British rhetoricians such as Campbell, Blair, and Whateley. Overall, Hōgetsu demonstrated a familiarity with Western scholarship that was new among the treatises of rhetoric published before his day. In fact, earlier works had generally been strongly indebted to a select number of Western works such as Bain's *English Composition and Rhetoric* and Quackenbos' *Advanced Course of Composition and Rhetoric*. In contrast to his predecessors, Hōgetsu was able to draw broadly from several fields such as linguistics, logic, and philosophy, lending increased credibility to his work.

10. Shimamura Hōgetsu, *Shin bijigaku*, 203.

11. Hattori Motohiko's *Shūjigaku* and Hagino Yoshiyuki's *Sakubunpō* had been the

only treatises of rhetoric to address the *genbun itchi* issue, even if only in a very superficial fashion. See Hattori Motohiko, *Shūjigaku*, 11; and Hagino Yoshiyuki, *Sakubunpō*, 30.

12. Hōgetsu had already brought forward this notion in an earlier article; see "Shōsetsu no buntai ni tsuite," in *Yomiuri shinbun*, May 9–10, 1898. In Yamamoto Masahide, *Kindai buntai keisei shiryō shūsei: Hassei hen*, 842–847.

13. The final editing and proofreading of the book were eventually carried out by Shōyō.

14. For an interesting discussion on the relationship between rhetoric and aesthetics, see Mattioli, *Studi di poetica e retorica*, 208–228.

15. Igarashi was among those, e.g., who acted as executors of Hōgetsu's will at the time of his death. See Sadoya Shigenobu, *Hōgetsu Shimamura Takitarō ron*, 169–186.

16. Igarashi Chikara, *Shin bunshō kōwa*. Other works on rhetoric by Igarashi include *Jōshiki shūjigaku; Jisshū shin sakubun; Sakubun sanjūsan kō;* and *Shūjigaku taiyō*.

17. Igarashi Chikara, *Shin bunshō kōwa*, 1.

18. Ibid., 10–11.

19. Ibid., 17.

20. Ibid., 38.

21. Ibid., 37.

22. Igarashi Chikara, *Bunshō kōwa*, 15.

23. Before discussing rhetorical figures, Igarashi addressed the clarity and accuracy of meaning and the purity of writing, including a treatment of dialects, foreign words, and special terms. He also cautioned against the indiscriminate mixing of *gabun* (high style) and *zokubun* (low style). See his *Shin bunshō kōwa*, 142.

24. Ibid., 185.

25. Among the remaining sections of the book, the third part dealt with the organization of writing, the fourth with the psychological and emotional elements of writing, and the fifth with the various types of style. Of particular interest was section seven, where Igarashi discussed the history of writing in Japan, providing an informative survey of the styles in use since the early developments of a writing system. Such a treatment was an important and welcome new addition to the treatises of rhetoric in Japan, which now began to be an integral part of the studies of national language and literature.

26. Anceschi, *Barocco e Novecento*, 231.

6. The Taishō Years

1. Quoted in Nishio Mitsuo, *Kindai bunshōron kenkyū*, 174.

2. Ibid., 174, 181. Several other scholars concur with this view. See, e.g., Morioka Kenji, *Bunshō kōseihō*, 379; Nishida Naotoshi, *Bunshō, buntai, hyōgen no kenkyū*, 52; and Kaneoka Takashi, *Bunshō ni tsuite no kokugogakuteki kenkyū*, 209.

3. Utsumi Kōzō (Getsujō), *Bunshō jikkō*, 311–312.

4. Mizuno Yōshū, *Gendai bunshō sahō*, 9.

5. Kayahara Kazan and Oda Masayoshi, *Gendai bunshō kōwa*, 22, 93.

6. See, e.g., Miyazaki Haruyoshi, *Gendai bunshō kōwa oyobi bunpan*, 1.

7. Sassa Masakazu, *Shūjihō kōwa,* 1–2.

8. Watanabe Yoshiharu, *Gendai shūjihōyō,* 7–9.

9. See, e.g., Uchiyama Shun, *Jisshū bunshō kōsei shūjihō;* Bunshō kōshūkai, ed., *Shinshiki bunshō sahō tebiki;* Mizuno Yōshū, *Gendai bunshō sahō;* Bunshō kōshūkai, ed., *Gendai sakubun kōwa;* and Kayahara Kazan and Oda Masayoshi, *Gendai bunshō kōwa.*

10. Among the works that retained a discussion of figures, see, e.g., Haga Yaichi and Sugitani Torazō, *Sakubun kōwa oyobi bunpan;* Fujii Mokuzō and Komuro Yoshizō, eds., *Gendai nijū meika bunshō sahō kōwa;* and Yoshida Kurō, *Bunshō sahō genri.* Haga and Sugitani, in particular, brought forth the idea that figures were necessary for good writing. The goal of figures was to express one's thoughts and feelings in a nonaffected fashion. No other major work until then had gone so far as to use this concept in a definition of rhetorical figures. On the contrary, "simplicity" had been a key word in the arguments of more progressive currents of thought such as realism and naturalism against the pomposity of style of classical modes of expression. Haga and Sugitani must have felt comfortable using this term in such a context, which illustrates how at the very end of the Meiji period the conflict between affectation and simplicity in writing, while still ongoing, had lost much of its power.

11. Mizuno Yōshū and Kayahara Kazan, e.g., also partially acknowledged the importance of rhetoric; see Mizuno Yōshū, *Gendai bunshō sahō,* 23; and Kayahara Kazan and Oda Masayoshi, *Gendai bunshō kōwa,* 92.

12. Something similar had already happened, e.g., in the United States, where rhetoric was now considered a part of English departments at several institutions around the country.

13. See, e.g., Inagaki Kunisaburō, *Kokutei tokuhon kyōjuhyō shūjihō oyobi toriatsukai;* and Yatsunami Norikichi, *Ōyō shūjigaku kōwa.*

14. E.g., Sawada Masatake's *Enzetsu bijihō* reached its eighth reprint edition by 1894; Komuro Shigehiro's *Jikken yūbengaku* reached its third by 1907; and Katō Totsudō's *Yūbenhō* was reprinted at least five times within one year.

15. Among the works that were clearly influenced by the elocutionary movement, see Matsumura Misao, *Enzetsu kinshin;* Tomioka Masanori, *Benshi hitsudoku enzetsugaku;* and Tankai Sanshi, *Seiji gakujutsu enzetsu tatsubenhō.*

16. Early discussions on language can be found in Hayashi Kohō, *Enzetsu shinpō* and Shibue Tamotsu, *Yūbenhō.*

17. Komuro Shigehiro, *Jikken yūbengaku,* 133–136.

18. Other works by Totsudō include *Enzetsu bunshō ōyō shūjigaku* and *Yūbenhō.*

19. To be precise, Endō had not been the first to call for a rhetoric that would concurrently discuss both written and spoken discourse. Yano Fumio had already suggested this possibility in his *Enzetsu bunshō kumitatehō* of 1884, and Totsudō had done the same in his *Enzetsu bunshō ōyō shūjigaku* of 1906.

20. On this point, Hara Shirō counters that studies of rhetoric never completely disappeared. Rhetoric continued to be taught at major universities until at least the beginning of World War II. See his *Shūjigaku no shiteki kenkyū,* 25.

21. See Miki Kiyoshi, "Yūbenjutsu no fukkō" (1939) and "Yūben ni tsuite" (1941), 373–375 and 458–468.

22. Hatano Kanji, "Retorikku no saisei" (1934), 7–23.

7. Rhetoric and the *Genbun Itchi* Movement

1. The four major varieties were *kanbun, wabun, sōrōbun*—which were already mentioned earlier—and *wakan konkōbun* (a style characterized by a combination of Chinese and Japanese elements).

2. For a discussion of these aspects of the movement, see Twine, *Language and the Modern State.*

3. Grayer Ryan, *Japan's First Modern Novel,* 82.

4. Quoted and translated in ibid., 118. *Aibiki* was a translation of Turgenev's "The Rendevous" (1850), a story from *Sportsman's Sketches.* According to Keene, in this translation "Futabatei stripped the language of the baggage of the traditional vocabulary, allusions, and rhetorical devices, bringing to Meiji literature the freshness of the colloquial as the medium for the intelligence and poetry of Turgenev." See Keene, *Dawn to the West,* 113.

5. Futabatei Shimei, "Yo ga genbun itchi no yurai" (1906). Quoted and translated in Twine, *Language and the Modern State,* 138–139.

6. Among Japanese scholars, Yamamoto Masahide should be mentioned for his lifetime commitment to the investigation of the *genbun itchi* movement; see the following pages of this chapter for a discussion of and quotations from his works. In the West, while many scholarly works have investigated the problem from different perspectives, Twine's study is probably one of the most exhaustive on the subject; see Twine, *Language and the Modern State.*

7. Hatano Kanji indicated that studies of rhetoric in Japan lost their raison d'etre with the rise of naturalism, therefore hinting at the antithetical nature of the relationship between naturalism and its role in the search for a modern literary language, and rhetoric itself. See Hatano Kanji, *Bunshō shinrigaku,* 8. The same position is held by Morioka Kenji, who also emphasized the conflictive nature of this relationship; see Morioka Kenji, *Bunshō kōseihō,* 379; and *Kindaigo no seiritsu,* 131. Hayamizu Hiroshi seems to agree with this view in that he also sees a paradoxical and impracticable coexistence between rhetoric's original definition of the "art teaching how to speak and write well" and the call of naturalism for the elimination of rhetorical embellishments. See Hayamizu Hiroshi, *Kindai Nihon shūjigakushi,* 7–8. Nishio Mitsuo underlined the decline of rhetoric at the end of the Meiji period as a result of a difference in goals and purpose between rhetoric and the literary trends in vogue at the time; see his *Kindai bunshōron kenkyū,* 174.

A few sources have acknowledged, however, the role played by rhetoric in the vernacularization process of the literary language, even if only in a very superficial fashion. Yoshitake Yoshinori has stated that rhetoric provided the necessary theoretical background to the literary undertaking of writers such as Futabatei Shimei and Yamada Bimyō; see Yoshitake Yoshinori, *Meiji Taishō no hon'yakushi,* 283. Similarly, Nishida Naotoshi has seen Western rhetoric as a response to the practical needs faced by Meiji writers in their search for a more colloquial literary style. See Nishida Naotoshi, *Bunshō, buntai, hyōgen no kenkyū,* 48. These works are nonetheless only very sporadic cases in Meiji literary criticism in which the relevance of rhetoric to the creation of a modern literary language has even been mentioned.

8. "Rhetorical" here is understood to mean the utilization of a special stylistic effect.

9. Twine, *Language and the Modern State,* 65–66, 270–272. Transliteration and English translations by Twine.

10. The Japanese equivalent, *"shūji,"* also seems to retain a comparable connotative neutrality. Other terms used at the time to indicate a special linguistic effect include *bijireiku, sōshoku, shūren, shūshoku, shikisai, bunsai, bunshoku,* and *aya.*

11. Nishi Amane, *Hyakugaku renkan* (1870), 90–91.

12. Nishi Amane, "Yōji o motte kokugo o shosuru no ron" (1874), 569–579.

13. Watanabe Shūjirō, "Nihon bun o seitei suru hōhō," in *Tōkyō akebono shinbun,* 3 September 1875; reproduced in Yamamoto Masahide, *Kindai buntai keisei shiryō shūsei: Hassei hen,* 154–156.

14. N. N., "Nihon bunshōron," *Kyōiku zasshi* 6–9 (May–July 1886); in Yamamoto Masahide, *Kindai buntai keisei shiryō shūsei: Hassei hen,* 343–345. "Danwa to bunshō to no itchi o yōsu," *Kyōiku zasshi* 11–13 (August–September 1886); in ibid., 346–350.

15. Fukuchi Gen'ichirō, "Bunron," *Tōkyō nichi nichi shinbun,* August 29, 1875; in Yamamoto Masahide, *Kindai buntai keisei shūryō shūsei: Hassei hen,* 151–153.

16. See his "Bunshōron" in *Tōkyō nichi nichi shinbun,* May 23–24, 1881; in ibid., 173–178. See also his "Bunshō no kairyō," in *Tōkyō nichi nichi shinbun,* January 27, 1887.

17. Kanda Kōhei, "Bunshōron o yomu," *Tōkyō gakushi kaiin zasshi* 7.1 (February 1885); in Yamamoto Masahide, *Kindai buntai keisei shiryō shūsei: Hassei hen,* 212–217.

18. Mozume Takami, *Genbun itchi* (Tokyo shoshi, 1886); in ibid., 265–289.

19. Washburn, *The Dilemma of the Modern in Japanese Fiction,* 89.

20. English translation in Twine, *Language and the Modern State,* 135.

21. Masaoka Shiki, "Jojibun," *Nihon* (January–March 1900); in Yamamoto Masahide, *Kindai buntai keisei shiryō shūsei: Seiritsu hen,* 203–209.

22. Takahama Kyoshi, "Genbun itchi," *Hototogisu* 3.7 (1900). See also Sakamoto Shihōda, "Shaseibun sadan," *Bunshō sekai* 2.2 (1907); and Itō Sachio, "Shaseibunron," *Shumi* 2.7 (1907). All reproduced in Yamamoto Masahide, *Kindai buntai keisei shiryō shūsei: Seiritsu hen,* 229–230, 624–628, and 665–676.

23. Keene, *Dawn to the West,* 226.

24. Tayama Katai, "Rokotsu naru byōsha," *Taiyō* 10.3 (1904); in Yamamoto Masahide, *Kindai buntai keisei shiryō shūsei: Seiritsu hen,* 516–519.

25. Tayama Katai, *"Sei* ni okeru kokoromi," *Waseda bungaku* 34 (1908); in ibid., 761–767.

26. Hasegawa Tenkei, "Genmetsu jidai no geijutsu" (1906); "Genjitsu bakuro no hiai" (1908). Both in vol. 57 of *Nihon kindai bungaku taikei,* 220–229, 230–243.

27. Miyake Yūjirō (Setsurei), "Bunshō higikōron," 2–5.

28. Katakami Tengen, "Shōsetsu no bunshō no shinmi," *Bunshō sekai* 3.1 (1908); in Yamamoto Masahide, *Kindai buntai keisei shiryō shūsei: Seiritsu hen,* 737.

29. Yano Fumio, *Nihon buntai monji shinron.*

30. See his lecture, "Bunshō no gobyū" (1889); reproduced in Yamamoto Masahide, *Kindai buntai keisei shiryō shūsei: Hassei hen,* 547–559.

31. Mozume Takami, "Genbun itchi no fukanō," in *Yomiuri shinbun,* December 17–19, 1902.

32. See, e.g., Tatsumi Kojirō, "Baku genbun itchi ron," *Gakkai no shishin* 2–4 (August–October 1887); and Kojima Kenkichi, "Bunshōron," *Bun* 2.6 (March 1889). Both reproduced in Yamamoto Masahide, *Kindai buntai keisei shiryō shūsei: Hassei hen,* 385–393, 529–534.

33. Kōyō had strong reservations about the *genbun itchi* style. See Ozaki Kōyō, "Genbun itchi to gikobun," *Kyōiku kōhō* 242 (1900); in Yamamoto Masahide, *Kindai buntai keisei shiryō shūsei: Seiritsu hen,* 253–254.

34. Tsubouchi Shōyō, "Meiji nijūninen bungakukai (omo ni shōsetsukai) no fūchō," in *Yomiuri shinbun,* January 14–15, 1890. Shōyō also made mention of Imamura Chōzen's *Bunshō tetsugaku,* a translation of Spencer's *Philosophy of Style* that appeared in 1889.

35. "Genbun itchi ni tsukite," *Teikoku bungaku* 3.7 (1897); "Shōsetsu no buntai," *Teikoku bungaku* 3.8 (1897). Both reproduced in Yamamoto Masahide, *Kindai buntai keisei shiryō shūsei: Hassei hen,* 782–784, 784–785.

36. Takayama Chogyū, "Meiji shōsetsu no dai ni ki," *Taiyō* 3.12 (1897); in ibid., 779–782.

37. Takeshima Hagoromo, "Genbun itchi tai, gazoku setchūtai," *Shōnen bunshū* 4.3 (1898); in ibid., 813–814.

38. Ōmachi Keigetsu, "Shōsetsu no shobuntai no tokushitsu," *Bungei kurabu* 4.5 (1898); in ibid., 818–822. Ozaki Kōyō and Kōda Rohan also called for a more polished literary language. See their respective articles, "Genbun itchi ron," *Shinchō* 3.6 (1905); and "Risōteki gengo o tsukure," *Bunshō sekai* 1.3 (1906). Both reproduced in Yamamoto Masahide, *Kindai buntai keisei shiryō shūsei: Seiritsu hen,* 542–543, 553–554.

39. The supposed lack of rhetorical refinement is one of the major criticisms of the style seen in one essay of the time; see Horie Hideo, "Genbun itchi ni taisuru hinan o bakusu," *Shinbun* 1.7 (1901); in ibid., 420–422.

40. Hattori Motohiko, *Shūjigaku,* 11.

41. Hagino Yoshiyuki, *Sakubunpō,* 30.

42. Quoted in Hayamizu Hiroshi, *Kindai Nihon shūjigakushi,* 168.

43. Takada Sanae, *Bijigaku,* 2.

44. Hattori Motohiko, *Shūjigaku,* 1.

45. Takeshima Hagoromo, *Shūjigaku,* 2.

46. Shimamura Hōgetsu, *Shin bijigaku,* 77.

47. Suzuki Sadami, *Nihon no "bungaku" gainen,* 294.

48. Miyake Yonekichi, "Genbun itchi no ron," *Bun* 1.10 (1888); in Yamamoto Masahide, *Kindai buntai keisei shiryō shūsei: Hassei hen,* 498.

49. Ueda Mannen, "Hyōjungo ni tsukite," *Teikoku bungaku* 1.1 (1895); "Kyōikujō

kokugogakusha no hōki shiiru ichi daiyōten," *Dai Nihon kyōikukai zasshi* 163 (1895). Both in ibid., 727–731, 732–741.

50. "Genbun itchi ni tsuite," *Gengogaku zasshi* 1.3 (1900); in Yamamoto Masahide, *Kindai buntai keisei shiryō shūsei: Seiritsu hen,* 225–229.

51. Yasugi Sadatoshi, "Kokugo no tōitsu to kokubungaku," *Myōjō* 5–6 (August–September 1900); in ibid., 244.

52. See, e.g., Sugimoto Mukō, "Genbun itchi sakubunpō," 29–34. See also Kutsumi Kesson, "Genbun itchi to shisō no seiton," *Shinbun* 1.7 (1901); Iwaya Sazanami, "Genbun itchi ni kansuru yo no keiken," *Shinkōron* 19.4–5 (May–June 1904); and Iwaya Sazanami, "Yomu hitsuyō wa aru," *Bunshō sekai* 3.15 (November 1908). The latter three reproduced in Yamamoto Masahide, *Kindai buntai keisei shiryō shūsei: Seiritsu hen,* 417–420, 525–538, and 774–775. An article that appeared in two subsequent issues of the journal *Kyōiku jiron* especially viewed rhetoric as the only way to elude the charge of verbosity. The author argued that "by applying the various rules of style such as the use of tropes and figures as taught by rhetoric, the *genbun itchi* style will ultimately acquire an aesthetic dimension." See Kamoashi Hidekatsu, "Genbun itchi no genzai oyobi shōrai," *Kyōiku jiron,* 597–598 (November 1901); also in *Kindai buntai keisei shiryō shūsei: Seiritsu hen,* 433–445.

53. Twine, *Language and the Modern State,* 206.

54. See chap. 9 of this volume for a discussion of this point.

55. Yamada Bimyō, "Jijo" (1887); in Yamamoto Masahide, *Kindai buntai keisei shiryō shūsei: hassei hen,* 362–367. For more information on this novel, see Yamamoto Masahide, *Kindai buntai hassei no shiteki kenkyū,* 528.

56. Yamada Bimyō, "Genbun itchi ron gairyaku," *Gakkai no shishin* 8–9 (February–March 1888); in ibid., 414–421.

57. Subettarō Koronda, "Omoitsukitaru koto sono ichi (genbun itchi)," *Yomiuri shinbun,* December 16–18, 1888; in Yamamoto Masahide, *Kindai buntai keisei shiryō shūsei: Hassei hen,* 508–511. Yamamoto Masahide has suggested that the author of this article was Bimyō himself. In ibid., 65.

58. Yamada Bimyō, "Genbun itchi kogoto," *Bun* 2.7 (1889); in Yamamoto Masahide, *Kindai buntai keisei shiryō shūsei: Hassei hen,* 534–537.

59. Yamada Bimyō, "Ware ware no genbun itchi tai," *Shigarami zōshi* 8 (May 1890); in ibid., 627–630.

60. Yamada Bimyō, "Genbun itchi tai o manabu kokoroe," *Iratsume* 56 (June 1890); in ibid., 631–633.

61. Among the first works to address the *genbun itchi* style, see Shimamura Hōgetsu, *Shin bijigaku;* and Takeshima Hagoromo, *Bunshō nyūmon.* Although not a rhetorical treatise, see also Takamatsu Bōson, *Meiji bungaku genbun itchi.*

62. See Takada Sanae, *Bijigaku,* 109. See also Hattori Motohiko, *Shūjigaku,* 33; Fuzanbō, ed., *Bunshō soshikihō,* 20; and Takeshima Hagoromo, *Shūjigaku,* 68. The terminology is rich and varied throughout the Meiji period: rhetorical figures are translated as *shūshoku* (Takada, Hattori), *washoku* (Fuzanbō), *shishi* (Igarashi), *tengi* and *jiyō* (Takeshima), *sōshoku* (Ōwada), and *shisō* (Shimamura).

63. Shimamura Hōgetsu, "Shōsetsu no buntai ni tsuite," *Yomiuri shinbun,* May 9–10, 1898. In Yamamoto Masahide, *Kindai buntai keisei shiryō shūsei: Hassei hen,* 842–847.

64. Shimamura Hōgetsu, "Genbun itchi no genzai, mirai," *Shinbun* 1.6 (October 1901); reproduced in Yamamoto Masahide, *Kindai buntai keisei shiryō shūsei: Seiritsu hen,* 404–406.

65. Shimamura Hōgetsu, "Genbun itchi no sannan," *Shinbun* 2.1 (February 1902); in ibid., 452–456.

66. Shimamura Hōgetsu, *Shin bijigaku,* 77, 79.

67. Shimamura Hōgetsu, "Isseki bunwa," *Bunshō sekai* 1.4 (1906). Reproduced in Yamamoto Masahide, *Kindai buntai keisei shiryō shūsei: Seiritsu hen,* 571–578.

68. Shimamura Hōgetsu, "Shin bunshōron," *Bunshō sekai,* 6.5–11 (April–August 1911); in ibid., 813–833.

69. "Ima no bundan to shin shizenshugi," 1–7. Kawazoe Kunimoto has also addressed this point; see his *Shimamura Hōgetsu: Hito oyobi bungakusha to shite,* 17.

70. Shimamura Hōgetsu, "Shizenshugi no kachi," 1–29.

71. Hasegawa Tenkei, "Hiyu no seimei to shizenkai," *Bunshō sekai* 1.8 (October 1906): 112–117; Katakami Tengen, "Shōsetsu no bunshō no shinmi," 739. In Yamamoto Masahide, *Kindai buntai keisei shiryō shūsei: Seiretsu hen,* 737–744.

72. Kosugi Tengai, "Geijutsu wa gikō shizen wa risō," 66–67.

73. Yoshida Seiichi, *Shizenshugi no kenkyū,* 323.

74. Tayama Katai, *Bibun sahō,* 54.

75. Tayama Katai, *Shōsetsu sahō,* 96.

76. Igarashi Chikara, *Shin bunshō kōwa,* 10.

8. From Old to New Artistry: Rhetorical Refinement as an Interpretive Paradigm

1. Haga Yaichi, "Kanbun no kihan o dasseyo," *Bunshō sekai* 1.3 (May 1906); Ueda Mannen, "Genbun itchi wa hatashite jōchō ka," *Bunshō sekai* 1.3 (May 1906). Both in Yamamoto Masahide, *Kindai buntai keisei shiryō shūsei: Seiritsu hen,* 554–556, 556–557.

2. Tsubouchi Shōyō, "Genbun itchi ni tsuite," *Bunshō sekai* 1.4 (June 1906); in ibid., 567–570.

3. Ōmachi Keigetsu, "Genbun itchi tai no ryūsei," *Taiyō* 13.1 (January 1907); Inoue Tetsujirō, "Genbun itchi wa teishumi da," *Bunshō sekai* 3.15 (November 1908). Both in ibid., 589, 771–774.

4. Kuwaki Gen'yoku, "Bunshō kyokugaikan," 79–81.

5. See, e.g., Horie Hideo, "Buntai tōitsu ga dekiru nara," 475–478.

6. Yamamoto Ryōkichi, "Sakubun no omoide," 69–72; Uchida Roan, "Bunshōjō no inakamono," 40–42.

7. "Sanjūkyūnen bunshōkai gaikan," *Bunshō sekai* 2.1 (January 1907); reproduced in Yamamoto Masahide, *Kindai buntai keisei shiryō shūsei: Seiritsu hen,* 606–610.

8. Nihon kindai bungakukan, ed., *Nihon kindai bungaku daijiten,* 222.

9. Shimazaki Tōson, "Shizen kara geijutsu o eru"; Takahama Kyoshi, "Shaseibunha

ga senkakusha"; Kubota Utsubo, "Gikō no sō to shin gikō"; Masamune Hakuchō, "Kyōmi mo nai sōsakunetsu mo nai"; Kosugi Tengai, "Geijutsu wa gikō shizen wa risō." All in *Bunshō sekai* 3.15 (November 1908):58–67. The issue also included Tokuda Shūkō's essay, "Fukuzatsu naru byōsha."

10. Shimamura Hōgetsu, "Torawarezaru buntai," *Bunshō sekai* 4.1 (January 1909); reproduced in Yamamoto Masahide, *Kindai buntai keisei shiryō shūsei: Seiritsu hen,* 784–786.

11. Igarashi Chikara, "Gojin wa ikanaru bunshō o manabu beki ka," *Bunshō sekai* 6.5 (April 1911); in ibid., 807–812. Much of the argument made in this essay can be found in the introductory section of his earlier treatise, *Shin bunshō kōwa.*

12. Kobayashi Aisen, *Shin bunshō no kenkyū.* Kobayashi Aisen was the pen name of novelist Katō Takeo (1888–1956).

13. It should be noted here that Tayama Katai posed the very same question; see his *Shōsetsu sahō,* 278.

14. Tokuda Shūsei, *Meiji shōsetsu bunshō hensenshi* (1914), 215.

15. Kamitsukasa Shōken, "Taishō sannen bungeikai no jigyō, sakuhin, hito," 51–52.

16. Nakamura Seiko, "Honnen no sōsakukai."

17. Chiba Kameo, "Taishō sannen bungeikai no jigyō, sakuhin, hito," 37–40.

18. Tanaka Jun, "Sōsakukai no genjō ni taisuru utagai," 98–101.

19. Nakamura Seiko, "Shin gikōha to wa?" 77–81.

20. Nakamura Seiko, "Futatabi gikōha ni tsuite," 60–63.

21. Nishinomiya Tōchō, "Iwayuru shin gikōhakan," 73–78.

22. Maeda Akira, "Atarashii jidai no hyōgen," 138–142.

23. "Bungei shingo jii," 17.

24. "Shinshin sakka jūgoshi no bunshō o hyōsu," 72–82.

25. Katakami Tengen, "Jiko no seimei no hyōgen," 54–58.

26. Tokuda Shūsei, *Shōsetsu nyūmon* (1918), 228.

9. The Revival of Oratory in Late Meiji Japan

1. Takada Sanae, *Bijigaku,* 1.

2. Hattori Motohiko, *Shūjigaku,* 1.

3. Gluck, *Japan's Modern Myths,* 111–112.

4. Ibid., 120.

5. Nakajima Kisō, *Enzetsu kappō,* 5.

6. Ozaki Yukio, "Yūben gairon," 34.

7. Noma Seiji, *Noma of Japan,* 128. See also Shashi hensan iinkai, ed., *Kōdansha no ayunda gojūnen,* 17.

8. See Komuro Shigehiro, *Jikken yūbengaku,* 1; Kokubo Kishichi, "Yūbenron," 33; Ashikawa Tadao, *Yūbenjutsu seishū,* 1; and Takeuchi Jō, *Atarashii gofunkan enzetsu o nere,* 5.

9. Sims, *A Political History of Modern Japan,* 101.

10. Ibid.

11. Gluck, *Japan's Modern Myths,* 231.

12. Aoki Tokuzō recollected several years later that the quality of students' speech

making at the beginning of the Taishō period was remarkably high. See Shashi hensan iinkai, ed., *Kōdansha no ayunda gojūnen*, 50.

13. Duus, *Party Rivalry and Political Change in Taishō Japan*, 118–119.

14. Ibid., 118.

15. Funao Isonosuke, "Sōdai yūbenkai hattenshi," 209–215.

16. Nagai Ryūtarō (1881–1944), a student at the time who would later become a politician, was instrumental in the establishment of the association. After a period of study in England, Nagai became a professor at Waseda.

17. On Noma and his interest in oratory, see Noma Seiji, *Noma of Japan*.

18. Ibid., 128.

19. Among the professors who supported Noma's idea were Ume Kenjirō, Miyake Yūjirō, and Iida Yasutarō; see ibid., 130.

20. Ibid.

21. See the preface to the first issue of *Yūben* (February 1910).

22. The price was set at twenty sen a copy; see Noma Seiji, *Noma of Japan*, 136. The last issue of *Yūben* was published in October 1939.

23. See Shashi hensan iinkai, ed., *Kōdansha no ayunda gojūnen*, 61.

24. Noma Seiji, *Noma of Japan*, 142.

25. Among these journals, see the *Kyōzon zasshi*, the *Hokushin zasshi*, and the *Ōmei zasshi*. On these journals, see Yamamuro Shin'ichi, *Meijiki gakujutsu genron zasshi shūsei bessatsu*, microfilm ed.

26. Several sources from this time offer evidence of a renewed interest in public speaking. See Mizuguchi Toshio, *Meibun to yūben*, 2; Tanaka Hozumi, "Yūben shiken," 108–113; Itō Jintarō, "Genron kin'atsu jidai no katsu rekishi," 173; Ashikawa Tadao, *Yūbenjutsu seishū*, 1; and Ashikawa Tadao, *Tsūzoku seinen yūben kappō*, 1. Mino and Sims have also pointed out the major role of public speaking in Ōkuma Shigenobu's electoral campaign of 1914; see Mino Noriyuki, *Saishin gofunkan enzetsu*, 5–6; and Sims, *A Political History of Modern Japan*, 135.

27. Kōdansha hachijūnenshi henshū iinkai, ed., *Kuronikku kōdansha no 80 nen*, 74; see also 66, 73. The success of *Yūben* led Noma to publish a second magazine, *Kōdan kurabu* (The Kōdan club) the following year. The idea of a second magazine had been proposed by Mochizuki Shigeru, who had helped considerably in the creation of *Yūben* and was now working at *Kokumin shinbun*. The aim of such a magazine was to provide written versions of old *kōdan*, stories and tales that traditionally had been read or chanted in theaters and storytellers' halls *(yose)*. *Kōdan* had served an important educational function in premodern Japan, contributing to the spread and consolidation of traditional ethical and cultural values, and Noma saw the publication of these stories as not only a means of attracting a large readership, but also as contributing to efforts by the government to improve popular education outside the framework of conventional learning. Compared to *Yūben*, *Kōdan kurabu* was much less scholarly in orientation, giving priority to entertainment and the rediscovery of popular culture. For this reason, some disapproved of its publication under the name of the Great Japanese Oratorical Society, and eventually it was put out under the name of a second

company, Kōdansha. A merger of the two companies in 1925 gave birth to the publishing house Dai Nihon yūbenkai kōdansha, which in 1958 became the present-day Kōdansha.

28. Ueda Mannen, "Kyōikujō kokugo gakusha no hōki shiiru ichi daiyōten," *Dai Nihon kyōiku zasshi* 163 (1895); reproduced in Yamamoto Masahide, *Kindai buntai keisei shiryō shūsei: Hassei hen,* 732–741; Tanaka Hozumi, "Yūben shiken," 109.

29. Ashikawa Tadao, *Yūbenjutsu seishū,* 1–2.

30. Miyake Yūjirō, "Yūben to shakai kyōiku," 41; Sassa Masakazu, "Gikai no benron, kentō no benron, mazu benron no kyōiku o hakare," 1–5.

31. See, e.g., Dai Nihon yūbenkai, ed., *Seinen yūbenshū;* Ashikawa Tadao, *Yūbenjutsu seishū;* and Ashikawa Tadao, *Tsūzoku seinen yūben kappō.*

32. Shiroyama Seiichi, *Yūben hiketsu: Enzetsuhō,* 252.

33. Itō Yōjirō, *Jitsuyō enzetsuhō,* 7.

34. Komuro Shigehiro, *Jikken yūbengaku,* 30.

35. Hoshina Kōichi, "Benronjutsu to gengo," 413–465.

36. In the early 1890s, see Shibue Tamotsu, *Yūbenhō,* 29–31; among later works, see Tsubotani Zenshirō, *Enzetsu tōron kihan,* 20–25; and Komuro Shigehiro, *Jikken yūbengaku,* 25–36.

37. Hori Tatsuo, *Sokusei yūben enzetsuhō,* 52.

38. Haga Yaichi, "Nihongo no hattatsu to benron," 2–4. It seems that while Haga viewed the lack of an oratorical tradition as one of the possible causes for the lack of linguistic unity, for Hoshina the very opposite was true—that is, the absence of a standard language had historically hindered the development of public speaking. Regardless of their different viewpoints, however, it is reasonable to think that a relationship of mutual necessity existed between public speaking and the achievement of linguistic unity. Speech making needed to employ the one variety of language that could be best understood throughout the country, and that same variety of language was in need of a form that would promote its employment over other dialects.

39. Ashikawa Tadao, *Yūbenjutsu seishū,* 120–124; Dai Nihon yūbenkai, ed., *Seinen yūbenshū,* 39.

40. See Sakaeda Mōcho, "Kokugo to benron," 85; Mukai Gunji, "Yūben ni tsuite," 95.

41. Ōmachi Keigetsu, "Shōsetsu no shobuntai no tokushitsu," *Bungei kurabu* 4.5 (1898); reproduced in Yamamoto Masahide, *Kindai buntai keisei shiryō shūsei: Hassei hen,* 818–822. Nishimura Shigeki, "Genbun itchi o ronzu," in *Tōyō gakugei zasshi* 18.238 (1901); in *Kindai buntai keisei shiryō shūsei: Seiritsu hen,* 374–380.

42. On the introduction of stenography, see Miller, "Japanese Shorthand and Sokki-bon," 471–487.

43. Uchida Roan and Tsubouchi Shōyō, *Futabatei Shimei,* vol. 2 (1909); quoted in Yamamoto Masahide, *Kindai buntai hassei no shiteki kenkyū,* 361. Inoue Tetsujirō, "Kokuji mondai sono ta ni tsuite," *Kokugo to kokubungaku* 11.8 (August 1934); in ibid.

44. Hayashi Shigeatsu, *Sokki sōsho: Kōdan enzetsushū;* see Kanda Sumiko, "Genbun itchi shijō ni okeru sokkibun enzetsu no kenkyū," 43–57.

45. See Shiozawa Kazuko, "Genbun itchi tai no seiritsu: Enzetsu sokki no hatashita yakuwari (1)," 91–124; and Shiozawa Kazuko, "Genbun itchi tai no seiritsu: Enzetsu sokki no hatashita yakuwari (2)," 27–54.

46. See Miyake Torata, *Nihon enzetsu kihan*, 83; and Kitaki Seirui, *Nihon enzetsu tōron hōhō*, 18, 43. *Nihon enzetsu kihan* contained a total of nine speeches, including Itagaki Taisuke's "Tōhoku shūyū no shui oyobi shōrai no mokuteki," Nakajima Nobuyuki's "Yūshisha ni tsugu," and Fukuchi Gen'ichirō's "Kaitakushi kan'yūbutsu no shobun awasete zaisei o ronzu." *Nihon enzetsu tōron hōhō* consisted of eight speeches, including Numa Morikazu's "Kokuseiron" and "Itagaki kun o mukau."

47. Rare instances of *de gozaimasu, da,* and *desu* can also be found.

48. See Sawada Masatake, *Enzetsu bijihō*, 154; and Nakajima Kisō, *Enzetsu kappō*, 239. *Enzetsu bijihō* comprised thirteen speeches, including Inoue Kowashi's "Kyōiku no hōshin," Inukai Tsuyoshi's "Chōsen no hanashi," and Suehiro Shigeyasu's "Naisei gaikō." These three speeches and Gotō Shinpei's "Shippei no hokenhō" are those that used the copula *de aru* most often. *Enzetsu kappō* contained eight speeches, including Itō Hirobumi's "Shisei no hōshin" and Ozaki Yukio's "Giin tokushoku hōan teishutsu no riyū." Except for the speeches by Itō, Ozaki, and the editor Nakajima Kisō, who all used *de arimasu* extensively, most of the speeches used *de aru*.

49. See, e.g., Chōutei Seisho, *Futsū enzetsuhō;* and Yoda Kiyomatsu, *Gakujutsu enzetsu tōronshū.*

50. Endō Takanojō, *Yūben to bunshō: Saishin kenkyū,* 6.

51. Abe Isoo, "Bunshō to enzetsu," 13–15.

52. Haga Yaichi, "Yūben to bungaku," 125.

53. Ayabe Den'ichirō, *Sokuseki ōyō sunkan yūben enzetsuhō,* 17.

Epilogue: Rhetoric and Modern Japanese Literature

1. Miyoshi and Harootunian, *Postmodernism and Japan,* xvii. This volume includes Miyoshi's "Against the Native Grain: The Japanese Novel and the 'Postmodern' West" and other interesting articles on the topic.

2. Fowler, *The Rhetoric of Confession,* 77.

3. Fujii, *Complicit Fictions,* 2.

4. Washburn, *The Dilemma of the Modern in Japanese Fiction,* 8, 17.

5. Ibid., 78–79.

6. Ibid., 14.

7. Tomi Suzuki, *Narrating the Self,* 31.

8. Kunikida Doppo, "Byōshō roku" (1908); quoted and trans. in Fowler, *The Rhetoric of Confession,* 90.

9. Kunikida Doppo, "Shizen o utsusu bunshō" (1906); quoted and trans. in Tomi Suzuki, *Narrating the Self,* 46.

10. Ibid., 39.

11. Fredric Jameson, "Foreword," in Karatani, *Origins of Modern Japanese Literature,* xii.

12. Karatani, *Origins of Modern Japanese Literature,* 47. On this point, see also Tomi Suzuki, *Narrating the Self,* 47.

13. Fujii, *Complicit Fiction,* 36.

14. Ibid., 38–39.

15. Ibid., 96.

16. Ibid., 109, 110; italics added.

17. Karatani, *Origins of Modern Japanese Literature,* 61.

18. Washburn, *The Dilemma of the Modern in Japanese Fiction,* 84.

19. Fujii, *Complicit Fiction,* 2–3.

20. Tomi Suzuki, *Narrating the Self,* 47.

Bibliography

NOTE: All Japanese-language texts were published in Tokyo unless indicated otherwise.

Abe Isoo. "Bunshō to enzetsu." *Bunshō sekai* 1.2 (April 1906):13–15.

Amagasaki Akira. *Nihon no retorikku*. Chikuma shobō, 1988.

Anceschi, Luciano. *Barocco e Novecento: Con alcune prospettive fenomenologiche*. Milano: Rusconi e Paolazzi, 1960.

Arisawa Shuntarō. *Meiji zenchūki ni okeru nihonteki retorikku no tenkai katei ni kansuru kenkyū*. Kazama shobō, 1998.

Aristotle. *Rhetoric*. Trans. John Henry Freese. Cambridge, Mass., and London: Harvard University Press, 1994.

Ashikawa Tadao. *Tsūzoku seinen yūben kappō*. Sanyūdō shoten, 1916.

———. *Yūbenjutsu seishū*. Dai Nihon yūbenkai, 1915.

Ayabe Den'ichirō. *Sokuseki ōyō sunkan yūben enzetsuhō*. Shinbukan, 1922.

Baba Tatsui. *The Life of Tatsui Baba (1885–1887)*. In vol. 3 of *Baba Tatsui zenshū*. Iwanami shoten, 1988.

———. "The Political Condition of Japan." In vol. 3 of *Baba Tatsui zenshū*.

———. *Yūbenhō*. Bunshōdō, 1885.

Bain, Alexander. *English Composition and Rhetoric*. London: Longmans, Green & Co., 1866.

Barilli, Renato. *Rhetoric*. Trans. Giuliana Menozzi. Minneapolis: University of Minnesota Press, 1989.

Bodman, Richard W. "Poetics and Prosody in Early Medieval China: A Study and Translation of Kūkai's *Bunkyō hifuron*." Ph.D. dissertation, Cornell University, 1978.

Bowen, Roger W. *Rebellion and Democracy in Meiji Japan: A Study of Commoners in the Popular Rights Movement*. Berkeley, Los Angeles, and London: University of California Press, 1980.

Braisted, William R. Meiroku zasshi: *Journal of the Japanese Enlightenment*. Cambridge, Mass.: Harvard University Press, 1976.

Brower, Robert H. "The Foremost Style of Poetic Composition: Fujiwara Tameie's *Eiga no Ittei*." *Monumenta Nipponica* 42.4 (1987):391–429.

———. "Fujiwara Teika's *Maigetsushō*." *Monumenta Nipponica* 40.4 (1985):399–425.

Brower, Robert H., and Earl Miner. *Fujiwara Teika's Superior Poems of Our Time: A*

Thirteenth-Century Poetic Treatise and Sequence. Stanford: Stanford University Press, 1967.

————. *Japanese Court Poetry.* Stanford: Stanford University Press, 1961.

Chance, Linda H. *Formless in Form: Kenkō, Tsurezuregusa, and the Rhetoric of Japanese Fragmentary Prose.* Stanford: Stanford University Press, 1997.

"Bungei shingo jii." *Bunshō kurabu* 3.4 (April 1918):17.

Bunshō kōshūkai, ed. *Gendai sakubun kōwa.* Tōseidō shoten, 1917.

————. *Shinshiki bunshō sahō tebiki.* Tōseidō shoten, 1916.

Chiba Kameo. "Taishō sannen bungeikai no jigyō, sakuhin, hito." *Waseda bungaku* 109 (December 1914):37–40.

Chōutei Seisho. *Futsū enzetsuhō.* Shūzandō, 1889.

Cicero. *De inventione.* Trans. H. M. Hubbell. Cambridge, Mass., and London: Harvard University Press, 1993.

————. *De oratore.* Trans. E. W. Sutton. Cambridge, Mass., and London: Harvard University Press, 1988.

Claiborne, Gay D. *Japanese and American Rhetoric: A Contrastive Study.* San Francisco: International Scholars Publications, 1993.

Cooper, Michael, ed. *They Came to Japan: An Anthology of European Reports on Japan, 1543–1640.* Berkeley: University of California Press, 1981.

Copeland, Rebecca L. *Lost Leaves: Women Writers of Meiji Japan.* Honolulu: University of Hawai'i Press, 2000.

Dai Nihon yūbenkai, ed. *Seinen yūbenshū.* Dai Nihon yūbenkai, 1914.

D'Angelo, Frank. "Nineteenth-Century Forms/Modes of Discourse: A Critical Inquiry." *College Composition and Communication* 35.1 (February 1984):31–42.

Day, Michael Joseph. "*Aimai no ronri:* The Logic of Ambiguity." Ph.D. dissertation, University of California at Berkeley, 1996.

Dilworth, David, and Umeyo Hirano. *Fukuzawa Yukichi's An Encouragement of Learning.* Sophia University, 1969.

Doi Tadao, ed., *Vocabvlario da Lingoa de Iapam.* Iwanami shoten, 1976.

Duus, Peter. *Party Rivalry and Political Change in Taishō Japan.* Cambridge, Mass.: Harvard University Press, 1968.

Endō Takanojō. *Yūben to bunshō: Saishin kenkyū.* Taisanbō, 1917.

Ettlich, Ernest Earl. "John Franklin Genung and the Nineteenth Century Definition of Rhetoric." *Central States Speech Journal* 17 (1966):283–288.

Fowler, Edward. *The Rhetoric of Confession: Shishōsetsu in Early Twentieth-Century Japanese Fiction.* Berkeley and Los Angeles: University of California Press, 1988.

Fujii, James A. *Complicit Fictions: The Subject in the Modern Japanese Prose Narrative.* Berkeley: University of California Press, 1993.

Fujii Mokuzō and Komuro Yoshizō, eds. *Gendai nijū meika bunshō sahō kōwa.* Mangandō, 1914.

Fukuchi Gen'ichirō. "Bunshō no kairyō." In *Tōkyō nichi nichi shinbun,* January 27, 1887.

Fukuda Hideko. *Warawa no hanshōgai.* Iwanami shoten, 1958.

Fukuzawa Yukichi. *Fukuzawa zenshū shogen.* In vol. 1 of *Fukuzawa Yukichi zenshū.* Iwanami shoten, 1958.

———. *Gakumon no susume.* In vol. 3 of *Fukuzawa Yukichi zenshū.* Iwanami shoten, 1959.

———. *Kaigiben.* In vol. 3 of *Fukuzawa Yukichi zenshū.* Iwanami shoten, 1959.

———. "Mita enzetsukai daihyakkai no ki." In vol. 4 of *Fukuzawa Yukichi zenshū.* Iwanami shoten, 1959.

Funao Isonosuke. "Sōdai yūbenkai hattenshi." *Yūben* 7.4 (April 1916):209–215.

Fuzanbō, ed. *Bunshō soshikihō.* In vol. 19 of *Futsūgaku zensho.* Fuzanbō, 1892.

Genette, Gérard. "Rhetoric Restrained." In *Figures of Literary Discourse.* Trans. Alan Sheridan. New York: Columbia University Press, 1982.

Genung, John Franklin. *The Practical Elements of Rhetoric.* Boston: Ginn and Co., 1887.

Gluck, Carol. *Japan's Modern Myths: Ideology in the Late Meiji Period.* Princeton, N.J.: Princeton University Press, 1985.

Golden, James L., and Edward P. J. Corbett. *The Rhetoric of Blair, Campbell, and Whateley.* Carbondale and Edwardsville: Southern Illinois University Press, 1990.

Group μ. *A General Rhetoric.* Trans. Paul B. Burrell and Edgar M. Slotkin. Baltimore, Md., and London: Johns Hopkins University Press, 1981.

Haga Yaichi. "Nihongo no hattatsu to benron." *Yūben* 8.14 (December 1917):2–4.

———. "Yūben to bungaku." *Yūben* 1.2 (March 1910):124–126.

Haga Yaichi and Sugitani Torazō. *Sakubun kōwa oyobi bunpan.* Fuzanbō, 1912.

Haga Yasushi. *Genron hyakunen: Nihonjin wa kō hanashita.* Kōdansha, 1985.

Hagino Yoshiyuki. *Sakubunpō.* Hakubunkan, 1892.

Hara Shirō. *Shūjigaku no shiteki kenkyū.* Waseda daigaku shuppanbu, 1994.

Hasegawa Tenkei. "Genjitsu bakuro no hiai" (1908). In vol. 57 of *Nihon kindai bungaku taikei.* Kadokawa shoten, 1972.

———. "Genmetsu jidai no geijutsu" (1906). In vol. 57 of *Nihon kindai bungaku taikei.* Kadokawa shoten, 1972.

———. "Hiyu no seimei to shizenkai." *Bunshō sekai* 1.8 (October 1906):112–117.

Hatano Kanji. *Bunshō shinrigaku.* Sanseidō, 1935.

———. "Retorikku no saisei" (1934). In vol. 1 of *Hatano Kanji zenshū.* Shōgakukan, 1990.

Hattori Motohiko. *Shūjigaku.* Kokugo denshūjo, 1891.

Hayamizu Hiroshi. *Kindai Nihon shūjigakushi.* Yūhōdō, 1988.

Hayashi Kohō. *Enzetsu shinpō.* Kurita Shintarō, 1888.

Honma Hisao. *Meiji bungakushi: Jōkan* (1927). In vol. 10 of Sasaki Nobutsuna, ed., *Nihon bungaku zenshi.* Tōkyōdō, 1994.

Hori Tatsuo. *Sokusei yūben enzetsuhō.* Daigakukan, 1906.

Horie Hideo. "Buntai tōitsu ga dekiru nara." *Nihon oyobi Nihonjin* 689 (September 1916):475–478.

Hoshina Kōichi. "Benronjutsu to gengo." In Yūben gakkai, ed., *Yūbengaku kōza.* Seikōkan shuppanbu, 1928.

Howell, Wilbur S. *Eighteenth-Century British Logic and Rhetoric.* Bristol, England: Thoemmes Press, 1999.

Ichikawa Takashi. "Edo jidai no bunshōron." *Kokugogaku* 15 (December 1953):32–40.

Ienaga Saburō. *Ueki Emori kenkyū.* Iwanami shoten, 1960.

Igarashi Chikara. *Bunshō kōwa.* Waseda daigaku shuppanbu, 1905.

———. *Jisshū shin sakubun.* Waseda daigaku shuppanbu, 1910.

———. *Jōshiki shūjigaku.* Bunsendō, 1909.

———. *Sakubun sanjūsan kō.* Waseda daigaku shuppanbu, 1913.

———. *Shin bunshō kōwa.* Waseda daigaku shuppanbu, 1909 (11th ed., 1924).

———. *Shūjigaku taiyō.* Shibun shoin, 1923.

Inagaki Kunisaburō. *Kokutei tokuhon kyōjuyō shūjihō oyobi toriatsukai.* Dōbunkan, 1912.

Ishida Tadahiko. *Tsubouchi Shōyō kenkyū.* Fukuoka: Kyūshū daigaku shuppankai, 1988.

Ishii Mitsuru. "Meiji shoki no enzetsu ni tsuite." *Gengo seikatsu* 99 (December 1959):46–52.

Ishii, Satoshi. "Buddhist Preaching: The Persistent Main Undercurrent of Japanese Traditional Rhetorical Communication." *Communication Quarterly* 40.4 (1992):391–397.

Ishikawa Hanzan. "Nihonjin no enzetsu." *Yūben* 5.1 (1914):55–62.

Ishikawa Mikiaki. *Fukuzawa Yukichi den.* Vol. 2. Iwanami shoten, 1932.

Itō Chiyū. "Genron kin'atsu jidai no jitsu rekishi (2)." *Yūben* 1.4 (May 1910):170–176.

Itō Jintarō. "Genron kin'atsu jidai no katsu rekishi." *Yūben* 2.3 (1911):172–175.

Itō Yōjirō. *Jitsuyō enzetsuhō.* Nagoya: Seikandō, 1889.

Itoya Toshio. *Josei kaihō no senkushatachi: Nakajima Toshiko to Fukuda Hideko.* Shimizu shoin, 1975.

Iwaki Juntarō. *Zōho Meiji bungakushi* (1909). In vol. 5 of Hiraoka Toshio, ed., *Meiji Taishō bungakushi shūsei.* Nihon tosho sentaa, 1982.

Kagawa Rinzō. *Fujin enzetsu shinan.* Osaka: Shinshindō, 1887.

Kamata Eikichi. "Keiō gijuku daigaku ni okeru enzetsu no enkaku ni tsuite." *Yūben* 1.2 (March 1910):126–129.

Kamei Hideo. *"Shōsetsu"ron: Shōsetsu shinzui to kindai.* Iwanami shoten, 1999.

Kamens, Edward. *Utamakura, Allusion, and Intertextuality in Traditional Japanese Poetry.* New Haven, Conn., and London: Yale University Press, 1997.

Kamitsukasa Shōken. "Taishō sannen bungeikai no jigyō, sakuhin, hito." *Waseda bungaku* 109 (December 1914):51–52.

Kanda Sumiko. "Genbun itchi shijō ni okeru sokkibun enzetsu no kenkyū." *Nihon bungaku* 19 (1962):43–57 (published by Tōkyō Joshi Daigaku).

Kaneoka Takashi. *Bunshō ni tsuite no kokugogakuteki kenkyū.* Meiji shoin, 1989.

Karatani, Kōjin. *Origins of Modern Japanese Literature.* Durham, N.C., and London: Duke University Press, 1993.

Katakami Tengen. "Jiko no seimei no hyōgen." *Bunshō sekai* 8.4 (March 1913):54–58.

Katō Totsudō. *Enzetsu bunshō ōyō shūjigaku.* Osaka: Sekibunsha, 1906.

———. *Tsūzoku kōwa oyobi riron oyobi hōhō.* Ryōgo shuppan, 1912.

———. *Yūbenhō.* Tōadō shobō, 1908.

———. "Yūbenron." *Yūben* 1.4 (May 1910):89–96.

Kawaoka Chōfū. "Meiji benron hattatsu shōshi." *Yūben* 2.1 (1911):45–62.

Kawatake Shigetoshi and Yanagida Izumi. *Tsubouchi Shōyō*. Daiichi shobō, 1988.

Kawazoe Kunimoto. *Shimamura Hōgetsu: Hito oyobi bungakusha to shite*. Nihon tosho sentaa, 1987.

Kayahara Kazan and Oda Masayoshi. *Gendai bunshō kōwa*. Nihon hyōronsha, 1919.

Keene, Donald. *Dawn to the West: Japanese Literature of the Modern Era*. New York: Holt, Rinehart and Winston, 1984.

————. *Essays in Idleness: The Tsurezuregusa of Kenkō*. New York and London: Columbia University Press, 1967.

Kenbō Gōki. "Meiji jidai no bungobun: Futsūbun ga dekiru made." *Gengo seikatsu* 74 (November 1957):32–41.

Kennedy, George A. *Comparative Rhetoric: An Historical and Cross-Cultural Introduction*. New York: Oxford University Press, 1998.

————. *A New History of Classical Rhetoric*. Princeton, N.J.: Princeton University Press, 1994.

Kikuchi Dairoku. *Shūji oyobi kabun* (1879). In vol. 20 of *Meiji bunka zenshū*. Nihon hyōronsha, 1928.

Kitaki Seirui. *Nihon enzetsu tōron hōhō*. Tōkyō shoshi, 1882.

Kitzhaber, Alfred R. *Rhetoric in American Colleges, 1850–1900*. Dallas: Southern Methodist University Press, 1990.

Kō Ryōji. *Taisei ronbengaku yōketsu*. Shōshodō, 1880.

Kobayashi Aisen. *Shin bunshō no kenkyū*. Nihon bunshō gakuin, 1913.

Kōdansha hachijūnenshi henshū iinkai, ed. *Kuronikku Kōdansha no 80 nen*. Kōdansha, 1990.

Kokubo Kishichi. "Yūbenron." *Yūben* 2.5 (May 1911):33–38.

Komuro Shigehiro. *Jikken yūbengaku*. Maekawa Bun'eikaku, 1903.

————. *Yūben kappō*. Shūbunsha, 1891.

Konishi, Jin'ichi. *A History of Japanese Literature*. Vol. 3. Trans. Aileen Gatten and Mark Harbison. Princeton, N.J.: Princeton University Press, 1991.

Kosugi Tengai. "Geijutsu wa gikō shizen wa risō." *Bunshō sekai* 3.15 (November 1908):66–67.

Kubota Utsubo. "Gikō no sō to shin gikō." *Bunshō sekai* 3.15 (November 1908):63–64.

Kuroiwa Dai. *Yūben bijihō*. Yoronsha, 1882.

Kuwaki Gen'yoku. "Bunshō kyokugaikan." *Nihon oyobi Nihonjin* 689 (September 1916):79–81.

Kyōeki kashihonsha, ed. *Kyōeki kashihonsha shoseki wakansho bunrui mokuroku*. Kyōeki kashihonsha, 1887.

LaCure, Jon. *Rhetorical Devices of the* Kokinshū: *A Structural Analysis of Japanese* Waka *Poetry*. Lewiston, N.Y.: Edwin Mellen, 1997.

Levy, Ian Hideo. *Hitomaro and the Birth of Japanese Lyricism*. Princeton, N.J.: Princeton University Press, 1984.

Lunsford, Andrea A. "Alexander Bain's Contributions to Discourse Theory." *College English* 44.3 (March 1982):290–300.

Lyons, Joseph A. *The American Elocutionist and Dramatic Reader.* Philadelphia: J. H. Butler & Co., 1874.

Maeda Akira. "Atarashii jidai no hyōgen." *Bunshō sekai* 12.11 (November 1917):138–142.

Maeda Tamon. "Enzetsu kanken." *Yūben* 1.1 (February 1910):77–82.

Masamune Hakuchō. "Kyōmi mo nai sōsakunetsu mo nai." *Bunshō sekai* 3.15 (November 1908):64–66.

Matsumoto Sannosuke and Yamamuro Shin'ichi. *Genron to media.* In vol. 11 of *Nihon kindai shisō taikei.* Iwanami shoten, 1990.

Matsumura Misao. *Enzetsu kinshin.* Shiseidō, 1881.

Matsuzaki Kin'ichi. *Mita enzetsukai to Keiō gijukukei enzetsukai.* Keiō gijuku daigaku shuppan, 1998.

Mattioli, Emilio. *Studi di poetica e retorica.* Modena: Mucchi, 1983.

McCullough, Helen Craig. *Brocade by Night.* Stanford: Stanford University Press, 1985.

———. *Kokin Wakashū: The First Imperial Anthology of Japanese Poetry, with 'Tosa Nikki' and 'Shinsen Waka.'* Stanford: Stanford University Press, 1985.

Miki Kiyoshi. "Yūben ni tsuite" (1941). In vol. 14 of *Miki Kiyoshi zenshū.* Iwanami shoten, 1967.

———. "Yūbenjutsu no fukkō." (1939). In vol. 15 of *Miki Kiyoshi zenshū.* Iwanami shoten, 1967.

Miller, J. Scott. "Japanese Shorthand and Sokkibon." *Monumenta Nipponica* 49.4 (Winter 1994):471–487.

Mino Noriyuki. *Saishin gofunkan enzetsu.* Osaka: Hattori bunkidō, 1926.

Miyake Torata. *Nihon enzetsu kihan.* Tōkyō shoshi, 1881.

Miyake Yūjirō. "Bunsho higikōron." *Bunshō sekai* 1.7 (September 1906):2–5.

———. "Yūben to shakai kyōiku." *Yūben* 2.1 (1911):39–41.

Miyamura Haruo. "*Goseibun* to *Kaigiben* no aida: Ishin no seishin o megutte." In Fukuzawa Yukichi kyōkai, ed., *Fukuzawa Yukichi nenkan.* Fukuzawa Yukichi kyōkai, 1974.

Miyatake Gaikotsu. *Meiji enzetsushi.* Seikōkan shuppanbu, 1926.

Miyazaki Haruyoshi. *Gendai bunshō kōwa oyobi bunpan.* Nihon shoin, 1922.

Miyoshi, Masao, and Harry D. Harootunian. *Postmodernism and Japan.* Durham, N.C., and London: Duke University Press, 1989.

Mizuguchi Toshio. *Meibun to yūben.* Kyōto: Kawai bunkōdō, 1909.

Mizuno Yōshū. *Gendai bunshō sahō.* Bakuaisha, 1917.

Moran, Joseph F. *The Japanese and the Jesuits: Alessandro Valignano in Sixteenth-Century Japan.* London and New York: Routledge, 1993.

Moran, Michael G. *Eighteenth-Century British and American Rhetoricians: Critical Studies and Sources.* Westport, Conn., and London: Greenwood Press, 1994.

Morioka, Heinz, and Miyoko Sasaki. *Rakugo: The Popular Narrative Art of Japan.* Cambridge, Mass., and London: Harvard University Press, 1990.

Morioka Kenji. *Bunshō kōseihō.* Shibundō, 1963.

———. *Kindaigo no seiritsu: Buntaihen.* Meiji shoin, 1991.

Morrison, John L. "The Absence of a Rhetorical Tradition in Japanese Culture." *Western Speech* 36.2 (Spring 1972):89–102.

Mozume Takami. "Genbun itchi no fukanō." *Yomiuri shinbun,* December 17–19, 1902.

Mukai Gunji. "Yūben ni tsuite." *Yūben* 1.1 (February 1910):92–95.

Mulderig, Gerald P. "Nineteenth-Century Psychology and the Shaping of Alexander Bain's *English Composition and Rhetoric.*" In James J. Murphy, ed., *The Rhetorical Tradition and Modern Writing.* New York: MLA, 1982.

Murata Shizuko. *Fukuda Hideko: Fujin kaihō undō no senkusha.* Iwanami shoten, 1959.

Murphy, James J. *Rhetoric in the Middle Ages: A History of Rhetorical Theory from Saint Augustine to the Renaissance.* Berkeley: University of California Press, 1974.

———. *A Synoptic History of Classical Rhetoric.* Davis: Hermagoras Press, 1983.

Nakajima Kanji. *Bunshō kumitatehō.* Kaishindō, 1891.

Nakajima Kisō. *Enzetsu kappō.* Hakubunkan, 1903.

Nakamura Akira, ed. *Nihongo no retorikku.* Chikuma shobō, 1983.

———. *Nihongo retorikku no taikei.* Iwanami shoten, 1991.

Nakamura Miharu, ed. *Kindai no retorikku.* Yūhōdō, 1995.

Nakamura Seiko. "Futatabi gikōha ni tsuite." *Waseda bungaku* 142 (September 1917):60–63.

———. "Honnen no sōsakukai." In *Yomiuri shinbun,* December 11, 1914.

———. "Shin gikōha to wa?" *Waseda bungaku* 141 (August 1917):77–81.

Namekawa Michio. *Nihon sakubun tsuzurikata kyōikushi: Meiji hen.* Kokudosha, 1977.

Nihon buntairon kyōkai, ed. *Buntairon nyūmon.* Sanseidō, 1966.

Nihon kindai bungakukan, ed. *Nihon kindai bungaku daijiten.* Kōdansha, 1978.

Nishi Amane. "Chisetsu." *Meiroku zasshi* 25 (December 1874). In vol. 1 of *Nishi Amane zenshū.* Munetaka shobō, 1960.

———. "Enzetsukai no setsu"(1877). In vol. 3 of *Nishi Amane zenshū.* Munetaka shobō, 1966.

———. *Hyakugaku renkan* (1870). In vol. 4 of *Nishi Amane zenshū.* Munetaka shobō, 1981.

———. "Yōji o motte kokugo o shosuru no ron" (1874). In vol. 2 of *Nishi Amane zenshū.* Munetaka shobō, 1962.

Nishida Naotoshi. *Bunshō, buntai, hyōgen no kenkyū.* Izumi shoin, 1992.

Nishinomiya Tōchō. "Iwayuru shin gikōhakan." *Bunshō sekai* 12.9 (September 1917):73–78.

Nishio Mitsuo. *Kindai bunshōron kenkyū.* Tōkō shoin, 1951.

Noji Junya. *Hanashi kotoba kyōikushi kenkyū.* Kyōbunsha, 1975.

Noma, Seiji. *Noma of Japan.* Kōdansha, 1934.

Nosco, Peter. "Masuho Zankō (1655–1742): A Shinto Popularizer between Nativism and National Learning." In Peter Nosco, ed., *Confucianism and Tokugawa Culture.* Princeton, N.J.: Princeton University Press, 1984.

Okabe, Rōichi. "American Public Address in Japan: A Case Study in the Introduction of American Oratory through the *Yūben.*" In Richard J. Jensen and John C. Hammerback, eds., *In Search of Justice: The Indiana Tradition in Speech Communication*. Amsterdam: Rodopi, 1987.

———. "The Impact of Western Rhetoric on the East: The Case of Japan." *Rhetorica* 8 (1990):371–388.

———. "*Yūben* in the Early Twentieth Century: A Case Study in the Promulgation of Western Rhetoric in Japan." *Speech Education* 7 (1979):1–12.

———. "Yukichi Fukuzawa: A Promulgator of Western Rhetoric in Japan." *The Quarterly Journal of Speech* 59.2 (April 1973):186–195.

Okano Takeo. *Meiji genronshi*. Ōtori shuppan, 1974.

Ōkubo Toshiaki. *Meirokusha kō*. Rittaisha, 1976.

Ōsawa Ichiroku. "Nihon yūbenjutsu." *Yūben* 6.7 (1915):78–93.

Oshima Kenji. "*Shōsetsu shinzui* to Bein no shūjisho: Sono moshashugi to risōshugi." *Kokubungaku kenkyū* 42 (June 1970):22–33.

Ōwada Takeki. *Sakubun kumitatehō*. Hakubunkan, 1893.

———. *Shūjigaku*. Hakubunkan, 1893.

Oxford, Wayne H. *The Speeches of Fukuzawa*. Hokuseido Press, 1973.

Ozaki Yukio. *The Autobiography of Ozaki Yukio: The Struggle for Constitutional Government in Japan*. Trans. Fujiko Hara. Princeton, N.J.: Princeton University Press, 2001.

———. *Gakudō jiden*. Osaka: Gakudō jiden kankōkai, 1927.

———. *Kōkai enzetsuhō* (1877). In vol. 1 of *Ozaki Gakudō zenshū*. Kōronsha, 1956.

———. "Yo ga hansei no yūben." *Yūben* 6.1 (1915):110–116.

———. "Yūben gairon." In Yūben gakkai, ed., *Yūbengaku kōza*. Seikōkan shuppanbu, 1928.

Perelman, Chaïm, and Lucie Olbrechts-Tyteca. *La Nouvelle Rhétorique: Traité de l'Argumentation*. Paris: Presses Universitaire de France, 1958.

Plato. *Gorgias*. Trans. W. R. M. Lamb. Cambridge, Mass., and London: Harvard University Press, 1991.

Quackenbos, George Payn. *Advanced Course of Composition and Rhetoric*. New York: D. Appleton and Company, 1854 (1885 ed.).

Quintilian. *Institutio oratoria*. Trans. H. E. Butler. Cambridge, Mass., and London: Harvard University Press, 1989.

Rabinovitch, Judith. "Wasp Waists and Monkey Tails: A Study and Translation of Hamanari's *Uta no shiki* (The Code of Poetry, 772), Also Known as *Kakyō Hyōshiki* (A Formulary for Verse Based on the Canons of Poetry)." *Harvard Journal of Asiatic Studies* 51.2 (1991):471–560.

Reid, Ronald F. "The Boylston Professorship of Rhetoric and Oratory, 1806–1904: A Case Study in Changing Concepts of Rhetoric and Pedagogy." *The Quarterly Journal of Speech* 45.3 (October 1959):239–257.

Rhetorica ad Herennium. Trans. Harry Caplan. Cambridge, Mass., and London: Harvard University Press, 1989.

Richards, Ivor A. *The Philosophy of Rhetoric*. New York and London: Oxford University Press, 1936.

Ricoeur, Paul. *The Rule of Metaphor: Multi-Disciplinary Studies of the Creation of Meaning in Language.* London: Routledge and Kegan Paul, 1986.

Rodd, Laurel Rasplica, and Mary Catherine Henkenius. *Kokinshū: A Collection of Poems Ancient and Modern.* Princeton, N.J.: Princeton University Press, 1984.

Rodgers, Paul C. Jr. "Alexander Bain and the Rise of the Organic Paragraph." *The Quarterly Journal of Speech* 51 (December 1965):399–408.

Ryan, Marleigh Grayer. *Japan's First Modern Novel:* Ukigumo *of Futabatei Shimei.* New York: Columbia University Press, 1965.

Sadoya Shigenobu. *Hōgetsu Shimamura Takitarō ron.* Meiji shoin, 1980.

Saitō Tsuyoshi. *Meiji no kotoba.* Kōdansha, 1977.

Sakaeda Mōcho. "Kokugo to benron." *Yūben* 1.1 (February 1910):84–87.

Sannomiya Torae. *Nihon yūben biji kihan.* Osaka: Yanagiwara Kihei, 1882.

Sanseibō Dōjin. *Dai Nihon yūbenshi.* Dai Nihon yūbenkai, 1916.

Saruta Tomoyuki. "Kindai izen shūjihō kenkyū no rekishi." In vol. 10, Suzuki Kazuhiko and Hayashi Ōki, eds., *Kenkyū shiryō Nihonbunpō: Shūjihō hen.* Meiji shoin, 1985.

Sasamori Junzō, ed. *Tōō gijuku saikō jūnenshi.* Tōō gijuku gakuyūkai, 1931.

Sassa Masakazu. "Gikai no benron, kentō no benron, mazu benron no kyōiku o hakare." *Bunshō kenkyūroku* 2.7 (1915):1–5.

———. *Shūjihō.* Dai Nihon tosho, 1901.

———. *Shūjihō kōwa.* Meiji shoin, 1917.

Satō Nobuo. *Retorikku kankaku.* Kōdansha, 1978.

———. *Retorikku ninshiki.* Kōdansha, 1981.

———. *Retorikku no shōsoku.* Hakusuisha, 1987.

Sawada Akio. *Ronbun no kakikata.* Kōdansha, 1977.

———. *Ronbun no retorikku.* Kōdansha, 1983.

Sawada, Janine Anderson. *Confucian Values and Popular Zen: Sekimon Shingaku in Eighteenth Century Japan.* Honolulu: University of Hawai'i Press, 1993.

Sawada Masatake. *Enzetsu bijihō.* Osaka: Aoki Sūzandō, 1888 (8th ed., 1894).

Seireishi. *Shakōjō no danwa to endanjō no yūben.* Ōkura shoten, 1910.

Seki Hidesaburō. "Masashige no yūben." *Yūben* 1.4 (May 1910):76–82.

Seki Ryōichi. *Shōyō, Ōgai: Kōshō to shiron.* Yūseidō, 1971.

Sekiyama Kazuo. *Sekkyō no rekishiteki kenkyū.* Hōzōkan, 1973.

Seto Ken'ichi. *Retorikku no chi.* Shin'yōsha, 1988.

———. *Retorikku no uchū.* Kaimeisha, 1986.

Shashi hensan iinkai, ed. *Kōdansha no ayunda gojūnen.* Kōdansha, 1959.

Shearer, Ned A. "Alexander Bain and the Teaching of Rhetoric." *Central States Speech Journal* 23 (1973):36–43.

Shibue Tamotsu. *Yūbenhō.* Hakubunkan, 1893.

Shimamura Hōgetsu. "Ima no bundan to shin shizenshugi." *Waseda bungaku* 19 (June 1907):1–7.

———. "Saikō shita koro no *Waseda bungaku.*" In *Yomiuri shinbun,* July 25–27, 1918.

———. *Shin bijigaku.* Waseda daigaku shuppanbu, 1902 (7th ed., 1922).

————. "Shizenshugi no kachi." *Waseda bungaku* 30 (May 1908):1–29.

Shimazaki Tōson. "Shizen kara geijutsu o eru." *Bunshō sekai* 3.15 (November 1908):58–59.

"Shinshin sakka jūgoshi no bunshō o hyōsu." *Bunshō kurabu* 3.5 (May 1918):72–82.

Shiozawa Kazuko. "Enzetsu no goi." In vol. 6 of Satō Kiyoji, ed., *Kōza nihongo no goi.* Meiji shoin, 1982.

————. *"Genbun itchi* tai no seiritsu: Enzetsu sokki no hatashita yakuwari (1)." *Kokubungaku ronshū* 12 (1978):91–124 (published by Jōchi Daigaku).

————. *"Genbun itchi* tai no seiritsu: Enzetsu sokki no hatashita yakuwari (2)." *Kokubungaku ronshū* 13 (1979):27–54 (published by Jōchi Daigaku).

Shiroyama Seiichi. *Yūben hiketsu: Enzetsuhō.* Osaka: Tanaka Taemon, 1887.

Sievers, Sharon L. "Feminist Criticism in Japanese Politics in the 1880s: The Experience of Kishida Toshiko." *Signs* 6.4 (1981):602–616.

————. *Flowers in Salt: The Beginnings of Feminist Consciousness in Modern Japan.* Stanford: Stanford University Press, 1983.

Sims, Richard. *A Political History of Modern Japan: 1868–1952.* New Delhi: Vikas Publishing House PVT Ltd., 1991.

Smits, Ivo. *The Pursuit of Loneliness: Chinese and Japanese Nature Poetry in Medieval Japan, ca. 1050–1150.* Stuttgart: Steiner, 1995.

Sōma Kokkō. *Meiji shoki no san josei: Nakajima Shōen, Wakamatsu Shizuko, Shimizu Shikin.* Fuji shuppan, 1985.

Sotozaki Mitsuhiro. *Ueki Emori to onna tachi.* Domesu shuppan, 1976.

Soviak, Eugene. "The Case of Baba Tatsui: Western Enlightenment, Social Change and the Early Meiji Intellectual." *Monumenta Nipponica* 18.1–4 (1963):191–235.

————. "An Early Meiji Intellectual in Politics: Baba Tatsui and the Jiyūtō." In Bernard S. Silberman and Harry D. Harootunian, eds., *Modern Japanese Leadership.* Tucson: University of Arizona Press, 1966.

Stewart, Donald C. "The Nineteenth Century." In Winifred Bryan Horner, ed., *The Present State of Scholarship in Historical and Contemporary Rhetoric.* Columbia and London: University of Missouri Press, 1990.

Sugaya Hiromi. "*Shōsetsu shinzui* to sono zaigen." *Hikaku bungaku nenshi* 9 (March1973):25–49.

————. *"Shūji oyobi kabun"* no kenkyū. Kyōiku shuppan sentaa, 1978.

Sugimoto Mukō. "Genbun itchi sakubunpō." *Shinbun* 1.2 (May 1901):29–34.

Suzuki Kazuhiko. "Tachibana Moribe no kokugo ishiki (1): *San senkaku* ni kanshite." *Yamanashi Daigaku gakugei gakubu kenkyū hōkoku* 10 (December 1959):21–29.

————. "Tachibana Moribe no kokugo ishiki (2): Bunshō senkaku ni kanshite." *Yamanashi Daigaku gakugei gakubu kenkyū hōkoku* 11 (December 1960):22–30.

Suzuki Kazuhiko, and Hayashi Ōki, eds. *Kenkyū shiryō Nihon bunpō: Shūjihō hen.* Vol. 10. Meiji shoin, 1985.

Suzuki Sadami. *Nihon no "bungaku" gainen.* Sakuhinsha, 1998.

Suzuki, Tomi. *Narrating the Self: Fictions of Japanese Modernity.* Stanford: Stanford University Press, 1996.

Takada Sanae. *Bijigaku*. Kinkōdō, 1889.

———. "Hanpō mukashi banashi" (1927). In vol. 98 of *Meiji bungaku zenshū*. Chikuma shobō, 1980.

———. "Shūji no gaku o sakan ni sezaru bekarazu." In *Yomiuri shinbun,* December 6, 1887.

Takahama Kyoshi. "Shaseibunha ga senkakusha." *Bunshō sekai* 3.15 (November 1908): 61–63.

Takahashi Yasumitsu. *Kindai no yūben*. Hōsei daigaku shuppankyoku, 1985.

Takaichi Yoshio. "*Shūji oyobi kabun* kaidai." In vol. 20 of *Meiji bunka zenshū*. Nihon hyōronsha, 1928.

Takamatsu Bōson. *Meiji bungaku genbun itchi*. Taiheiyō bungakusha, 1900.

Takeshima Hagoromo. *Bunshō nyūmon*. Ōkura shoten, 1907.

———. *Shūjigaku*. Hakubunkan, 1898.

Takeuchi Jō. *Atarashii gofunkan enzetsu o nere*. Yūben kenkyūsha, 1926.

Tanabe Masao. "*Bunshō senkaku* no buntaironteki igi." *Kokugakuin zasshi* 60 (August 1959):61–67.

Tanaka Hozumi. "Yūben shiken." *Yūben* 1.2 (March 1910):108–113.

Tanaka Jun. "Sōsakukai no genjō ni taisuru utagai." *Bunshō sekai* 12.7 (July 1917):98–101.

Tanaka Sumiko, ed. *Josei kaihō no shisō to kōdō*. Jiji tsūshinsha, 1975.

Tanimoto Tomeri. "Bunshō to wa nani ka," *Nihon oyobi Nihonjin* 689 (September 1916):42–52.

Tankai Sanshi. *Seiji gakujutsu enzetsu tatsubenhō*. Gakuyūkan, 1894.

Tayama Katai. *Bibun sahō*. Hakubunkan, 1906.

———. *Shōsetsu sahō*. Hakubunkan, 1909.

Teele, Nicholas. "Rules for Poetic Elegance: Fujiwara no Kintō's *Shinsen Zuinō* and *Waka Kuhon*." *Monumenta Nipponica* 31.2 (1976):145–164.

Todorov, Tzvetan. *Theories of the Symbol*. Trans. Catherine Porter. Ithaca, N.Y.: Cornell University Press, 1982.

Tokuda Shūkō. "Fukuzatsu naru byōsha." *Bunshō sekai* 3.15 (November 1908):59–61.

Tokuda Shūsei. *Meiji shōsetsu bunshō hensenshi* (1914). In vol. 24 of *Tokuda Shūsei zenshū*. Yagi shoten, 2001.

———. *Shōsetsu nyūmon* (1918). In vol. 24 of *Tokuda Shūsei zenshū*. Yagi shoten, 2001.

Tōkyō teikoku daigaku, ed., *Tōkyō teikoku daigaku*. Kokusai shuppan insatsusha, 1942.

Tomioka Masanori. *Benshi hitsudoku enzetsugaku*. Senshindō, 1882.

Tsubotani Zenshirō. *Enzetsu tōron kihan*. Hakubunkan, 1903.

Tsubouchi Shōyō. "Bijironkō" (1893). In vol. 11 of *Shōyō senshū*. Daiichi shobō, 1977.

———. "Kaioku mandan." (1925). In vol. 12 of *Shōyō senshū*. Daiichi shobō, 1977.

Tsukahara Tetsuo. "Bunshō kenkyūshi: Meiji igo no bunshō kenkyū." In Morioka Kenji, et al., eds., *Sakubun kōza* 4. Meiji shoin, 1968.

Twine, Nanette. *Language and the Modern State: The Reform of Written Japanese*. London and New York: Routledge, 1991.

Uchida Roan. "Bunshōjō no inakamono." *Nihon oyobi Nihonjin* 689 (September 1916):40–42.

Uchiyama Kametarō. *Jitchi enzetsu hikki*. Kyōto: Kaishindō, 1887.

Uchiyama Shun. *Jisshū bunshō kōsei shūjihō*. Jitsugyō no Nihonsha, 1913.

Utsumi Kōzō (Getsujō). *Bunshō jikkō*. Bunseisha, 1910.

Valignano, Alessandro. *Historia del principio*. Trans. Michael Cooper in *They Came to Japan: An Anthology of European Reports on Japan, 1543–1640*. Berkeley: University of California Press, 1981.

Waseda daigaku daigakushi henshūjo, ed. *Waseda daigaku hyakunenshi*. Vol. 1. Waseda daigaku shuppanbu, 1978.

Washburn, Dennis C. *The Dilemma of the Modern in Japanese Fiction*. New Haven, Conn., and London: Yale University Press, 1995.

Watanabe Yoshiharu. *Gendai shūjihōyō*. Jinbo shoten, 1926.

Welch, Patricia Marie. "Discourse Strategies and the Humor of *Rakugo*." Ph.D. dissertation, University of Michigan, 1988.

Wolfe, Katherine J. "Towards a History of Classical Japanese Rhetorics and Their Recognition in American Composition Studies." Ph.D. dissertation, Texas Christian University, 1994.

Yamada Tatsuo. *Kōkai enzetsu yūben tōronhō*. Shūgakudō, 1907.

Yamamoto Masahide. *Genbun itchi no rekishi ronkō: Zokuhen*. Ōfūsha, 1981.

———. *Kindai buntai hassei no shiteki kenkyū*. Iwanami shoten, 1965.

———. *Kindai buntai keisei shiryō shūsei: Hassei hen*. Ōfūsha, 1978.

———. *Kindai buntai keisei shiryō shūsei: Seiritsu hen*. Ōfūsha, 1979.

Yamamoto, Masao. "The Aesthetic Thought of Shimamura Hōgetsu." In Michael F. Marra, ed., *A History of Modern Japanese Aesthetics*. Honolulu: University of Hawai'i Press, 2001.

Yamamoto Ryōkichi. "Sakubun no omoide." *Nihon oyobi Nihonjin* 689 (September 1916):69–72.

Yamamuro Shin'ichi. *Meijiki gakujutsu genron zasshi shūsei bessatsu*. Microfilm ed., Nada, 1987.

Yanagida Izumi. *Meiji shoki no bungaku shisō*. Vol. 2. Shunjūsha, 1965.

———. *Wakaki Tsubouchi Shōyō*. Shunjūsha, 1960.

Yano Fumio. *Enzetsu bunshō kumitatehō*. Maruya zenshichi, 1884.

———. *Nihon buntai mōnji shinron*. Hōchisha, 1886.

Yatsunami Norikichi. *Oyō shūjigaku kōwa*. Keibunkan, 1914.

Yoda Kiyomatsu. *Gakujutsu enzetsu tōronshū*. Tōkyō tosho shuppan, 1897.

Yoshida Kurō. *Bunshō sahō genri*. Bunshūdō shoten, 1926.

Yoshida Seiichi. *Shizenshugi no kenkyū: Jōkan*. Tōkyōdō, 1955.

Yoshitake Yoshinori. *Gendai buntairon*. Kyōdō shuppan, 1969.

———. *Meiji Taishō no hon'yakushi*. Kenkyūsha, 1959.

Index